Praise for *Among the Remnants*

A story of faith, hope, family and inspiration….of a little boy whose childhood was stolen, who went on to become one of America's greatest leaders and teachers in the field of Senior Care… who now is dedicated to telling his story to young people.

STEVEN BARAL
Vice President, Holocaust Center for Humanity, Seattle
Executive Board Member, American Society for Yad Vashem

This warmly personal memoir is an encounter with a fortunate Jew, who embodies in his personal life the continuity with the rich Jewish traditions of *menschlichkeit* and *edelkeit*.

Gortler's most vivid account of the Displaced Person's life from June 1945 to June 1951 is rich with the insights of a future social worker and keen observer of human foibles. This is an important story that is just beginning to be told.

Among the Remnants is a moving reminder of suffering but also an affirmation of life's lessons viewed through a learned and soulful man.

This a book that every young social worker, rabbi, or aspiring organizer needs to read.

RABBI HAIM DOV BELIAK
Chaplain, Skirball Hospice, Encino CA
Executive Director, Friends of Jewish Renewal in Poland

Josh Gortler explains how he developed Kline Galland Center into one of the nation's premier Jewish adult services agencies. But the book offers far more: a story of surviving the Holocaust, the five years in DP camps in Germany that influenced the man he would become, and coming to America. Josh tells his story with grace and intelligence in his own distinctive voice.

HOWARD DROKER
Historian
Co-author of *Family of Strangers: Building a Jewish Community in Washington State*

This book makes it clear that one can dwell on one's misery, or use the experience to become a better person and speak for understanding and tolerance. From beginning to end, I was on a journey with Josh, and I was unable to put the book down.

PETRA HEUSSNER-WALKER
Honorary Consul, emerita, of the Federal Republic of Germany
Director of the Seattle Eric M. Warburg Chapter,
American Council on Germany

This autobiography represents an invaluable addition to the literature of those "remnants" of World War II Europe who spent their youth and early adolescence on the run, in war-torn Europe. [Josh's] rise from refugee to one of American health care's most respected and honored executives offers countless life lessons.

SETH B. GOLDSMITH
Professor Emeritus of Health Policy and Management
University of Massachusetts at Amherst
Author of *The Rabbi of Resurrection Bay*

This memoir is engaging and insightful and teaches both world history and Seattle Jewish history. With a pioneering spirit, Josh takes us through his personal timeline, narrating us on his life's journey and giving us a sense of the endless tools he used for his own survival and education to become one of the most compassionate and effective leaders that Jewish Washington has ever seen.

LISA KRANSELER
Executive Director
Washington State Jewish Historical Society

Engagingly written with humor, insight and erudition. A truly enjoyable read. From DP camp scamp to a community builder, pillar and mentor. Josh's description of becoming a *mentsh* as a Displaced Person was especially rare and very moving. The footnotes are excellent.

ELLIOTT PALEVSKY
CEO Emeritus, River Garden Senior Services, Jacksonville FL
Scholar of Yiddish Language and Literature

For almost 20 years, not really knowing why, I have drawn on the courage, compassion and strength of my friend Josh. After reading his book I now understand that I was drawing from the love, resilience and appreciation of life. This book has humbled me beyond words to be called his friend and honored to witness the sharing of his journey for generations to come.

ERIC PETTIGREW
Representative, 37th Legislative District (Seattle)
Washington State Legislature

Josh takes us on a journey that crosses borders and continents where we experience the best and the worst of humanity. His story depicts the consequences of a world filled with hate and one man's indomitable will to better himself. A stunning example of the difference one man can make.

DEE SIMON
Executive Director, Holocaust Center for Humanity, Seattle

Josh Gortler's memoir *Among the Remnants*, co-authored with the skillful Gigi Yellen, illuminates one individual's experiences within the brutal swath of 20th century history. From Josh's childhood trauma during the Holocaust, the reinvigorating of a Jewish life and spirit in displaced persons camps, to his incredible journey through a career of service to others, *Among the Remnants* presents enduring lessons in resilience, humor, faith, and compassion.

JULIA THOMPSON
Education Resource Coordinator
Holocaust Center for Humanity, Seattle

Among the Remnants

Among the Remnants

JOSH GORTLER'S JOURNEY

by Joshua H. Gortler, MSW, DHL
with Gigi Yellen

coffeetownpress

A Coffeetown Press book published by Epicenter Press

Epicenter Press
6524 NE 181st St. Suite 2
Kenmore, WA 98028.
www.Epicenterpress.com
www.Coffeetownpress.com
www.Camelpress.com

For more information go to: www.epicenterpress.com

Design by Rudy Ramos
Cover photographs: John Froschauer, photographer (lower right). From the
2013 Powell-Heller Conference for Holocaust Education at Pacific Lutheran
University; (center) Holocaust Center for Humanity, Seattle Washington.

"Holocaust survivor: Remember the cruelty when considering today's displaced
people," by Jerry Large / Seattle Times staff columnist, Local News, April 27,
2017, reprinted by permission of The Seattle Times.

"Holocaust Survivor Puts Things in Perspective" reprinted by permission of
Capitol Hill Times (Pacific Publishing)

ISBN: 9781603817196 (hard cover)
ISBN: 9781603816885 (trade paper)
ISBN: 9781603817141 (ebook)
Printed in the United States of America

Dedicated to my beloved wife
Sarah Gortler, a true *eishes chayil,*
who has been at my side for the best six decades
of my journey.

Table of Contents

APPENDIX

PREFACE

As I reached my 81st birthday, I began to reflect on my life.

Some people get to live a neatly ordered life. You're born into a community. You spend your childhood and youth in that community. You marry, have children, and settle down there. You build a career. You contribute to the community's life. This was the world as my family had known it for generations.

But this is not how I started. My childhood and my youth were robbed. My family life during my childhood was focused on trying to avoid getting murdered.

A few years prior to my birth, a *soneh Yisroel*[1] was already trying to change the world. He did change the world. Unfortunately, in his idea of how to make a perfect world, the Jews were the main evildoers, and should be destroyed. He insisted on what he called "the final solution to the Jewish problem." Millions of people followed his ideas.

I was born into a family of Jews, into the world he changed forever.

My parents, my brother, and I managed to survive in places that were not our homes during the years known as World War II, while the famous battles were raging, and the infamous concentration camps were burning bodies by the hundreds every day.

---

1   Yiddish, meaning Jew-hater

After the war ended, I was blessed to emerge into a world that I would help change for the better. I would dedicate my life's work to creating real solutions for the kinds of problems that all people face in the declining years of their lives.

I have not only managed to make my own new family, but I have also had the privilege of helping to create a new environment of kindness and comfort. I have dedicated my life's work to the service of people experiencing difficult times.

It's true that wars have occurred throughout the centuries. But has there ever been a war with a country whose leader was obsessed not so much with winning and gaining territory, but with eliminating human beings? Perhaps Hitler would have won the war if he had not spent so much energy on the destruction and the annihilation of the Jewish People. Throughout the centuries, there have been plenty of tyrants. In my opinion, Hitler surpassed them all. But we Jews as a People survived.

THE THREE KEYS

Now, at 81, I look back and I say, what is the key element in life? I think life is really guided by three key elements.

One is *mazel*—luck. You have to be in the right place at the right time. Within moments, it can go one way or another.

Another key element is what I refer to as *hashgacha pratis*[2]: God's special intervention for an individual or a family. I think that *hashgacha pratis* played the key role in how I survived, in how I immigrated to the United States and managed to reclaim the spiritual inheritance of my childhood and youth, for myself, my family, and the community I eventually came to call home.

The third key to a successful life is to find a partner who is really a true partner—a person who walks with you every step of the way, where the two, as they say, become one. I was fortunate to find my true mate in my wife, Sarah. We have been walking these steps together for sixty years and counting. We made our important decisions together. We have moved and worked, not contradicting each other, but *b'lev echad*, with one heart.

This is where I am today. These philosophies— *mazel*,[3] *hashgacha*

---

2   Hebrew/Yiddish, meaning individually supervised, watched over, guarded from harm
3   Usually translated as "good luck," literally refers to the stars in alignment

pratis, and finding the right partner—have shaped who I am and what I have done in my lifetime. As our Sages say, "The rest is commentary. Go and study."

As you follow my life's journey in the pages of this book, you see the points along the way where these three keys have come together to make me into the person I have become. It wasn't easy. But I am satisfied with the result.

A SENSE OF PURPOSE

How do you overcome adversity and make the best from it? God gave you a lemon. And you could *kvetch* that lemon—complain about it—or you could make lemonade. It's a cliché, but it's true. People who came out of the experiences I went through, and those who have experienced other adversities, could put their heads in the sand and become pessimistic. They could say that life is not worth living, and just mark off their days rather than doing something with them.

The path that I took is a lot more than just marking off days. I marked my days with purpose. I intended to reach something higher than simply acquiring wealth, or honor, or position.

My path has been to achieve that purpose through my family life, and through my community's life. I now see the impact that I have made on the children, the grandchildren, the great-grandchildren. They are contributors to society and to the wider world.

It was a big decision for Sarah and me to leave the comfort of New York, the little *shtetl*⁴ we were in—where we had friends and colleagues surrounding us all the time—and get on an airplane and come to Seattle, Washington, a place that we thought of as the end of the world.

It was a big decision to take on a dysfunctional organization that had virtually no community support. It was my job to create enthusiasm among the lay leadership. Together, we created one of the leading eldercare agencies in the country. That was *mazel,* it was *hashgacha pratis,* and it was hard work, not only for Sarah and me, but also for the leadership of the community that became our home.

---

4   Yiddish term, meaning "small village." Commonly used to denote a close-knit Jewish community in prewar Eastern Europe.

HASHGACHA PRATIS, AND DOING THE WORK

After receiving my master's degree in social work from Yeshiva University in 1960, I accepted a position at the Jewish Community Center in Englewood, New Jersey, to complete my second year of internship. My title was Youth Activities Director. After two years, I was promoted to Program Director, which was actually the second highest position in the agency.

From Englewood, I was recruited by the Flushing, New York YMHA (Young Men's Hebrew Association) and United Help to be the director of their Older Adult Center. This was an innovative position combining services to the population at the Y with services to Holocaust survivors housed in two nearby high-rise buildings.

Then, in 1969, I was recruited by the Seattle Jewish community to become the Executive Director of a very small home for the aged that served seventy people, with a total budget of $250,000 a year.

Seattle is where I settled, at last, and where I have managed to fulfill my sense of purpose. During my tenure of "double chai[5] + one" (37) years, with various titles (Executive Director, Executive Vice President, and Chief Executive Officer), we were able to build a world-renowned facility with a total budget of $35,000,000 dollars. After stepping down as CEO, I created a foundation, with an endowment fund to ensure that programming can continue into the future. I became the first president of the Kline Galland Foundation.

The Kline Galland Center became a training ground for medical staff, social work staff, and physical and occupational therapy students. Today, it is considered one of the leading geriatric centers in the country.

POINTING NORTH

I had a certain teacher at Yeshiva University—one of the most dynamic teachers I ever had. Rabbi Gorelick. Rabbi Gorelik was a maverick. A real, real maverick. I may not remember the *Toisfos*[6] he taught, I may not remember the *Gemara*[7] he taught, but I remember one thing. It will always stay with me: You've got to know where you're going.

---

5   *Chai* = life, in Hebrew, where each letter also has numeric value. The two letters that spell *chai* add up to 18. This is why 18 and multiples of 18 are often used as an amount of a charity donation, or in other references to health and life.
6   Medieval rabbinic commentaries on the Talmud
7   Traditional name for Talmud

Rabbi Gorelik wore a cap. Not a baseball cap. In Yiddish it's called a *kashkett*. It's a hat with a *dashek*. A *dashek* is a visor. *A hittl mit a dashek*, a hat with a visor. The visor always points straight ahead.

He used this hat to teach us this important truth.

You don't walk around in circles. You need a direction. Think of the hat as a compass. The *dashek* points North.

I'll never forget, he said, "Find a direction and go for it. The *dashek* points you there." That was Rabbi Gorelik's philosophy.

I wear that kind of hat a lot. It always points me where I'm going.

Have a compass in life. It points to North. And once you find your North, you're no longer lost.

Joshua H. Gortler
March 2020
Seattle, Washington

FOREWORD:

Listening to Josh's Voice

To the reader: Photos, documents, the words of colleagues and friends—these tell part of the story, but the conversations we recorded over the better part of three years form its heart.

Josh's spoken English flows with a graceful Yiddish lilt. In print, his native language infuses his speech with more than tones of voice. Josh's vocabulary reflects his lifelong encounter with the diversity of Jewish tradition.

Josh's name in itself is a story. Quite apart from the American assimilation tale of a name changed and re-changed (which he recalls in the chapters about his first days in Phoenix and at YU), the job of matching the pronunciation with the spelling of Josh's birth name poses a challenge all its own.

On his identification documents, Josh's childhood name might read "Szia," or "Szija," or even "Shia," pronounced "Shee-ah." This is, in fact, the pronunciation (in the distinctive accent common to the Jews of his parents' home region) of an affectionate nickname, the second half ("shu-ah") of the Hebrew name "Yehoshua," Joshua. His Hebrew name, Yehoshua Tzvi, was the name of his maternal grandfather.

To allow consistency for the reader of Josh's story, we have chosen to retain the spelling "Szia," and hope that the reader will hear it as "Shee-ah," the sound Josh heard spoken by the tender voices of his mother and father.

In Josh's references to religious law and texts, and to the holidays of the Jewish year, the reader will find that he alternates between different traditional styles in the pronunciation of Hebrew terms. These are pronunciations associated with the geography of the Jewish diaspora.

As a child of Yiddish-speaking Polish Jews, Josh's native pronunciation of Hebrew is Ashkenazic. But it was the Sephardic pronunciation that became the accent of the nascent State of Israel. An Israeli accent is sometimes described as "Sephardic."

Josh toggles between these two traditions as he tells his story because his formative educational experiences—the ones he lovingly recalls in this memoir—came to him in the DP camps of Europe. There, his teachers included both European rabbinic scholars who spoke Hebrew in the Ashkenazic way, and speakers of Modern Israeli Hebrew.

Josh describes his relationship with his beloved Sarah as *b'lev echad* – with one heart. Whether he says *echad* (Sephardic) or *echod* (Ashkenazic), this open-hearted memoir serves as a lasting tribute to this precious partnership, and to the inspiring inheritance Josh so lovingly bequeaths to his reader.

This life story embodies Josh's faithfulness to the Fifth Commandment: to honor one's father and one's mother. As he tells it, his parents were the people who, with the help of the Almighty, kept him in life, and sustained him, and enabled him to reach this season of the publication of this memoir.

Josh, thank you for inviting me to listen, and to work with you on this most extraordinary life story. I have done my best to bring your voice onto these pages.

Gigi Yellen
Seattle
March 2020
Nisan 5780

PART ONE

A KID ON THE RUN

My hometown of Tomaszów. *Courtesy of the Holocaust Center for Humanity, Seattle.*

CHAPTER 1
A "Wild Thing" Under Mother's Shawl
TOMASZÓW LUBELSKI, POLAND
May 3, 1936 – September 5, 1939

In August of 1936, the victories of Jesse Owens, the gifted African American athlete, smashed Hitler's racial superiority claims at the Berlin Summer Olympic Games. Unfortunately, one talented athlete's success could not stop Germany's dictator and his murderous Nazi war machine from tearing apart the lives of millions of people, including my family.

Probably no one was thinking about the upcoming Olympics in the little *shtetl* known as Tomaszów Lubelski in southeastern Poland, on the day I was born there, on May 3, 1936, to a middle-class Jewish couple, Josef and Estera Gortler. Tomaszów was near the border between Poland and a part of the Soviet Union now called Ukraine. The closeness of that border would soon prove critical to the survival of my family—my brother, Monyik[8], born in 1934, my parents and myself. Little did my parents know, on May 3, 1936, that three years later, they would be running for their lives across that border, with this baby and his big brother, away from the only place they had ever called home.

We were hardly alone. The makers of the documentary film *Saved by Deportation* describe the situation this way:

Prior to the outbreak of the Second World War, 3 million three hundred thousand Jews lived in Poland By 1945 only 300,000 survived. Of the survivors, approximately 80% escaped the Holocaust as a result of Stalin's

---

8   Polish for "Moshe," my brother's Hebrew name

deportation deep into the Soviet Union....In 1940, a year before the Nazis started deporting Jews to death camps, Joseph Stalin ordered the deportation of approximately 200,000 Polish Jews from Russian-occupied Eastern Poland to forced labor settlements in the Soviet interior. As cruel as Stalin's deportations were, in the end they largely saved Polish Jewish lives, for the deportees constituted the overwhelming majority of Polish Jews who escaped the Nazi Holocaust.[9]

My mother, Estera Balsenbaum, was also born in Tomaszów. Jews in Tomaszów have a long and rich history, dating back to the 1600s. Just before World War II, the Jewish population of Tomaszów was approximately 6,000, which was approximately half of the town's inhabitants.[10]

The Balsenbaums were businesspeople, involved in wholesale food distribution to the Polish army, hospitals, and other institutions. My mother's father, Szia Balsenbaum, would go early in the morning to the wholesale markets, and then sell produce and other groceries to his customers.

The area around Tomaszów was a place of dense forests.

My father, Yosef Gortler, was born in Krasnobrod, a smaller *shtetl* nearby. The Gortlers of Krasnobrod had been involved in the lumber business for generations. In his work, my father would meet with woodsmen in the forest and give them orders for the types of tree trunks he wished to purchase. He prepared the trunks for shipping by rail, from a station near Tomaszów. When my father married my mother, they established a home in Tomaszów, where my father continued in the family lumber business.[11]

My mother had a business of her own. She was an expert seamstress and dressmaker, and a smart manager. She employed about 15 women or young girls in her workshop in the front room of our house.[12] They made men's underwear and shirts, as well as women's clothing. The business was especially active around the Jewish holidays in spring and fall, when people, especially the men, would want new clothing. She made her own patterns from each customer's measurements, using the fabric that they would bring her.

---

9   "Saved by Deportation" introductory note, on website https://www.kanopy.com/product/saved-deportation

10 https://sztetl.org.pl/en/towns/t/51-tomaszow-lubelski/99-history/138161-history-of-community

11 Sarah Gortler, interview with Gigi Yellen, April 4, 2019, reporting on conversations with her mother-in-law

12 *Ibid.*

Her skills with a scissor would prove handy in my childhood. She taught me how to sew, and to this day I still know how.

Early each morning, my mother would make breakfast for my father, my brother Monyik, and me. Although she employed a girl to take care of us during the work day, she would never leave the cooking to the girl. She preferred to do it herself. She would often come back out of the shop during the day to keep an eye on us.[13]

My father was one of seven siblings, the children of Rabbi Yaakov Gortler and his wife, Chana. Before I was born, a fire in their house had killed my grandmother.[14]

My father was the only one of his siblings who survived World War II.

All of my father's siblings were religiously observant, and continued the Orthodox Jewish practices of the family, except for one: Eliezer. He dropped his religious practice when he married a woman named Regina from a secular family in Zamosc, the nearest big *shtodt* (a city, not a *shtetl*). Eliezer and Regina settled in Zamosc, and became known in the family as the non-religious ones. Regina had attended *gymnasia*, the secular high school in Zamosc. They did not educate their kids in traditional Jewish study. Nevertheless, it was their son, Yehuda, who braved incredible odds to reunite the remnants of our family after the war.

My father and his siblings did receive some secular education, but it did not include *gymnasia*. My father was schooled in a traditional Jewish educational institution, known as a *yeshiva*.

Aunt Regina talked about my grandfather Yaakov as "the fanatic." He was a businessman, this grandfather. But he was also considered one of the respected elders of the community, a *dayan*.[15] They referred to him as Rav[16] Yankele. People would come to him to resolve disputes, because the Jews of these communities didn't go to the secular courts, they went to the *besdin*, the religious court.

Yaakov Gortler refused to go to his son Eliezer's wedding to Regina, because she was not going to cut or cover her hair, she was not going to go to the *mikvah*—the ritual bath—and she wasn't going to keep kosher.

Eliezer wound up being killed by a falling tree in Siberia. As a deportee

---

13 *Ibid.*
14 *Ibid.*
15 Judge in a rabbinic court; decides issues of Jewish law
16 Title of respect, short for "rabbi"

in a labor camp, he was assigned to a job he was not qualified to do. Regina and their three children managed to survive the war. Their journey to their new life included the legendary refugee ship "Exodus." Regina became an Israeli, known by her Hebrew name, Rivka.

My mother was probably schooled at home. She learned basic Yiddish writing, and fluency in praying in Hebrew (*davening*), and how to read the *Tzena u'Re'ena*, the Bible in Yiddish translation, which was used primarily by women. They called Hebrew language "*ivreh*"; and their phrase for reading Hebrew was "*leynen ivris.*"

My Yiddish name was Szia (Yehoshua Tzvi in Hebrew), named for my maternal grandfather. While my brother was called by his Polish name, I never was given one. Prior to the invasion of Tomaszów by the Nazis, we lived a very comfortable and wholesome Jewish life. I was a typical three-year-old, with my own ideas. I was a "*vilde chaya,*" or "wild creature," as my mother called me.

But from 1939 to 1945, I had to totally hold that energy in. I was not allowed to raise my voice, not allowed to speak, or even to cry. I was certainly not allowed to walk where I wanted. We were always hiding. Even when we were in Tashkent, in the *kolkhoz* (the Muslim communal farm where we were given refuge), we had to keep a very, very low profile. Can you imagine what it was like to be a spirited seven-year-old with limitations like that?

But as my mother told me years later, I had a brief chance to be a normal, mischievous little boy, before we had to flee our home.

Once, my father brought home a live turkey for Rosh Hashana. Being the rambunctious three-year-old that I was, I decided that this turkey would be an excellent opportunity for a horseback ride. So, I climbed on that turkey. The turkey did not appreciate the weight on its back. It jumped on me and poked me in my left temple, right next to my eye. I almost lost my eyesight. I still have the scar.

On another occasion, this three-year-old went to a *bris milah*—a celebration of the *mitzvah*[17] of circumcision—and was very impressed with the skills of the *mohel*, the ritual circumciser. According to my mother, I came

17 Jewish Religious commandment. The well-known terms "bar mitzvah" (for boys) and "bat mitzvah" (for girls) mark the age at which the religious commandments become one's adult responsibilities, and no longer one's parents'. Circumcision, a commandment incumbent on a boy's parents, is only one of over 600 mitzvahs.

Tomaszów Outdoor Market, May 1938. *Unknown photographer, courtesy of the Holocaust Center for Humanity, Seattle*

home, marched into the kitchen, took out a sharp kitchen knife, and wanted to perform the *mitzvah* on one of my friends, to make him *glatt* kosher.[18] Luckily for all those concerned, the adults intervened, and the boy was saved.

All this changed in September of 1939, when German Nazi troops overtook Tomaszów Lubelski.[19] We Jews were forced to leave our comfortable homes. And so began our extraordinary life of trying to survive.

There was a fierce air battle near our town. Tomaszów received a major air attack. Most of the buildings in the town were destroyed. Our house was seriously damaged.

It was morning. My brother and I were home with our parents. We heard sirens. We heard bombs very nearby.

My brother and I started running with our parents as the bombs kept falling. We were running toward the homes of other relatives in the town. Our father was carrying whatever belongings he was able to grab. My mother wanted to protect our eyes from seeing the devastation. She used a shawl to cover our faces so that we would not see the horror, the dead people in the street. Like an eagle protecting her chicks with her wings,

18 Kosher by the strictest standards
19 https://worldhistoryproject.org/1939/9/17/first-battle-of-tomaszow-lubelski

our mother covered us, her two young offspring.

We ended up staying in some relatives' house. Every time our mother tried to comfort us, she would start by humming the song *Rozhinkes mit Mandlen.* Then she would sing it with words, to help us close our eyes and fall asleep to the beautiful *Rozhinkes Mit Mandlen.*

The title of the song means "raisins and almonds." The words ask, "What is going to be your profession, little one? A very beautiful profession. You're not going to be a shoemaker or a tailor. You're going to deal with fruits and spices." Spices, in Jewish tradition, are symbols of beauty. Shoemaker and tailor shops don't always smell so beautiful. The idea of the lullaby is that you will grow up to have the best of everything: spices, sweet flavors, delicacies, dreams. Despite the fact that you are in terrible exile, you will grow up to be surrounded with beautiful things.[20]

This lullaby was engraved in my mind, from the days of bombing in Tomaszów through the years of hiding out in Siberia and Uzbekistan, and on through our lives in the Displaced Persons camps. To this day, I still remember the sound of my mother's sweet voice.

The Germans succeeded in occupying Tomaszów. We were forced to leave our relatives' home under Nazi guard. We were gathered in a central holding place, to be shipped out to the Zamosc ghetto.

The following story was related to me by my Aunt Regina (Rivka), wife of my father's brother Eliezer. This is what she told me about my grandfather Yaakov, my father's father, whom she affectionately referred to as Rav Yankele:

When we were all crowded into this central gathering place in Tomaszów with our few belongings, my grandfather insisted that the women separate themselves from the men[21]so that he could put on *tallis* and *tefillin* (prayer shawl and phylacteries) for morning prayers. Since the women refused to separate from the men in such a tightly crowded place, my grandfather took his *tallis* and *tefillin* and left. I was told that he was later found hanging from a tree.

---

20 Often mistaken for an ancient folksong, the music and lyrics to this song were composed by Abraham Goldfaden for the 1880 Yiddish play *Shulamis*. It is understood to express both a mother's prayer for her child, and the exiled Jewish people's longing for return to the land of Israel.

21 According to the Orthodox Jewish practice of my grandfather, a man's prayers could not be said in close proximity to a woman.

CHAPTER 2

From a Ghetto, Across a Border

ZAMOSC TO RAVA-RUSKA
Fall and Winter, 1939

We were incarcerated in the ghetto at Zamosc. I have no idea how we got to Zamosc, but that's what my parents told me. We were forced to live in extremely tight and unsanitary conditions. We spent the cold Polish winter in that crowded ghetto with other Jews. The adults were forced into slave labor, to help the Nazi machine in their war efforts. Suddenly I, this *vilde chaya*, this lively little three-year-old boy, had to be kept quiet, forbidden to utter a peep. We survived on boiled potatoes, and, if we were lucky, a piece of bread.

Years later, my mother told my wife Sarah how terrible the conditions were in this ghetto and labor camp. They were so terrible that her teeth fell out, one by one. She could just take her fingers and pull. My mother never told me this herself. She always wanted to protect me.

Because she became ill in the labor camp, my mother reluctantly sent my brother and me to stay with a Polish woodman's family. It was terrible for her to let us out of her sight. When she and my father were able to escape the labor camp, she refused to be separated from us children again. She told Sarah what she had decided: "If I have to die, I want my children to be with me." Over the years, my mother developed an enlarged heart, so that everything she tried to do was difficult. She only managed to live as long as she did because of her strong will and her fierce commitment to protecting her family.[22]

---

22 Sarah Gortler, interview with Gigi Yellen, April 4, 2019, reporting on conversations with her mother-in-law

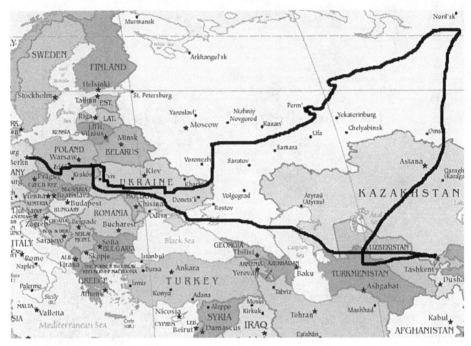

Gortler family journey *(graphic courtesy Holocaust Center for Humanity, Seattle, from Josh's presentation)*

Through my father's connections with the Gentiles outside of the ghetto, we were able to escape that place. Some of these connections must have sheltered and guided us in the direction of the border. Zamosc and Tomaszów were very close geographically to the border between Poland and Soviet Ukraine. One border city, Rava-Ruska, was originally in Poland. It was occupied first by the Germans, and then reoccupied by the Russians. We were able to cross the border into Russian-occupied Rava-Ruska by walking, and by horse and buggy.

Opposite: Document: Shia Gortler. *Courtesy of the United States Holocaust Memorial Museum, Washington DC.*

SHIA GORTLER

(This record is not available on the web.)

Sex: Male

Patronymic Name: Iosifovich

Date of Birth: 1934

Place of Birth: Liubel'skaia gub., G.Tomashev

Libelskiy region, Tomashev city

Address: L'vovskaia obl. Rava-Russkii, Rava-Russkaia

Lvovskiy region

Sentence: prib. na spetsposelenie v Arkhangel'skuiu obl. 25.07.40. Rovdinskii r-n, Matveyevka. Osv. so spetsposeleniia po amnistii 00.09.41

Assigned for temporary residence in Matveevka [village], Rovdinskiy district, Arkhangelskiy region on July 25th, 1940 with amnesty until June 9th, 1941

Education: 1 klass

Nationality: evrei

Source: Baza dannykh "Pol'skie spetspereselentsy v Arkhangel'skoi obl."

Database: "Polish temporary citizens in Arkhangelskiy region"

SOURCE

Title: [Subset of data from Perpetuating the Memory of the Victims of Repression]

Description: Electronic data regarding Jewish GULAG victims extracted from data compiled by "Memorial" in Moscow

Document from United States Holocaust Memorial Museum, Washington DC

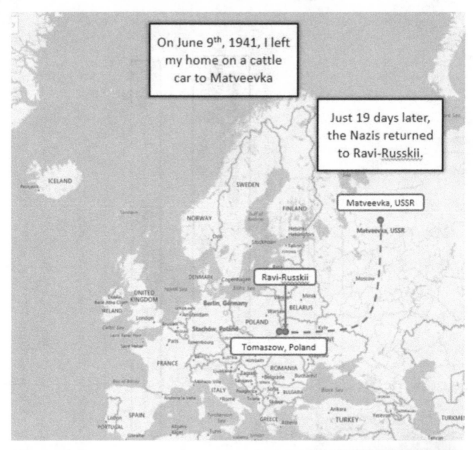

On June 9th, 1941, I left my home on a cattle car to Matveevka

Just 19 days later, the Nazis returned to Ravi-Russkii.

Matveevka, USSR

Matveevka, USSR

Ravi-Russkii

Berlin, Germany

Stachów, Poland

Tomaszow, Poland

Above: map of the beginning of our journey. Right: typical scenes in Rava-Ruska. From Joshua's presentation. *Courtesy of the Holocaust Center for Humanity, Seattle.*

CHAPTER 3

RAVA-RUSKA

Winter and Spring 1940

THOSE WELCOMING RUSSIANS

What I remember from Rava-Ruska is being in a big hall with hundreds of people, sleeping on a dirt floor. There were no "quarters" for us to live in.

People just poured into this place. It was like a military camp. There was no fence. There was a boundary, but I cannot recall what kind of boundary, between us and German-occupied Poland.

Russian soldiers played an accordion and sang Russian melodies. They were welcoming us! They were not like the Germans that we were afraid of. The Russians were very friendly to the refugees, or to the escapees, whichever you want to call us. That's where I first heard the sounds of the Russian language, and picked up a few words, like *khlyeba*, meaning bread. For food, boiled potatoes were a big item. They used a big pot to boil hundreds and hundreds of potatoes. We just ate the potatoes cooked, unpeeled.

FACING DEATH ON THE ROAD OUT OF RAVA-RUSKA

From Rava-Ruska, we once again began our journey to…somewhere. None of us knew where.

We were loaded onto horse-drawn wagons. It was a caravan of wagons, with several families in each one. The wagon consisted of a platform, with maybe a two-foot-long wooden plank along the edges, with the back and front left open. It was like a flatbed truck, with four poles sticking up from

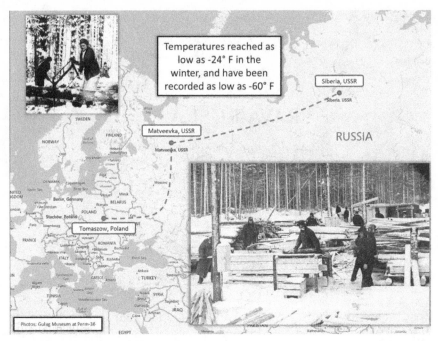

Temperatures reached as low as -24° F in the winter, and have been recorded as low as -60° F

Siberia, USSR

Siberia, USSR

Matveevka, USSR

Matveevka, USSR

RUSSIA

SWEDEN

NORWAY

FINLAND

DENMARK

UNITED KINGDOM

Berlin, Germany

BELARUS

POLAND

Stachów, Poland

Moscow

FRANCE

Stachów, Poland

Tomaszow, Poland

ROMANIA

ITALY

GREECE

TURKEY

SYRIA

TUNISIA

IRAQ

EGYPT

Photos: Gulag Museum at Perm-36

Forced labor in Siberia. From Joshua's presentation. *Courtesy of the Holocaust Center for Humanity, Seattle*

the corners of the truck bed. *Shmattes* (rags, worn out blankets or burlap) were stretched around the poles.

Each wagon was pulled by one old, tired, skinny horse, driven by a tired, overworked *balagala* (Yiddish for wagon driver). There were no roads. The wagon was pulled through the *blohtteh* (the mud) by this poor horse. Periodically, the wheels would sink into the *blohtteh*, and the horse couldn't pull. All the men, and also the bigger kids, would go out and push the wagon. They themselves would end up to their knees in the mud. The women would walk alongside. The little children were the only ones left in the wagon.

Once, somewhere in our travels, before the poor horse could stop, one of the other wagons turned over. Three people were killed in front of our eyes. Our mother, who was walking alongside us, quickly climbed back into our wagon, grabbed her shawl, and covered our eyes. But I had already seen the dead people. There were two children and a woman. The whole wagon had turned over, and everything they had fell onto these poor people.

People from other wagons came over and lifted and disconnected the horse. They buried the people who died right there. Years later, my mother told Sarah that the people who were killed were from a very religious family. She wondered how it was that this little family had perished, while we Gortlers escaped with just a few scratches.

We were a few days and nights in this wagon, until we reached a railroad depot where the Russians put us onto railroad cars. *Wagonnen,* we called them, Yiddish for wagons. We sat in those for a few days until a locomotive came and started moving us east, to Siberia.

In 2017, while my grandson Yosef was reading through archives at the US Holocaust Memorial Museum in Washington DC, he found a document that verified the following information: on July 25, 1940, we were assigned to go to a Siberian village, Matveyevka, with amnesty—meaning permission to stay there—until September 6, 1941.

A NARROW ESCAPE

How fortunate we were to leave Rava-Ruska when we did. According to historical documents,[23] not long after the date of our departure from Rava-Ruska, the Germans reoccupied that town. The Jewish inhabitants were forced to dig trenches, and all the Jews were massacred. They were shot. Those that were still alive were told to shovel dirt over the corpses of their neighbors, friends and relatives. Then they themselves were shot.

Near Rava-Ruska, the Belzec extermination camp began operations in March of 1942. By December of that year, the crowded conditions in the Rava-Ruska ghetto had led to the spread of typhus. But Jews who managed to survive the disease died anyway: they were labeled as "sickly," and murdered. Between December 7th and December 11th, during a four-day Nazi "*Aktion*"[24] in Rava-Ruska, 6,000 to 7,000 Jews were either shipped by train to their deaths in Belzec, or murdered in their beds.[25]

By that time, my family and I were long gone. We had been transported by train, in cattle cars, deep into Siberia. Imagine if we had not been sent to Matveyevka.

---

23   http://www.holocaustresearchproject.org/ghettos/rawaruska.html
24   Targeted murders officially sanctioned as euthanasia by Nazi Germany
25   *op.cit.*

CHAPTER 4
SIBERIA
Summer 1940 – Spring 1942

In Siberia, we refugees spoke Yiddish among ourselves, and Russian with the guards and their people.

The adult men were forced to work as lumberjacks, even though most of them had no such experience. Many Jews lost their lives because of falling trees, including my uncle Eliezer, who was somewhere else in Siberia. Many more of these so-called lumberjacks were injured and maimed by falling trees. Fortunately, my father had some knowledge of falling trees, thanks to his work in the lumber business. As he told me later, he escaped these dangers many times.

There were no sanitation facilities. When people had to relieve themselves, they had to do so in the open, behind a tree. Food was very scarce. Again, we ate boiled potatoes and a piece of dark bread when we could get it. This was the main source of nutrition.

The open fire in the hut was also used to melt snow and ice, which became our drinking water. Disease was very common: diphtheria, tuberculosis, and of course malnutrition. Many people, including my father, became temporarily blind, and had to be led around by others. They were like the walking dead. It turned out that this was because we were exposed to very little vitamin D. The older boys would trap wild birds, kill them, extract the livers from the birds, and feed the livers to people, which helped restore their eyesight. How did they know this would work? I have no idea.

The winter temperatures in Siberia would drop to outrageous lows. Temperatures reached as low as minus 24 degrees Fahrenheit in the winter. According to some reports, temperatures in Siberia have been recorded as low as minus 60 degrees (as I found out later, thanks to research for my presentations at the Holocaust Center for Humanity). The extreme cold of Siberia left many people with frozen fingers and toes, which had to be amputated. I saw people with no thumbs, and no fingers.

Years later, while I was watching the movie *Dr. Zhivago,* I felt that bone-chilling cold again, as the wagons on the movie screen traveled across the same terrible snow.

Under the law in the Soviet Union, any kind of religious practices were prohibited. As a result, Jewish boys who were born in Siberia during that period were not circumcised. Prayer was prohibited. I remember seeing Jewish men huddle in clandestine groups, with the prayers led by one person who knew them by memory. They had no prayer books, so others would repeat after him. I saw people on the lookout making sure that the Soviet guards would not see what they were doing.

CHAPTER 5
From Cold to Hot, A Confusing Train Trip: Siberia to Tashkent
Springtime, 1942

When I was about five and a half, late in 1941, the German army—the Nazis—were moving deeper into Soviet Union territory. Unbeknownst to us refugees in Siberia, the Soviets had decided that it was time to move us out. Maybe it was because of the battles between the Soviets and the Germans, or perhaps it was because the Germans were moving into Soviet territory at such a fast pace.

Sometime in the spring of 1942, when the cold was getting less harsh, Soviet army trucks arrived at Matveyevka with Russian-speaking soldiers in them. They piled us into the trucks and moved us away from the huts where we had found shelter. They drove us to the closest railroad junction, where we were piled into what we called *wagonnim*, the railroad cattle cars. There was some straw on the floor, but no seats. No hygienic accommodations. No heat. There were no provisions for food. In the middle of the *waggon*, there was an open metal potbelly stove. We sat for several days at the junction, not moving. Ours was one of about half a dozen *waggonnim*.

Out of nowhere, a black locomotive showed up, and the wagons started to move! The progress was very slow; some people were actually out in the fields, collecting wood and whatever they could find to eat, mostly potatoes or turnips. Someone actually found a few loaves of black bread. They must have either stolen it from the peasants or traded it for the few valuables we had left.

As the wagons started to move, the people in the fields started running back to the wagons. People inside put out their hands to catch these individuals. As the wagons moved faster, there was a chain of people putting out their hands, as adults inside the wagon held them in place to keep these people from falling out. Not everyone ended up in their original wagon. They climbed into any wagon they could get on. Some people were left behind. Families were broken up. That didn't happen to anybody in my wagon that I remember.

My father was one of those people in the field at the time. I still remember the fear I had that he might not make it back into the wagon. *Hashgacha pratis*—it was God's intervention— that he made it back into the same wagon we were in. He even carried some food. He was an amazing person to provide us with food to sustain us throughout the journey.

As the train picked up speed, I noticed the ground was covered with white snow. I could hear the sound of the locomotive, and I could see the black smoke coming out of the chimney. Looking through the peepholes of the wagon, I could see the path created by the moving locomotive, with snow piling up on each side of the tracks. When we watched *Dr. Zhivago*, and that scene with the train going across the snow came on, I actually exclaimed to Sarah, "This was what it was like!"

After a few days of traveling, the train stopped again. The locomotive left, and there we were, abandoned on the tracks in our wagons, in the middle of nowhere, waiting for another locomotive. The able-bodied men jumped out of the wagons and into the fields. They dispersed to look for food, water, and whatever else they could bring in.

Peasants in the fields noticed the train. Some actually helped bring something to us. Others turned their backs and said ivrieskies," Jews," in a derogatory tone. There was another term that was more derogatory: *parkhaty ivreiskies*, "disgusting Jews."

After a few days of idle sitting, a black locomotive that had other wagons attached to it would come and schlep our wagons to another destination. This happened three or four times. After about a month of this back and forth, we arrived outside of Tashkent, in Uzbekistan.

We sat at the freight train depot for several more days, before broken-down trucks showed up. We were loaded onto those trucks, and after several hours on the road, we arrived in a kolkhoz.

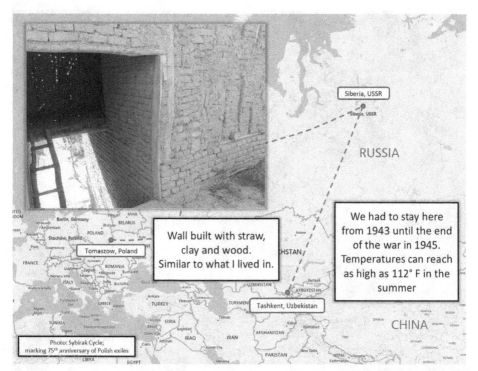

Map with Kolkhoz Hut. *Courtesy of the Holocaust Center for Humanity, Seattle.*

Kolkhoz is a communal village, like a kibbutz.[26] But it wasn't a village of Jews. We had come from Siberia to the Muslims. The whole kolkhoz was Muslims, Uzbek Muslims. I remember these women covering their faces completely. The men wore what looked to me like big yarmulkes. This experience felt very strange to me.

Soviet soldiers and some militia—police, and other uniformed men of some kind —had met us at the station and loaded us onto wagons to bring us to the kolkhoz. Now they moved us into primitive straw huts. They put two or three families in each hut.

The temperature was extremely hot compared to the freezing temperatures in Siberia. We had traveled from the springtime in Siberia to the summertime in Tashkent.

---

26   Israeli communal farm

A ceramic bowl, about the size of a cereal bowl, that my parents obtained in the kolkhoz around 1943. They carried this bowl back to Poland, to Germany, to three DP camps, across the Atlantic Ocean on a boat to New Orleans, and a train ride to Phoenix. It is now in my possession in Seattle. 2019. *Photo by Luci Varon*.

CHAPTER 6
In The Kolkhoz
1942-44

At this time, I was still a little boy, so what I remember from this period is from the point of view of a child between six and eight years old. We were refugees in the kolkhoz, outside of Tashkent. People let us in to their community, sort of. We lived in very primitive housing.

Kolkhoz, I later learned, is a compound word in Russian, meaning collective ownership. These collective farms were creations of the Soviet Union, starting around the time of the 1917 Revolution. They were to replace the labor arrangements where the serfs were beholden to aristocratic landlords, and indeed, to replace the economy of private property itself.

The Muslims who lived there were very kind to us. I would go out to the fields, where shepherds were milking their goats, carrying a little bowl. I kept that little bowl. It was given to us when we arrived at the *kolkhoz.* I still have it today.

I remember one shepherd who saw me. I must have been this pitiful, sickly-looking, dejected child, carrying my little bowl. He motioned for me to come over. I watched the way his fingers moved, milking the goat. He filled my bowl with milk straight from the udders. The milk was warm, and I took a sip right then and there. The rest I brought back to my family, so everyone else could have a taste, too.

I was so different from that shepherd, so unconnected to his world. And yet he took pity on me. To this day I remember the kindness he bestowed on me.

The kolhoz was just outside of Tashkent. In that city, there was a long-established Jewish community. Looking back on that time, I'm surprised, and, frankly, angry to realize that there was no interaction between us Jewish refugees and that community. Despite the fact that our Jewish tradition teaches us to welcome the stranger, and to extend our hand to those in need, I saw no such *chesed*—kindness—extended to us from our fellow Jews. Compare this treatment to what the American Jewish community does for its refugees now! In fact, compare it to the treatment my family and I received when we arrived in America. Between the Jewish communal professionals and the generous Jewish volunteers, we were welcomed and escorted every step of the way. I must say, I was disillusioned by the experience, or rather, lack of any kind of experience, with the Jews of Tashkent.

FOOD

My father, *alav hashalom*[27], would always gravitate towards where food would be available. For example, in the kolkhoz, my father worked in the bakery. He was able to sneak bread out.

It was a bread like pita. They would throw it onto the hot bricks, where it would attach to the sides of the oven, and when it was done, it would fall down. They would bake the bread on the hot bricks.

A river ran straight through the kolkhoz, dividing the village in two. We lived on one side of the river. The bakery was on the other side. The river was used for everything. We bathed in the river. We washed the few clothes we had in the river. We drank from the river. The river was everything. It was our lifeline.

CLOTHING, SHELTER, AND THE VALUE OF A SCISSOR

We had a little hut made out of mud. All four of us lived in this mud hut. We slept on straw that we had to collect. As for going to the bathroom, there were no toilets. We would go outside. When we were lucky, a couple of newspapers would end up in the kolkhoz, and we would take pieces of that and use it as toilet paper. But most of the time we would use either a leaf or a stone to clean ourselves.

My mother's skills as a seamstress, making dresses and shirts, were

---

27   Hebrew for "peace on him"

put to good use. The only tool she carried with her were scissors. Those scissors were part of her well-being, in a way.

Once, in a hut near our own, there was a lot of noise, and they tried to keep the kids away from the commotion. They called on my mother to come, and so she grabbed those scissors and ran to the other place. As kids, we were curious. So we looked in, and saw the birth of a child. My mother was using her scissors to cut the umbilical cord. At the time, I had no idea what an umbilical cord was. They needed to cut it. These very "sanitary" scissors, used for cutting clothes, carried through Siberia; they were the instrument used to help the births in the kolkhoz. My mother: the lady with the scissors.

In the kolkhoz, we were afflicted with many diseases. Diphtheria and tuberculosis were very common. However, the most memorable disease with which I was afflicted, which even today I have residual issues with, is malaria. Malaria was also very common in the kolkhoz. At the onset of the disease, you become extremely cold; no matter how many blankets and covers are placed on you, you shiver uncontrollably. Hours later, your body temperature reaches a hundred and three degrees or higher, which is when you begin to have convulsions. Sometimes, the entire family was sick at once, and no one was available to help us.

Malaria was treated with quinine. I had to line up in a straight row with other children, waiting for a nurse with a very large syringe. In my eyes, this needle looked to be a foot long. She would stick the needle into the buttocks, from one child to the next, without even wiping it down. It is a miracle that none of us were infected with anything worse. Actually, I don't really know if that was the case.

Years later, when I was at Yeshiva University, there was a blood drive. Of course, all the YU guys were eager to participate in this lifesaving event. I, too, tried to participate. They took a sample of my blood, but they quickly informed me that I was not eligible, because there was lingering residual evidence of malaria in my blood.

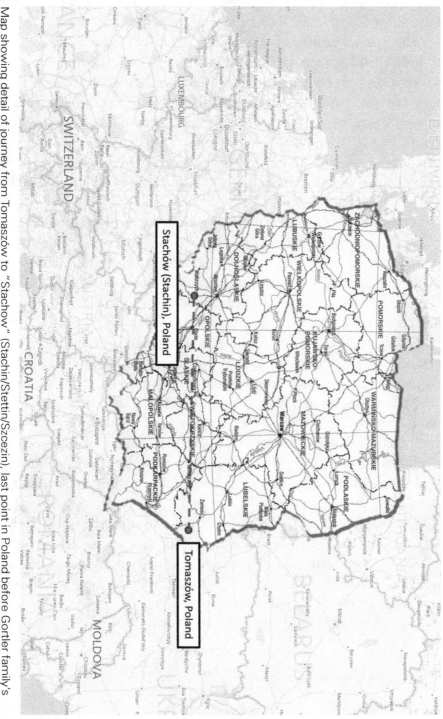

Map showing detail of journey from Tomaszów to "Stachow" (Stachin/Stettin/Szcezin), last point in Poland before Gortler family's illegal crossing into postwar Germany. *from Joshua Gortler's presentations, courtesy of the Holocaust Center for Humanity, Seattle.*

Stachów (Stachin), Poland

Tomaszów, Poland

CHAPTER 7

Uzbekistan to Tomaszów:
Going "Home"
MAY 1945

In May of 1945, the news of the defeat of Germany finally reached the kolkhoz. Perhaps someone from the Muslim community there was able to obtain a newspaper from Tashkent and bring the news to the village. The war was over. The Germans had surrendered.

The local authorities gave the refugees a choice: we could remain in the kolkhoz or return to our place of origin. For us, there was no question. We were going home. Home, to Tomaszów Lubelski in Poland.

GO HOME?

We loaded up the few belongings we had. We were able to get a peasant with a wagon to take us from the kolkhoz to Tashkent. There, we would board a train going to Poland. With all the chaos after the war, nobody had us purchase tickets to get onto any passenger train. The mode of transportation was similar to what had brought us to the kolkhoz: Cattle cars, or wagons.

Just as before, we had no idea how long this journey would take or where this part of the journey would end. But we knew that our goal was Tomaszów. *Mein shtetele*[28] *Tomaszów*.

We sat on the floor of this cattle car for a few days, not moving. We were

---

28 "My little town" Affectionate and nostalgic, the phrase *mein shtetele* invokes the title of a heartrending Jewish song of longing for another lost *shtetl*, Belz.

able to get several days' food supplies from the local people in Tashkent. We had no idea how long the wait would be before we would move.

A black locomotive finally attached to the cars, and our wagon was at last part of a long train going somewhere. We were on our way out of Tashkent.

After a few days of traveling, the wagons with the refugees were detached from the transport and moved to the side of the main rail depot. The waiting began again. Where we were, no one knew.

We needed water but no one offered us any. There was a huge pump that brought water to the locomotives. We would take some of the containers that we had, and the adults would go towards the pumps and fill up buckets of water and bring them into the wagon for drinking. I know that we didn't get sick from this dirty water, and I have no idea why. It was the unpurified water that was used to pump into the locomotives to create steam. That was our drinking water.

Days would go by. Another locomotive would show up, move the wagons from the side track onto the main line, and attach them to another freight train that was going…somewhere. West? North? South? We had no idea.

Sometimes, after traveling for a day or two, we would come back to the same place where we had started. We could recognize the scenery! I don't think the people in charge of moving the refugees had any idea where they were going, either.

Finally, after several weeks of this, in the heat of summer, the train arrived in Poland. I don't remember any border crossing experience. If there was one, we certainly didn't go through any security. We ended up in a freight train depot.

Now that we were in Poland, we were able to board a real train to Lublin, which was the closest train station to Tomaszów. People were getting into trucks, buggies, wagons, whatever was there, to make their way to their shtetl of origin.

We traveled in the back of a truck from Lublin to Tomaszów, a trip of some 80 miles. It took us almost a full day, as all the roads had been destroyed by the German Luftwaffe. Of course, we were hoping that our neighbors would welcome us with open arms, would open the doors for us.

THIS DID NOT HAPPEN.

Of course, we had thought of Tomaszów as home. Where else? We tried going back to our house. But our house had strangers living in it, and they weren't about to give it back to us. The neighbors didn't want us back. What are you doing here? That was their attitude. There was a lot of anti-Semitism from people who my parents had thought were their friends. There was a complete changeover in attitude towards Jews, even from people who knew us, after the war. They were the same old neighbors, but now they were so different.

It was obvious that the *polaks* resented these Jews who were still alive (*parszywsky zhid*, I heard them say in Polish, words that meant "disgusting Jews," like the insults we had heard shouted at us in Russian on that strange train ride from Siberia to Tashkent). These citizens of our hometown had already claimed the Jews' homes and their businesses for themselves. They were happy with their new Polish way of life, which is to say, a life without Jews.

Among the refugees, conflict and friction took hold, especially between the Jews and the non-Jews. You should understand that a lot of the non-Jews found homes very quickly, because they were able to go back to their country of origin. But Jews did not seem to have any country of origin.

We had been at home in Poland, or so we thought. Our country had been attacked, and its people had fought back. But the war had unleashed old hostilities. Now we were the objects of that hostility. Jews were not wanted back in Poland.

WE HAD BEEN REPLACED.

My parents knew that we would have to find a new home. We would become refugees, "displaced persons." We stayed temporarily somewhere in Tomaszów, but not in our old house, that's for sure.

My father and a number of his old business associates were able to convince the Tomaszów and Krasnobrod municipalities that they should restart a lumber business in that area. They obtained a loan. But they used the money instead to move, secretly, out of the area, into Stettin (Szcezin).

Sometime in June of 1945, we arrived in Stettin. We had no documents. My parents had managed to convert those *zlotys* [29]from the business

---

29 Polish currency

Entrance to the Jewish cemetery at Tomaszów.

Dog at Cemetery, Tomashóv.

Inside Jewish cemetery, Tomaszów.

Left: To the Jews of Tomashóv, 1623-1943" "Yehudei Tomaszów" [in Hebrew] Sculpture at Jewish cemetery Tomaszów.

All photoscourtesy of Moshe Blockman, grandson of Joshua Gortler. Photographed on his visit to Poland, ca. 2012-13.

loan into American currency, which was then used for bribes. They knew that the dollar would be accepted anywhere on the black market.

They purchased a truck. They hired a driver. In the dark of night, they loaded a few families into the truck, and bribed the guards on both sides of the border. In the heat of summer, we kids were hidden under blankets.

THE GOAL WAS TO GO WEST. TO BERLIN.

Berlin at that time was divided into four zones, each occupied by one of the Allied countries who had defeated the Nazi regime: the Russian, British, French, and American zones.

Our goal was to reach the American zone.

We crossed the Polish border into the Russian zone.

My parents paid off the Polish guards.

We crossed the Russian zone by bribing the Russians. We crossed the French zone by bribing the French guards, and then the British guards. We finally reached our goal: the American zone in Berlin.

We were now officially "DP's": Displaced Persons. The official designation would entitle us to housing, food, clothing, and education. We would begin our lives anew.

For the next five years—until I was 15—we would be living in DP camps. Like any adolescent boy, my experiences between the ages of 9 and 15 shaped me. I can't emphasize enough how important the DP camps were for me. I became who I am in the DP camps.

PART TWO

A DISPLACED PERSON IN CAMPS

Föhrenwald. Originally built for slave
laborers. In the center of the photo, the
Bamidbar Theater. This is where the
Gortler family lived from 1949-1951.

Right: Street view, Föhrenwald.

*Courtesy of the Holocaust Center for
Humanity, Seattle.*

CHAPTER 8
DISPLACED
1945

It's easy to forget that the organization known as the United Nations didn't even exist until 1945. The United States President, Franklin D. Roosevelt, coined the term "United Nations" in a 1942 speech declaring unity among the countries known as the "Allied Powers," which worked together to defeat Hitler's Germany and the countries that supported it, known as the "Axis Powers."

In May of 1945, one month after America and its allies declared victory in Europe, the official UN charter was signed by 50 countries.

That charter wasn't even ratified until October of 1945.[30] But meanwhile, there was a great deal of work to do. Some 11 million people had been displaced by the war.

Four of these 11 million displaced persons were my parents, my eleven-year-old brother, and me, a nine-year-old kid.

The Allies—the United States, England, France and the Soviet Union (Russia)— assigned the care of these Displaced Persons to the new United Nations Relief and Rehabilitation Agency (UNRRA), but it was the Allied military forces themselves that got the work started. They improvised Displaced Persons camps, "DP camps," whenever and wherever they could. These camps provided shelter, food, clothing, education, health care, and a sense of community for people who had been torn away from

---

30   https://www.un.org/en/sections/history/history-united-nations/

their homes, their loved ones, and even their nationalities, as a result of the war.

By the end of 1945, there were hundreds of DP camps. Most were set up in Germany and Austria, but there were DP camps in Italy and other European countries, and even one in Mexico.[31]

We lived in three different DP camps, all in Germany, between June of 1945 and June of 1951: Schlachtensee, near Berlin, 1945-1947; Ludendorff Kaserne, near Neu Ulm, 1947-1949; and Föhrenwald, near Munich, 1949-1951. During these six years bridging my late childhood and early adolescence, I learned everything from how to eat with a fork, to how to read and write, to how to celebrate my family's traditional holidays.

After each war, there are displaced people. In most instances, after the war is over, and some semblance of peace occurs, the refugees, or displaced people, find themselves back in their country of origin.

In most instances.

The Jews, however, who found themselves in the DP camps after the Second World War, were people who nobody wanted. Poles hated the Jews. Czechoslovakians hated the Jews. Romanians hated the Jews. Austrians hated the Jews. No matter what country these Jews had come from, there was no way back.

Strangely, Germany was probably the most hospitable of all after the war. The German government accepted responsibility for what had happened. Jews who remained in Germany after the DP camps closed made new homes there. In recent years, there's been a revival of Jewish life in Germany. Some of today's German Jews are the children and grandchildren of the DPs, who have helped reestablish a community.

Right at the end of the war, from 1945 to 1947, Jews like us found ourselves in a precarious situation, asking, where will we go? It wasn't the first time Jews asked that question. I think of the song "Vu Ahin" ("Where can I go?"). It was written right before World War II. Ironically, the man who wrote the words to that song was murdered in a Nazi concentration camp.[32]

---

31 https://www.yadvashem.org/articles/general/displaced-persons-camps.html
32 http://holocaustmusic.ort.org/music/yiddish-tango/

CHAPTER 9
My DP Camp Years Begin
Berlin, Germany (Schlachtensee)
1945-1947

We arrived, undocumented, in Berlin, in June of 1945, after a couple of days pressed together with other families in the back of the truck. My father and his companions had bought that truck and hired a non-Jewish driver, with the promise that if we arrived at the destination we wanted, the truck would be the driver's compensation. This was a driver who had crossed the border before, and knew what was at stake. He knew what to do with our parents' cash.

The cash, in the hand of that driver, bribed border guards to get us out of Poland, into Germany, and finally into the American sector in Berlin. We kids had obeyed our parents' instructions, spending the two-day trip huddled under blankets in the summer heat, to avoid being seen. We traveled back roads, or no roads at all, and we didn't travel at all during the day. We drove only at night, to avoid detection.

My brother was eleven. I had just turned nine.

At last we could emerge. Under the midday sun, our truck rumbled into a camp called Schlachtensee. More people on trucks were coming in, too, from other areas, and other countries. When we climbed down, everybody had to first stand in a long line. All the Gortlers had with us was one wooden suitcase, tied together with ropes. Inside, just a handful of clothes, and the bowl we had schlepped from Tashkent.

We were assigned a room in a three-story building that had once been German soldiers' barracks. Each floor had a long hallway. One room, empty except for four green American army cots, was assigned to my parents and my brother Monyik[33] and me. It's amazing that we were not only still alive, but still together.

Everybody received an itchy green wool army blanket. There were no sheets. We also received a metal container—it might have been something that the American armed forces were eating from—and one utensil: a spoon, fork and knife all in one. I kept that metal container for a long time. My mother even schlepped it to America.

You'd think the first thing we would want were showers. But we probably had showers once a month. I think Americans have a real obsession—and I'm part of it, because I'm also an American—with needing a shower, needing to be clean. We really did smell! We wore the same clothes. We were also infested with lice all over, body and clothes.

Before we were even allowed to go to our rooms, we were disinfected. We were put into a big room, with people under the supervision of the American army. Men and women had to go to different places. We lowered our pants, and this guy pumped white powder all over us. They had a pump-like machine that spewed some white stuff. It smelled terrible. But it disinfected us—it killed the lice.

THIS ISN'T FOR DRINKING?

The first time I ever saw a urinal was when I came to Berlin. It was a long trough. All of us kids started to drink the water from it!

What did we know? We were accustomed to drinking water from a river. We would just put our face in the river water, and we would drink. Or we would cup our hands and pick it up: *SLURRRPPP.*

When we were on the run, we had no utensils, and we had no running water. When we were in Siberia, we would kneel down by the river, and drink with our hands. We would lap it up.

So, when I came to the first DP camp, in Berlin, and saw the urinal, I put my face into the water. Not even just my hands! My whole face! And I drank. Everybody did! Then we realized, Oh my gosh! This is where people empty out their bladder!

The men among us, my father and the others, they might have had running water before the war, so they knew what to do with it. But the kids? Not in Rava-Ruska, or Siberia, or Tashkent, and certainly not on

---

33   Polish version of "Moshe"

those long train rides. We had never seen running water. Water came from melting snow and ice, and from rivers, that's what I knew.

THIS IS HOW WE EAT?

Here I am, at nine years old, never before exposed to using eating utensils. I didn't know how to use a knife or a fork or a spoon. Well, spoons, yes, we had wooden spoons in Siberia, where we ate soup. But a knife? We never had anything that we needed to cut. You had a potato, you'd take it with your hands and you'd eat it. A fork was totally foreign to me. I had no idea how to use it. Right hand? Left hand? How do you cut? When we were on the run, an adult might have had a knife, but there was one knife for everybody. Someone would cut up the food, whatever we had.

The food in the Berlin DP camp was communal food. We didn't have our own kitchen. We didn't receive rations. We all went to a dining hall together. You took the dish that you received on arrival, you stood in line to fill up this container that had compartments in it, then sat down and ate.

It was not a kosher setup, that's for sure. That was one of the complaints: we didn't eat non-kosher meat. The people in charge said, okay, if you don't eat it, then don't eat it. This is what we have. The people who prepared the food were DP residents. The food came in from UNRRA, the UN refugee agency.

GUARDS

The Berlin DP camp was guarded by former Nazi police! State police! Right away, that was seen as a problem. The result was something like a revolt in the camp.

My family, we had escaped, and had been on the run, but think of how it felt for the people who had been in the concentration camps. We spoke to people who had survived in Dachau, and other concentration camps. When they saw the German police with the uniforms, there was an absolute uproar.

Then the Americans came in. The American MPs took over guarding the camp. They wore the American uniform, with very, very shiny helmets, almost like a mirror. We kids were impressed. They had the letters MP on their arms. That meant "military police," but we didn't know that.

We Jews had nicknames for everything, and MP was "Moishe Pisher." When we talked about the MPs, "Oh, there's *Moishe Pisher* coming." To

Map of journey to Berlin, with four photos overlaid. *Courtesy of the Holocaust Center for Humanity, Seattle.*

Photo insets (from lower left): Lower left: My father Josef Gortler (right) with my mother's brother, Chaim Balsenbaum, an actor, DP camp. Upper left: children and women outside a window, DP camp. Upper right: My brother Monyik's secular studies class, DP camp (Monyik is seated, second row, third from left, looking at camera) Lower right: Me (far left) with yeshiva classmates and teacher, DP camp. *Courtesy Joshua Gortler collection*

pish, in Yiddish, means to pee. *Moishe* was just a really common name to us, like Joe. So, this was definitely little boy humor! Joe the pisher. Or we would say "MP" was "*Moishe Parakh.*" *Parakh* is a Yiddish word meaning something like "boils," some skin disease. Basically, these were names that meant, "These are not our favorite people."

They weren't Nazi guards, but any kind of uniformed guards were a source of continued pain and anxiety for people who had survived being ordered around by a hostile military. For people who had been incarcerated, or worse, these uniformed soldiers must have felt more intimidating than comforting.

CHAPTER 10
My Home: Three Camps
June 1945 – June 1951

Berlin, Germany (Schlachtensee) Arrived, *undocumented, June 1945*
Neu Ulm, Germany (Ludendorff Kaserne), *September 1947-August 1949*
Munich, Bavaria, Germany (Föhrenwald), *September 1949-June 1951*

We spent nearly two years in Berlin. I don't remember much of those years at all. But I do remember the end of those two years. We were taken by American army trucks to a train station and sent on to a new camp, Ludendorff Kaserne, in Neu Ulm, Germany. Our truck driver was a black American soldier. This was the first time I had ever seen a person of that color. I was eleven.

Berlin was a transit camp. There was no going out of the camp, no trading with the locals. There were no kids I could really associate with. I couldn't tell you the names of kids from Berlin. One good thing that did happen in Berlin was that Monyik and I were able sit on a real motorcycle. Actually, it's only because someone, maybe a soldier, snapped a picture of us that I know we even sat on that cycle. We never actually rode the thing.

It was in Neu Ulm that my formal schooling really began. I remember a bunch of names from that time, especially one family: Pesach, Rivka, and Ephraim Nadler. Rivka and my brother Monyik were a pair. Pesach was my age, and he was my best friend. Ephraim was a little younger than us. They later immigrated to Palestine from the DP camp.

In Neu Ulm, my life began to resemble a more normal boyhood: I banged up my knees playing soccer with a can. I got sick and went to the infirmary. I fell down and broke my nose. I got to be the one who went to the bakery with the cholent, the special stew warmed overnight for Sabbath lunch.

The Berlin camp didn't leave much of an impression on me. As far as I know, very little happened there, very little schooling, just a little Torah learning. I don't remember any secular classrooms, but I do remember that Berlin was the place where I took the first step toward my future as a literate person.

LEARNING TO READ AND WRITE MY OWN NAME

When we first got to Berlin, I did not know how to read in any language. I had seen letters—Russian letters on signs in the kolkhoz and in Siberia, Hebrew letters on the pages of a siddur my father used—but no one had ever shown me what to do with them, or even what my own name looked like spelled out on a page.

At the DP camp in Berlin, that was the first lesson I received. I don't remember who gave me that lesson. I think I was part of a group.

Before we were even taught the whole alphabet, we were taught to recognize our names in both Roman letters and Hebrew letters. There would be ID cards and other documents with our names on them, so we needed to know this right away.

They first trained our eyes to recognize the printed letters of our names.

But how was my name spelled? Szia? Shiia? Szja? Transliterating from Yiddish meant it was spelled in multiple ways, which presented a problem to me. I had to learn to recognize them all.

After that, they trained our fingers to write our names ourselves. Then, they began to teach us the alphabets, and the reading and writing skills that the letters made possible.

I had an explosion of education. I was ten years old when the light bulbs went off in my mind. I suddenly realized I could put together the letters on a page to make a word. I learned that putting words together is reading. Suddenly, I could not only count with my fingers but I could also write numbers on a page, and I learned that this was arithmetic.

By 1949, when I turned thirteen and became a *bar mitzvah*, I had learned to read and write, but only the bare minimum. By that time, I had learned how to *daven*, and how to read Hebrew. I knew a little bit of Israeli geography. I had a very minimum understanding of science and arithmetic.

CHAPTER 11
She'arit Ha'pleita[34]:
The Surviving Remnant Goes to School
1945-1951

EDUCATION IN THE DP CAMPS

There were two distinct educational systems in the camps. One was religious, and one was secular.

For us boys, the religious education was based on the old East European model, the *cheder*,[35] or *Talmud Torah*,[36] where the teachers, all men, were referred to as *melamed (literally, "teacher")*, or *rebbi*.[37] The language of the classroom was Yiddish. These teachers would be older men, with yeshiva[38] backgrounds. The *melamed* ran the younger children through the classic language drills, starting with the letters of the Hebrew alphabet and adding their vowel sounds. In a singsong voice, they would repeat the pattern: vowel, consonant, "sound." *Kometz alef "aw." Kometz beis "baw."*

The rebbi taught the older boys Chumash, Mishna, and eventually Gemara.

In the religious school, boys were required to wear a head covering in class. The secular school, on the other hand, discouraged the wearing of any head covering in class.

---

34 Hebrew. "surviving remnant" (Sephardic pronunciation), a Biblical phrase
35 Yiddish, from "room" in Hebrew. Pronounced khey'd'r. A one-room school.
36 Literally, "teaching Torah," Hebrew
37 Affectionate version of rabbi, meaning teacher
38 Rabbinical school

The secular education was based on the *Tarbut* (cultural) model developed by the pioneers of the rebirth of Hebrew as a modern spoken language in the land of Israel. The teachers were called, in Hebrew, *moreh* (male) or *morah* (female). The language of the classroom was Modern Hebrew (*Ivrit*). The subjects were science, math, geography, especially the geography of the land of Israel, and history. The Tarbut classes were coed.

The Tarbut school was where we were taught to recognize and write our names using the Roman alphabet.

The main emphasis of DP camp education was this Tarbut approach. Hebrew became sort of the binding language, because you had kids who came into the camp speaking many different languages: Hungarian, Russian, Polish, other Slavic languages, German, Yiddish. With a shared language, we could begin to learn to communicate with one another.

Some children attended only one kind of school. But our parents insisted on enrolling us in both.

ZIONISM IN OUR CAMP SCHOOLS

In the DP camp secular schools, our teachers came to us from the growing Jewish communities in Palestine, where they spoke Modern Hebrew. Most of these teachers were secular Jews, meaning they were not religiously observant. They taught the Hebrew language, and the Hebrew Biblical books of the Pentateuch, Prophets, and Writings (*Tanach*) as simply the history of our people.

There were also teachers among the European survivors who had taught, prior to the war, in a similar way, in the Tarbut School systems in Europe. These teachers imparted the same philosophy: Jewish texts as a people's history.

Only a few decades earlier, Hebrew had been mostly an academic language, like ancient Greek or Latin. But Hebrew had been resurrected as a modern language as part of the Zionist movement, one of many national liberation movements born in the late 19th century.

For many of these Jewish national liberation activists, religion was considered an antiquated limitation on human freedom. The worldview of these early Zionist pioneers (*chalutzim*), born and raised in Russia, was inspired by the Marxist and Communist philosophies that were prevalent at that time. Speaking Hebrew was an expression of affiliating with a Jewish national movement.

Using the language was part of the physical renewal of the Jew as a complete person. How could this body be renewed? How could it exchange the pale look of a man of the study hall for the tanned, muscular body of a farmer? This was how we were to go about building the identity of what we understood as the new Jew.

Yes, we were living in historic times. We were made to understand that it was not just each of us, but the Jewish people as a whole, that had survived.

WE USED OUR EDUCATION TO MOVE ON

In our classes we never said, "We don't need this education." We were all hungry for learning.

As for my group of friends from that time, I didn't maintain contact with most of the boys. It was a new life when I came to the United States. My new connections would be the Yeshiva University crowd, my peers in high school, college, grad school, people in my professional world.

The only one of the DP guys that I did keep in contact with for many years, was a fellow named Goldstein. He went into the nursing home business in the Los Angeles area and became an extremely, extremely wealthy person.

The DP camp was just one phase of my life. I talk more about it today, when I do my presentations, than I talked about it during my entire high school, college and grad school career. We were too busy making it in America to dwell on the past. We had nothing in common. Some were religious, some were not religious. We were there for only a short period of time. We were close, and then each one moved on.

THE TWO BOOKS IN MY
DP CAMP LEARNING THAT MEANT THE MOST TO ME

Both of the books that made the biggest impression on me from that time were part of my religious education. One was *Mesillas Yesharim* (The Path of the Upright), by the 18th century Rabbi Moshe Chaim Luzzatto, a book that teaches proper behavior. I thought *Mesillas Yesharim* was the best book I was ever taught. I thought, "That's ethics, that's how a person should behave."

The other book was *Tanya*, by Rabbi Shneur Zalman of Liadi, the first Chabad Rebbe.[39] With a name that's hard to translate—*Tanya* is a

---

39 *Chabad* is an acronym in Hebrew meaning "wisdom, comprehension, knowledge. "*Rebbe*" suggests "spiritual guide." (vs. "Rabbi" suggests "teacher.")

Secular school. Boys and girls together. I am close to the back. An Israeli *shaliach* is the teacher of Zionism. Other teachers, many Israeli, taught math, reading, history, science, geography. Note the shabby condition of the "school building" where I got my first education. Courtesy of the *Joshua Gortler collection.*

Talmudic word meaning "it was taught"—it is a spiritual guide, in the mystical tradition, published in 1797. Tanya is used by the Lubavitch ("Chabad") Hasidim all the time.

Today, I look at all my religious books that I have acquired through the years. They include four sets of Talmud, and two sets of Soncino translations of Tanach and Gemara.

In my retirement, I continue to faithfully attend a weekly Gemara *shiur* (class). In this way, as in so many others, I see that I became who I am in the DP camps.

A FAMILY TRADITION:
MY FATHER'S CREATIVE ARITHMETIC SOLUTION

Elementary math was very challenging for me. I had a very difficult time memorizing the multiplication tables. My father taught me the multiplication table on my fingers. If you knew how to multiply up to five, from five on I used my fingers for multiplication.

The "Gortler method" lives on in Memphis, where my grandchildren have learned it.

I can still do multiplication on my fingers, like my father taught me. I hold my hands under the table. Of course, now I use my calculator. For a person like myself—I work with budgets, large numbers—the calculator, even the adding machine, is a tremendous asset.

In my life, I have earned a master's degree. I've been awarded an honorary doctorate. I've had a successful professional career, and executive positions. But the basics, I have had difficulty with, because during my most formative years, I had no formal basic education

READING

Reading was also difficult, of course. In a normal life, we take an infant and we begin to read to them, and they begin to learn words. But for me, from ages three on, there was no such "normal life." There were certainly no children's books anywhere near me. We were on the run. There were *siddurim*,[40] but I had no idea how to read them. I saw Russian books, but it looked like Greek to me. I have never learned how to read Russian or Polish.

BOOK LEARNING

I was learning the Hebrew alphabet and the Latin alphabet at the same time. I was learning that one language goes from right to left, and the other goes from left to right. Now, which is what? I'm ten, eleven, twelve years old, and I'm supposed to know both of those. I am totally confused.

There was so much stuff going on all at once, and it's like my brain cells were fighting with each other.

STREET LEARNING

At the same time, I was learning coping skills. Running out and finding apples. Hustling chickens. Going out to the farms, making deals, selling stuff. Bartering with chocolate and cigarettes. I was smoking; everybody was smoking. In some ways, were like the kids in Mark Twain's *Huckleberry Finn*.

After all we had been through, we were developing *chutzpah*. All these years, I hadn't strayed far from my parents, but now I had a chance to discover what I could do on my own. We kids were finally free to start discovering the world.

---

40   Daily prayer books

We really lived so many lives in the same body. We went to school, and we lived a rebellious life, just surviving by having a little business, stealing stuff, finding out what we could get away with. And oh, we played, too. After all, we were kids.

LEARNING TO PLAY SPORTS IN THE DP CAMP

We learned how to play soccer. It was called football. We had no football. We used a can—there were no balls. The can was our ball.

Finally, we were able to get a real ball into the camp. I had never seen a ball before. Where would I have? With a Russian kid? A Ukrainian kid? I don't remember that. The Russian kids were not going to play with a Jew kid.

YIZKOR: REMEMBERING

Two ideas dominated the education of the children among the remnants in the DP camps. One was Zionism, which was taught and instilled in the classroom, exclusively in the secular education program.

The other idea was to remember what had happened to us. The adults did not want to upset us, but they wanted to make sure that the newer generations would not forget the experience that, from the 1950s on, came to be known as "The Holocaust."[41] In just about every public place in the DP camps—the shuls, the theatre (in <u>Föhrenwald</u> there was a large auditorium), in the schools – there was a memorial. There were no monuments, but there were signs in Hebrew that said "*yizkor*" or "*zachor*" ("remembrance" or "remember"). Those words were actually posted on the signs, with the number six million.

These hand-made signs were far from any professional work. Sometimes you would see a wooden box, with a black piece of cardboard, or a black piece of plywood; inside, the letters were not written, but cut out. Behind the cut-out, there would be a light bulb, which was always on. This wasn't the official Ner Tamid, the ritual light above the holy ark in a synagogue. Anywhere you went in the camp, you saw these signs that read "*yizkor*" or *zachor*, and the number six million.

We didn't dwell on it in the classes; we did not even talk about it, at least that I remember. But in public places, there was always this remembering.

---

41   https://english.stackexchange.com/questions/106031/who-coined-the-term-holocaust-to-refer-to-the-nazi-final-solution-for-the-je

This is a picture of me (second from right) with three other boys in Berlin, 1947.
The older kid is probably sixteen or seventeen. The other kids may be eight or ten,
or eleven like me. We are all in the same class, studying the *alef-beis*. That was the
religious school. This photo was shot by an American soldier. They had cameras, and
they came back and gave these pictures to the kids. They were a very, very big deal,
these pictures. *Courtesy of the Joshua Gortler collection.*

The signs would often include the term *she'arit ha'pleitah*, or *she'aris
ha'pleitah*, a Hebrew phrase which translates as "the surviving remnant."
That phrase comes from the Prophets. When Ezra and Nehemia came back
with the Jewish people from their exile in Babylonia, to rebuild the Holy
Temple, they were the surviving remnant. The theme was remembering,
and not forgetting.

Despite the fact that the adults didn't want to talk about it with the
children, the murder of the six million was in your face. Still, in neither
of the school systems—Tarbut or Yeshiva—did we ever discuss anything
called "The Holocaust."

THERE WERE NO SOCIAL WORKERS FOR THE CHILDREN

We knew we were among people who had been through what we'd
been through, more or less. We DPs identified different levels of suffering
among ourselves. While our family had been on the run before we got to
the DP camp, others had been in Auschwitz and other death camps. We

were considered as the ones who suffered least. We had managed not only to survive but also to stay together.

But even though I may have been one of those who suffered the least, here I was, nine or ten years old, and I didn't even know how to use a fork. I didn't know how to read. I didn't know any arithmetic, not even one plus one.

As a child, it was in your face that you shouldn't forget what you had just been through, but there was no one helping you learn the tools to cope with what had happened to you or your family.

Nevertheless, I saw something that would influence me to make the professional choice that eventually directed my life. I saw social workers. They came in with the Vaad Hatzalah (an American Orthodox Jewish organization working for the spiritual rehabilitation of the survivors), and with the Red Cross, and they tried to restore the broken bones, so to speak, of the spirits of the remnants—the dry bones, to use the metaphor from the Book of Ezekiel. To restore this spirit, and give us some tools for recovery, they worked with the adults.

They did not work with the kids. We children never had the social worker come and say, "Tell me your story, let's talk about your suffering." Never.

Just as I had to acquire essential skills at a relatively late age, people in late life often find themselves unprepared for the challenges they have to face. As a social worker in service to the geriatric community, I have been able to use my experiences to help people and their families, as other people have helped me and mine.

In my professional opinion, it could have been a whole different life for many of us if we had talked about it then. But the wounds and the pain were so great that, anyway, you couldn't talk about it yet. Really, this whole work of remembering "The Holocaust," and writing stories about it, and hearing the testimonies of survivors—that came much, much later. It was the 1960s and 70s by the time people were willing to start talking about it and writing it down.

WHO LIVED IN THESE DP CAMPS?

Each camp was a little village, with a community center, a library, schools, and a clinic staffed by Jewish and German physicians and nurses. There were also emissaries from the Jewish communities in Palestine.

They were there to give to all who wanted to immigrate to our ancestral homeland the language and practical skills they would need to do so, despite the British blockade against such immigration.

Our last camp, Föhrenwald, was all-Jewish. Both Neu Ulm and Föhrenwald felt like little *shtetls*.

But some of the DP camps put together refugees from different backgrounds. The camp in Berlin was definitely a mixture, not a strictly Jewish camp.

When Jews and non-Jews were together, there was a lot of tension. Old hostilities, new jealousies, frayed nerves, undiagnosed PTSD—you name it, it came out as tension among the refugees. Was there antisemitism from fellow refugees? You bet.

The non-Jews were mostly refugees from various countries who had for some reason ended up in Germany. Some were prisoners of war, some were laborers who had been enslaved by the Germans. These were mainly men, unlike the Jewish refugees, who were families with children, or children without families at all.

After the war, the non-Jewish DP camp residents were able to return home to the countries they had come from. Some of them, however, sought to emigrate, and eventually wound up in Canada, the United States, and South America.

We Jews always felt the tension between ourselves and the non-Jews in the DP camps.

GERMAN JEWS, EAST EUROPEAN JEWS, AND OTHER CLASHES

In the book *Our Crowd*,[42] you see in the immigration patterns of the United States something like what we saw in the DP camp. The German Jews didn't want anything to do with the Polish Jews in the United States; in Germany they didn't associate with East European Jews. They considered us to be uneducated. The German Jew was a "sophisticated" person, with music and Western culture, who considered the East European Jews way below them.

In the DP camp, we had a hard time agreeing on most things, with so many different groups of Jews together.

One of the reasons all the schooling was in Hebrew was because we were all talking different languages. One of the reasons for changing from a

---

42 Stephen Birmingham, *Our Crowd*. Harper & Row, 1967.

communal kitchen to distributing food for every person to cook for themselves was because we couldn't agree. How could you agree? The Hungarians wanted goulash and the Romanians wanted *mamaliga*. The Ashkenazi and the Europeans wanted matza balls and gefilte fish. There were so many cultures in the DP camps, it was amazing that we didn't kill anyone among ourselves after the war, because we couldn't agree on anything.

In fact, there were fights, but the fights consisted of verbal attacks on one another. The Polish Jews' manner of speech was mocked as *vooss vooss* ("What? What?"). The Germans were *yekkes*. The Hungarians had a different name. Each group had a way of downgrading the others verbally. There was a lot of verbal fighting, but it was only words.

There were no major crimes that I can recall in the DP camps. Stealing was common, but as for fights, kids always fight amongst themselves, anyway.

I did see some physical fights among the adults in the DP camps. These occurred when survivors from the Nazi death camps (such as Auschwitz or Buchenwald) identified an individual as a former *kapo*.[43] The Jewish DP police force would physically break up these fights. Sometimes they would isolate the *kapo* in the camp's makeshift jail, for his own protection.

WHY THE PHOTOGRPAHER WAS THE
MOST POPULAR PERSON IN THE CAMP

Family pictures had all been lost. People needed to create new family histories, so new pictures were essential.

Maybe the photographer had been a professional photographer before the war. But whether he was a professional or not, he was the most popular person in the camp! He had his own equipment. In each camp, the photographer would set up shop in the square.

Lines and lines of people would wait to take pictures of themselves to send to relatives, saying that they had survived. Pictures were hung up on posters, with messages, to say, "I'm alive, can anybody recognize me, can you connect? I'm from this and this town, and this is what I look like."

The messages would be printed in the camp newspapers and passed by hand from one DP camp to another.

---

43   A Jewish death camp inmate whose job it was to keep the other inmates in line. Kapos frequently treated their fellow prisoners brutally to protect themselves from their Nazi captors.

A CAMPERS' GOVERNMENT

The camp residents established, in a very short time, a very sophisticated and organized system of self-governance. Leadership jobs were created for the DP residents. Elections were held.

There were regional meetings. A "region" might be an area the size of King County, Washington. Most of the DP camps were in Bavaria, so the conferences would take place in Munich.

My father was one of the representatives of Föhrenwald.

Szia and Monyik on Motorcycle, Berlin.
Courtesy of the Joshua Gortler collection.

DP CAMP COMMUNICATIONS: THE PA SYSTEM AND THE RADIO

I first used a library—the *biblioteka*— in Neu Ulm. Each camp had a library, which contained books and magazines in many languages. Most of them were in Yiddish or in Hebrew, in publications from the Jewish communities in British-controlled Palestine.

In the camp library, there would be one radio. This radio was connected to a public-address (PA) system, with loudspeakers throughout the camp.

During the day, music would be played on the radio over the PA system. This was the first time that I actually heard classical music and American jazz. Also on the radio were news programs, with bulletins in German, Hebrew, and Yiddish. These were read by DP camp residents over the PA system.

The shortwave radio picked up stations from all over the world. From Palestine, we would hear news in Hebrew twice a week on *Kol Yisrael La'Golah*[44]. Other news, we would hear on the BBC. The camp announcer would translate from English into Yiddish, and we would hear the English in the background.

---

44 "The Voice of Israel to the Exile" or "to the Outside World" (Hebrew)

Camp announcements on the PA system might be in several languages: Yiddish, Polish, German, Russian, Hebrew. They would announce market days, weddings, the start of Shabbos. Before an announcement, they would say, "*Achtung, achtung.*"[45]

On Friday afternoon, a siren would sound over the PA system when Shabbos, the Jewish Sabbath, was about to start. Usually, the Orthodox residents managed to prevent the playing of music or announcements over the PA system on Shabbos. It was on a Friday afternoon that I first heard the chanting of a *haftorah* (the weekly reading from the Prophets, traditionally read in synagogue on Sabbath morning), coming over the loudspeakers from a broadcast on *Kol Yisrael La'Golah.*

NEWSPAPERS: SEARCHING FOR THE LOST

There was a newspaper in Yiddish in Föhrenwald. In fact, practically every DP camp had a newspaper. In the early days, they were handwritten; later, they were typed and mimeographed.

The newspapers always included a listing of survivors, the remnants of families and communities, looking for one another, trying to reunite. Those lists were also posted, like those posters after 9/11 in New York, so the lists of names were plastered on walls. These were seen everywhere in all the DP camps. Between the posts and the newspapers, that's how people searched for their family. "Do you know Yankel from Krasnobrod? His father was Moshe Beryl...." That kind of information.

The names of the camp newspapers tell us so much. In Föhrnwald it was called "*Bamidbar*"—Hebrew for "In the Desert," or "In the Wilderness" (also the name for the Torah Book translated as "Numbers"). Other newspaper names included "*Noch die Sreifah*"—After the Destruction. "*Unser Hoffnung*"—Our Hope. *Unser Welt*"—Our World. "*Vie die Regeborn*"—From The Reborn.

Newspapers would make the rounds of the camps, carried by hand, by individuals on trucks, motorcycles, trains, and on foot.

It was through the newspaper network that my cousin Yehuda found us in the DP camp, when he came back from the ship *Exodus.*

---

45   "Attention, attention!" (German)

CAMP FOOD: FROM COMMUNAL KITCHEN
TO "HOME COOKING"

At first, all DP camp food was prepared for all of us residents in one communal kitchen. These were the kitchens that had, not long before, been used to prepare food for the Nazi soldiers. The food preparation presented several kinds of problems. That's why the communal kitchen situation did not last for very long.

Before we started getting raw food to cook for ourselves, people would come to the communal kitchen with a little container and carry the food back to their place to eat. The container looked like a kettle, with a handle. Four people's amount of food would fit inside this can, which was maybe half the size of an office wastebasket, about 2 feet square.

Three times a day, we would go get our food. In the morning, we would get a couple of rolls that were baked, and some milk, and a hot beverage. That all fit into the container. The larger meal was at noon. Potato soup was a big item. Some turnips would be in the soup. Meat was unheard of. Sometimes we would get a slice of cheese, or some butter.

Butter? Now that I think of it, it was Crisco. We didn't even know what it was. Butter arrived in the camps much later. Dinner might be some black bread, a piece of cheese, yogurt—yogurt was a big thing. What we really enjoyed was what we called "*shmeteneh*," bread with some sour cream (*shmeteneh*) on top.

There was almost a rebellion over complaints about the taste and the appearance of the food. There was a unanimous decision (very difficult to achieve among Jews, but on this there was no dissent) that the "DP-niks" wanted raw food to be distributed, so they could prepare their own. This distribution of food also solved the problem of *kashrus* (keeping kosher).

Ration cards were printed and distributed to each family. Several times a week the food would be distributed.

This is where my father played a role. His job, called *magaziner*[46], was to organize the food and its distribution. He was one of several men and women in charge of this work.

Most of the food was shipped from the US, from the Department of Agriculture, through the surplus food and commodities program. This is

---

46 Stock room specialist

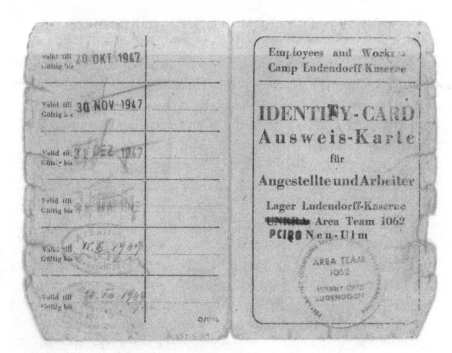

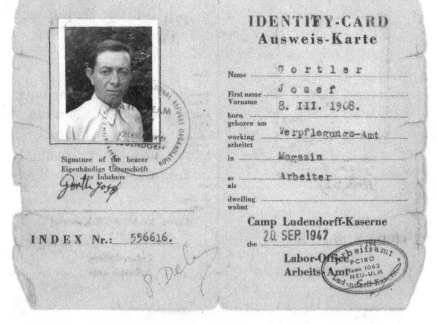

Front and back photos of Yosef Gortler's ID card, which says "Magazin," meaning he worked in the warehouse. *Courtesy of the Joshua Gortler collection.*

how I was first introduced to the wonders of peanut butter, Crisco, and tuna fish in cans.

We had never heard of fish going into a can! How did it get into the can? My mother would take the tuna fish and make gefilte fish; she cooked it with carrots and the sugar we had from our provisions.

THE AMAZING PEANITSCH BUTTER

Peanut butter was something none of the refugees in the DP camp had ever heard of or tasted. But it was very, very handy. I can recall, as though it were yesterday, how we used the peanut butter: we used it in the wintertime to insulate the windows, because it hardened! It was soft and gave the windows a good finish, closing up the holes in the walls so the cold air could not get in.

There's a Yiddish expression: *A yid kin gefinnen an eitza*—a Jew can find a solution. Take peanut butter and use it to insulate the little place where we were living: now that's resourceful.

Did we ever eat it? We tasted it, but it didn't go very far. It was not a taste that we knew or liked. My mother would call it "peanitsch." Peanitsch butter.

For many years, I didn't look at peanut butter as food. When my kids were getting peanut butter and jam sandwiches, Sarah would make me something else. As the years went on, I finally allowed myself to occasionally eat peanut butter on a cracker for an afternoon snack.

THE COMMUNAL OVEN FINDS A HIGHER PURPOSE

It's ironic that that same communal kitchen we had rejected, the one that had served the German Nazi soldiers, turned into a place that served our religious purposes. We used it every week, even after we began to cook for ourselves.

On Friday, all of us who kept kosher would put our cholent pots into that communal oven, to cook overnight so we could have our warm stew for Sabbath lunch. In observance of our tradition's prohibition of cooking on Shabbos, we would arrange for a guy to find wood and heat up this huge, huge oven on Friday. On Shabbos, the guy would use a *lopetteh*, meaning a shovel, the long-handled tray like pizza makers use, to take out the pots. There were ID's to mark whose pot was whose.

SHELTER

We were four people in one room about the size of a tiny office. We would unfold our four cots at night to sleep. During the day, we would fold them up and store them against the wall, so we could walk around. We ate our meals on a table we set up out in the hallway.

CLOTHING

There was a distribution of clothing, because we had very little with us. Most of the clothing we wore was second-hand. The shoes were always second or third hand, hand-me-downs, sent to us refugees in the DP camps.

When we would tear a hole in our pants, someone—probably my mother—would make from a remnant of cloth some kind of a patch, a *latteh*, and sew it on. Sometimes, our clothes consisted of more *lattehs* than the original material. (It's ironic: today, teenagers pay a fortune for torn jeans with holes in the knees!)

I'M A 12-YEAR-OLD WITH A SIZE 5 FOOT, AND A SIZE 10 SHOE

You would get a pair of shoes, and they weren't your size, so you would fill in with *shmattehs* (rags) on the top, to make it smaller, to fit your foot. That way, one pair of shoes could be used for a whole family. For a while, Monyik and I shared one pair of shoes. My father had boots, *shtiefel,* that were not part of the distribution. The *shtiefel* were something like gold on the black market. Since my father had access to the food, he had used some of that to buy the boots.

BOOTS AND KINDNESS

A true act of kindness is connected to those boots. After a long and complicated search, my cousin Yehuda was able to contact us in Föhrenwald. He arrived in the DP camp with no shoes. His feet were covered with *shmattehs*. Without blinking an eye, my father removed his brand-new *shtiefel* that he had purchased from a German soldier for several cartons of cigarettes—a very high price—and gave them to Yehuda.

My father never mentioned this story to me. It was on one of my visits to Israel that Yehuda himself shared with me this fantastic act of kindness.

How did Yehuda even get to us there at Föhrenwald? He did it with grit and determination, and with the help of the network of newspapers and handwritten posters.

YEHUDA'S JOURNEY FROM THE "EXODUS" SHIP TO US

My cousins and my aunt were on the original 1947 *Exodus*, the ship that went to Palestine as part of the illegal immigration movement known as *Aliyah Bet*, to break the British Blockade. This was the incident made famous in the novel *Exodus* by Leon Uris, later the movie of the same name that starred Paul Newman.

Palestine at that time was under the British Mandate. Starting in 1939, the British government severely limited Jewish immigration. Most of the Jews who tried to escape persecution in Europe by returning to this land of their ancestors were prevented from entering. Even after the war, most of the ships that brought the refugees from DP camps to Palestine were sent to Cyprus, and the people were put into holding camps.

One of these ships was the *Exodus*. In 1947, the people on this ship were stopped by the British blockade, in the Mediterranean Sea, before they could enter the territory of Palestine. They were forced off the ship, placed on British warships, and taken first to France, where they refused to get off. The ship kept going, back to Germany, where they were unloaded and placed into DP camps. My cousins were on that ship.

I learned even more about my cousins' *Exodus* story from my grandson, Fozzie, born in 2006. Fozzie, whose Hebrew name is Yoav, is named for my father Yosef. It means so much to me that this treasured piece of my

Rachel Gortler Wallach, my cousin. L: as a teenager in Emden, Germany; R: as an adult in 2019, Israel. *Courtesy Facebook, via Alisa Blockman, posted by Sharon Staller Wallach*

family's story has been rescued thanks to the work of one who is inheriting it two generations later.

Fozzie interviewed my Israeli cousin Rachel, Yehuda's sister, for a school project. From that interview he learned that Rachel, when she was a twelve year old kid—not much older than Fozzie at the time—was among those who led the demonstrators in hunger strikes on the *Exodus*.

It was when they wound up in the DP camp Emden, in Germany, that Yehuda took it upon himself to find his family. He was the only man in the family, after all. He had just his mother and his two sisters; his father, my Uncle Eliezer, had been killed by the tree in Siberia. So it was Yehuda who set out to search for living relatives. He sent messages with people who were traveling from camp to camp, asking them to check the lists of survivors for his family's names.

He found Gortler, my father, in Föhrenwald. Yehuda probably hopped from one truck to another, from DP camp to DP camp, to get to us in Föhrenwald.

Can you imagine? All he had was the name: Josef Gortler, Föhrenwald. No ticket on a train, no bus, he just hopped onto those trucks and got to Föhrenwald. No address. No phone number. This was decades before the invention of cell phones or email. And still he managed to connect with my father.

Hashgacha pratis! I believe Divine protection kept my cousin safe. I mean, how in the world? Maybe even today, someone is desperate enough to consider saying, I've got an uncle in a faraway place, I've never been there, but I'm going to that place to find my uncle. I'm just going. People like my cousin did exactly that.

Think of the adventures, and the chances that were taken! You needed a pioneering spirit, a willingness to go where you had never gone before.

A SPIRIT OF ADVENTURE

Did this kind of spirit influence my approach to life and work? It could be.

Upon reflection, I realize I myself was so adventurous then. I'm so timid now: before I go anywhere, I check five times if I have the right address, and the right directions. I check Google maps. I get very edgy before I travel. I don't sleep the night before. This all started after I got to the US. "*Reise-fever*," my mother used to call it, "travel fever."

We took so many chances. Even beyond the adventures we as young people would be expected to pursue, think of my parents, at their stage of life, taking a chance on a move to a whole new world.

Think of coming to the United States, to some city pronounced FEE-nix, but when they saw it spelled out, they called it "FAW-nix." None of us spoke English. True, we knew we would be met by people at the train, but we had no idea who would be meeting us, or where. We didn't know what would happen to us when we got to this "FAW-nix." We had no idea. We took a chance, and hoped that it would work out.

THE HISTORIC UN PARTITION VOTE
THAT MADE POSSIBLE THE STATE OF ISRAEL

The PA system brought us two life-altering experiences, making us witnesses to history.

We, who had suffered so much just for being Jews, were privileged to experience, over the camp PA system, the live broadcasts of the November 1947 UN vote for the Partition of Palestine into Jewish and Arab states, and the May 1948 Declaration of Independence of the State of Israel.

We knew that *Eretz Yisrael*[47] was our ancestral homeland. A Jew's prayers and holidays are based on that land: its seasons, its produce, its places. Even today, we continue to use the words and observances that have come to us through generations of our people, as a collective memory of the Jewish people in its land.

The Judaean hills, the city of Jerusalem: these had been overrun many times, creating the Jewish diaspora in which we were still living. Our leaders and scholars had kept alive the understanding that, no matter where else we might live, we were a people in exile. But with the exile of most of the People of Israel came the dream of returning to the place we knew as Zion. By the time I was born, that dream had survived for some two thousand years.

The Hebrew word "Zion"—meaning Jerusalem, or the land surrounding it, but literally, a marker, or a sign—is found in the Psalms, and in the books of our Prophets. Our Sages wrote the hope for a return to Zion into the central parts of our daily prayers. Even the sweet lullaby my mother comforted me with in our early days on the run carries the story of a longing for this return.[48]

---

47   Hebrew term, meaning "The Land of Israel "
48   *Rozhinkes Mit Mandlen*

And that is why, in the DP camps, we were Zionists. We were all for the creation of a Jewish state in our ancestral homeland. We had spoken the words "Zion" and "Jerusalem" every day, we and our parents and their parents before them. And we understood that, long before Germany's Nazis had torn up our lives, a movement called Zionism had been bringing brave Jews to build new farms and towns in Eretz Yisrael.

So on that Saturday night, November 29, 1947, when the United Nations General Assembly voted on a resolution to end the British Mandate in Palestine and partition the territory into two independent states, Jewish and Arab, we knew we were listening to history.

We were in Ludendorff-Kaserne, in Neu Ulm. The PA system announcer said "Achtung" about five or six times, so we knew something major was going on in the world. Everybody came out from the barracks, listening intensely to the loudspeakers. The radio was a live broadcast, probably from the BBC, with commentary from the DP camp's local announcers.

We held our breaths as we listened to the vote. No one in this huge crowd made a sound.

Then the announcer spoke the numbers we were waiting for: 33 votes in favor, 13 against, 10 abstentions. Partition passed! And the entire camp broke into spontaneous singing of the Hatikva, the song that became Israel's national anthem.[49] The title of the song means "the hope."

After the Hatikva, we sang the song of the Partisans, "*Zog nit keynmol az du geyst dem letstn veg*"[50] ("*Never say that this is the end of the road*") and then everybody started dancing the hora. We danced and danced.

That night, there wasn't a single person who stayed in the barracks. Everybody was outside.

WHY THIS MOMENT IN HISTORY MATTERED TO US

We were Jews. Although we had so recently been chased out of the places our families had called home for generations, and although we were exhausted and confused, surrounded by barbed wire and uncertain of our futures, we knew that this UN vote was about our people's first homeland, the land of our people's dreams. People like my cousin

---

49   https://knesset.gov.il/holidays/eng/hatikva_eng.htm
50   http://holocaustmusic.ort.org/places/ghettos/vilna/zog-nit-keynmol/

March of young Zionists in support of the creation of the State of Israel.

We are either in the camp, or just outside the camp, at Neu Ulm, in November 1947 or in early 1948.

The boy in the second row of the photo, blowing the shofar, is me, age 11. (I still blow shofar. I blow shofar great! I used to blow shofar all the time!)

You can see the kind of pants that I wore. They were not all the way down to the ankles. Knickers, they call them. That's what we had. With high socks. And these hats, called a hittel mit a dashek—a hat with a visor.

I know it's a secular class in the marching photo, because there are girls and boys, and the first row is carrying Herzl's picture. We were learning to be Zionists.

We were taught by Israelis. We were always marching: "yemina, yemina, yemina, smola!" So we were trained: "right, right, right, left!" Or "One, two, three! One! One! One, two, three!": "Achat, shtaim, shalosh! 'khat! 'khat! 'khat shtaim shalosh! ('khat was the left.)

My brother isn't in the march picture. We kind of ran in different circles. He was a little older. In the DP camps, there were so many kids, we did not have to stick together.

Courtesy of the Joshua Gortler collection. Photographer: either American soldier or camp photographer.

Yehuda and his family had risked their lives – many had sacrificed their lives – to resettle there and make that ancient home ours again.

This moment made me feel proud. As far as I could tell, everyone in the DP camp felt the same way. We finally had a place that we could call a permanent Jewish home. Every Jew would be welcome in Israel. Any Jew who wanted to live there could become a citizen automatically.

A BARBED WIRE FENCE AROUND OUR CAMP

Today, Jewish kids go to camp in the summer for adventures and learning. For me, the DP camp provided adventures, yes, and my first learning in an actual school—with some serious limitations.

The camp was surrounded by barbed wire. There was a gate that would open and close, with two guards who let you in and out. In the early stages, there wasn't much freedom of movement. You would have to sneak out, or sneak in. You couldn't just say, "I'm going to town for a few minutes."

Later on, when the Jews living in the camps took over control and started running the camps themselves, it became very easy to get out. It was more difficult to come back. You had to show that you belonged, that you were a camp resident.

CAMP MONEY? THE REAL CURRENCY WAS CIGARETTES, CHOCOLATE, COFFEE

There was no normal currency to pay the people who worked in the camps. Actually, there were two official currencies, sort of. In the early days—from 1945 to 1947—there was the Deutsche (German) Mark, which was absolutely useless. Nobody wanted to have it.

There was a special currency issued by the occupying United States Armed Forces: AMC. These bills were blueish, and not very large.

Then there was the black market.

On this illegal market, people were using a different terminology for currency. The American dollar was a very, very big item. It would be accepted anywhere in Europe. The American dollar was known as *weiche*—soft money.

Gold coins, silver, these were *harde*—hard money.

Diamonds, these were called *kniplach*—buttons. They made it easy to carry a lot of value in a very small space.

My parents and my aunt and uncle, like most of the other DP-niks, made use of the black market.

In the DP camps, there was a humongous black market going on. Black market was *the* place. The authorities in the camps accepted the black market as a way of life.

The people who were employed in the camps, whether as a cook or a cleaner or a police guard, were paid with cigarettes. Some of these people were Jewish camp residents. Some were local Germans. The more "sophisticated" your job, the more you earned. So, if you were an office worker or if you were a doctor, or a nurse, or a teacher, you got a higher pay of cigarettes.

Cigarettes were the basic mode of bartering with the outside world, too. With a pack of cigarettes, you could sneak out of the DP camp and go down to a farm and buy some apples, some other fresh food.

People also got paid in chocolate, and in cans of coffee.

Eastern European Jews did not drink coffee a lot. But the Germans loved the coffee, and the chocolates, and the cigarettes. The chocolate, cigarettes, and coffee were the biggest bargaining tools when we went out.

WHERE DID ALL THOSE GOODIES COME FROM?

US Army surplus provided these goods. The chocolate would come in a bar about ten inches long, in a waterproof box. They were rations that were given to the soldiers in battle.

UNDERCOVER MEAT. LITERALLY.

Today, we have kosher meat markets. We can even buy nice, neatly packaged cuts of kosher chicken in the supermarket.

In the DP camp, we would have to sneak in live chickens. No telling where we found those chickens in our wanderings outside the camp. We would put on a big coat (a *paltan*), oversized, with chickens inside it. Let's say you were a size medium. When you went to get clothing, you'd ask for it in 3 to 4 times your normal size. Nothing fit anyway, so it didn't look too unusual.

Sometimes, people would even sneak in a whole cow! The cow would be covered in *shmattehs*. Several guys would walk, with the cow all covered, between them.

The camp administration's Jewish police force knew what was up. But there were also the American MPs, and they would periodically check for illegal activity. Remember how we called the MPs "Moishe Pisher"? We'd warn each other: "*Moishe Pisher kummt!*"[51]

In the middle of the night, the *schochet*[52] would *schecht*[53] the smuggled cow.

A crier would announce where to find the meat, and whether it was kosher. He'd shout, "*Fleisch in finftsn block*" (Meat in Number Five Block) when he meant "There is nonkosher meat tonight." Or he would shout, "*Fleisch in dritten block*" ("Meat in Number Three Block") if it was kosher.

EVERYBODY HAD A SIDE BUSINESS, INCLUDING ME

We were a group of about ten kids who would run around together. We were like the kids in *Oliver Twist*!

Everybody had some kind of business on the side. Mine was ice cream, which we called *lodeh*. We kids managed to find milk and eggs, and we used our parents' rations of sugar. We would load that up in a baby carriage that we found.

How did we even learn skills like how to make ice cream? I have no idea. Somebody in my group of kids obviously watched some grownup, and that's how we made it. We knew you needed eggs and milk and ice, and we put the salt in the ice and churned. And we made some money! Learning life skills, like how to work as part of a team, how to do business, even how to sneak a chicken into the DP camp, those just became natural for us.

There was plentiful food in the Bavarian area. One kid would climb a tree, shake the tree, and we would fill our clothes with apples, peaches, pears. Some we would eat there, and some we would bring back to the camp.

About twice a week there was a bazaar in the camp, like today's farmers' markets. We kids would have a stand there. It was all stolen goods. We would find stuff outside the camp, bring it inside, and sell it.

This was Germany after the war: the country was devastated. People were hungry. Who asked for permission from the people who owned the fruit trees? We weren't the only ones who were going around selling and bartering stuff. The money system had collapsed. The only thing you could use for money was something you could hold in your hand.

---

51   "is coming" (Yiddish)
52   Kosher slaughterer
53   Slaughter according to kosher rules

B'nai Akiva yeshiva (religious) school, Neu Ulm. Lower left corner: my best friend Pesach. We were always together. I'm right behind him. *Photographer unknown. Courtesy of the Joshua Gortler collection.*

My group of Yeshiva boys and teachers. Note the menorah poster near the ceiling. At its top, the word "Yizkor." A light bulb has been hung above it.

The large sign on the wall reads "It is forbidden to talk during prayer time." *Courtesy of the Joshua Gortler collection.*

LIVE IT UP, KIDS!

Our parents wanted us to experience life! The Germans had been defeated. The kids had the freedom. The kids could do no wrong.

There were kids with no siblings. No parents. Those were the first in Germany to be recruited into the building of the kibbutzim in Palestine. That kid in both the book and the movie *Exodus*, the Sal Mineo character, Dov Landau:[54] these were those kids. The ones who had parents, like me, their parents would not easily give them up.

Right after the war, the Jews felt emancipated. Here's an example: Nobody paid for trains. Once, I was in a train station, and saw Jews running over the tracks to catch the next train. The trainmaster was yelling at them. The Germans were yelling, "Don't do that!"

The kids were yelling, *"Hitler Hitler ist kaput!"* The response came back, *"Yawohl, aber ordenug muss dach zein."* ("Yes, but order, there must be.")

ME, THE WILD THING, RELEASED

From 1939 to 1945, this *vilde chaye*—this wild animal that I was—had to hold in my impulses, even in the kolkhoz. It's true that we only had to pass as non-Jews for a very short time, right after we escaped from Tomaszów—but still, it was hard! Even when we were living in the kolkhoz, once we stepped outside of there, we found we were hated in Russia by the peasants, so we had to behave in a certain way. Don't call too much attention. Keep a low profile.

Now, in the DP camps, the children had all the freedom that had been taken away from us.

I was set free in the DP camps.

---

54   A scrappy young orphaned resistance fighter, DP camp resident, survivor of Nazi brutality

CHAPTER 12
JEWISH HOLIDAYS ENTER MY LIFE
1945-1951

Jewish holidays? Before the DP camps, I had no idea they existed. We were in Soviet Russia. We were in Siberia, the Tashkent area, Rava-Ruska. Religion was outlawed in Soviet Russia. Where would I have seen the holidays? How would my family have been able to observe them?

Now, in the DP camp, I was like a sponge, trying to catch up on eleven years of education and exposure to my people's culture.

I HAD ALMOST NO JEWISH PRAYER EXPERIENCES
AT ALL BEFORE THE DP CAMP

The DP camp was the first time we were really unafraid to show that we were Jews. Before that, we had hidden our Jewish identities.

Back in the kolkhoz, I had watched my father and a few other men gather for what I now realize was *davening* with a *minyan*.[55] I had noticed that they were watching carefully to make sure no one could tell what they were up to. But now, being a Jew was open and encouraged. We were encouraged by the *shlichim*[56] from Israel; by the Lubavitchers[57] who came from New York to Europe to work with us;

---

55   Saying Jewish prayers with the required quorum
56   Outreach workers
57   Lubavitchers = a sect of Orthodox Jews dedicated to helping other Jews become more religious. The name comes from the Russian town where the sect was founded. Its leadership is now based in New York.

by the Va'ad Hatzalah[58]; and by the American Jewish chaplains and the Jewish soldiers.

MOST JEWS IN THE CAMP WERE NOT OBSERVANT

People may think that all the Jews in the DP camps celebrated everything, but I would say most were not observant.

These non-observant Jews questioned the existence of God. Where was God when all of these atrocities happened? Why didn't He intervene? If there is a God, they would say, His eyes were closed while we, and our loved ones, were being displaced and murdered. On Shabbat, they would smoke in the streets. They would use transportation, in and out of the camp. A person who observes Jewish law would know that these things are forbidden on the Sabbath. There were not many vehicles that ran around in the camp itself, but there were taxis that Jews ran outside the camp. If you wanted to go to Munich, or wherever you wanted to go, you got a taxi. The taxis ran on Shabbos.

WHY I FELT BOUND TO STAY OBSERVANT

My parents were observant. But while we were on the run, they weren't able to observe Shabbos and the Jewish holidays. Finally, now that we were in the DP camp, this became once again a central part of my parents' lives.

To this day, I remember the taste of my mother's cholent, the warm Shabbos stew that I often had the privilege of bringing home from the camp's communal ovens. I can almost taste her canned-tuna gefilte fish. I remember her challah.

We would go to shul (synagogue) on Shabbat. Now, my parents could make sure that I received an excellent religious education. I was inspired to continue with this tradition.

SHABBAT[59]

Shabbat, the weekly observance of the Sabbath, was sort of a mixed bag in the camp. Friday night, a siren would sound, to indicate that

---

58 A rescue and relief organization created originally to rescue rabbis and their students during World War II, but expanded postwar. https://www.jewishvirtuallibrary.org/vaad-ha-hatzalah accessed 07/21/19

59 *Shabbat*, the Sephardic and Israeli pronunciation, is pronounced, and written, *Shabbos* among Ashkenazim like Josh's family. His use of "Shabbat" here is indicative of his dual Zionist-religious education.

Shabbat was here. That was necessary, because not everyone had a clock to know what time to *bentsch* (Yiddish for "to bless," meaning, here, "to light Sabbath candles") to begin the Sabbath observance. Those that were observant went to shul.

There's an old Jewish joke we tell about ourselves. If there are two Jews stranded on an island, they need to build three synagogues: one for you, one for me, and one that neither one of us would set foot in. The truth behind the joke was evident in the DP camps.

There were over a dozen different synagogues in the camps where I lived: the Ashkenazic, the *nusach sfard, nusach Ari* ("Lubavitch"), and several other little *shtiebels.* [60]

On Shabbat morning, there were the *hashkama* ("dawn") *minyanim* for the early risers, and for the latecomers, their own later services. All the synagogues had a *mechitzah* (separation) between men and women. I don't recall any Reform or other non-Orthodox services. What about the assimilated German Jews? I don't remember any shuls of their style in the DP camp.

CHANUKAH: A SECULAR HOLIDAY
WITH RECYCLED MENORAHS

Chanukah was taught in the secular classes. That's where we learned the whole story of the Maccabees. The *brachos*—the blessings over the candle lighting—we learned from the teachers in the religious school.

Chanukah is actually not a major holiday in the Jewish religious calendar, but it was definitely a major holiday in the camp. It was kind of like Chanukah in the United States: a secular holiday.

They didn't talk about any miracles: God's miracle of intervention, the miracle of the one-day jar of oil that burned for eight days, none of that. They talked about the victorious Maccabees, the whole idea that we are no longer going to be victims. We're going to have our own country. Palestine would be a Jewish state. We were going to have soldiers. The Maccabees were kind of the ideal that all of us kids should strive to be.

There was a Chanukah play—in Hebrew, because all the secular classes were in Hebrew. I was in this play about the Maccabees, but our play was

---

60 *Shtiebel* = very small synagogue serving a close-knit community. Pronunciation, and certain prayers, differ from community to community within different Jewish traditions. *Nusach ari* and *nusach sfard* are two of those prayer traditions.

not just for the fun of it. This was part of the acculturation of the Jewish children in the DP camps. We were being taught to think of ourselves as victorious. To have a sense of pride, and not to carry the self-image of being a victim, after what we had all been through. Little could I have imagined that, more than sixty years later, I would have a granddaughter, born at Chanukah time, whose name would reflect this pride. Her name is "Orli," a Hebrew name that means "a light to me."

As for lighting the Chanukah lights, we had recycled menorahs! We took potatoes and cut them in half, then cut out a little hole in the half-potato. In the hole we would put a little oil or even the Crisco that we received (which was not kosher at the time!)—anything that could burn. Then we took some cotton and made a little wick, and dipped it into this stuff. This was what we would light.

The first night, we would have one cut potato: one half, we used as the *shammas*[61], and one was the first candle. And on down the line for eight days: two potatoes, three potatoes....

We lit these potato candles in the school. But nothing was wasted! We decided to make latkes from those potato menorahs, but we didn't have a *ribaizen*—a potato grater. How could you make a potato grater? We took a can, whatever can we could find. We cut the can in half. Then we took a nail, and we made holes in the tin. We used those holes on the other side as a grater.

Adults, kids, we all did this. It's like those craft projects you find in the American Boy Scout and Girl Scout handbooks. But the only craft project handbooks we had were in our heads.

PURIM

Purim is the Jewish calendar's early spring carnival holiday, when we read the Book of Esther ("The Megilla"). It's a favorite holiday for children, with costumes and noisemakers and fun food. You might think that, like now, we in the camps would have celebrated Purim—a story of the Jews' victory over a murderous political figure—by mocking the defeated Nazis. But the experience was too fresh, and the grief was too deep, for us to make fun of such things.

The Megilla was read, we kids played with noisemakers, and ate

---

61   "helper" candle that lights the sacred ones

hamentaschen, the traditional triangle-shaped pastries. (They just had poppy seed filling, none of the fancy fillings we have now.) Some kids put on a mask, but we did nothing fancy with costumes.

PESACH[62]: THE PRECIOUS JAFFA ORANGES

The first time that we actually got oranges: now, there's a Pesach memory. Jaffa oranges. I had never before had an orange in my life. That was a very big treat.

Somehow, for Pesach, there were a few crates of Jaffa oranges that ended up in the camp. There would be just one or two oranges for the whole family. We would very gently open the orange up and take each section apart: a little bit to this person, a little to that one. We wouldn't eat a whole orange just like that, the way we do today. For us in the DP camp, oranges were like gold! This kind tasted different than the oranges we get in the US today. It was a big orange. Very juicy. Just to touch it, to get my fingers on it, was very special. My mother taught me how to peel it.

We had the orange for the seder. At the end of the seder, we each got one little section of orange, and it tasted just wonderful. Just wonderful. We were told that these oranges came from Palestine. From Jaffa. From the Holy Land. In Hebrew, they were called *tapuchei zahav*, golden apples.

They were handing the oranges out very carefully. We carried them delicately, feeling the texture. I'd never felt a texture like that before.

A VERY SPECIAL WINE

We made our own wine. I remember my father making it for Pesach.

We got *rozhinkes*, raisins. We did not get grapes, but we were able to get *rozhinkes* from the CARE packages that came to the DP camp. From the *rozhinkes*, we made homemade wine.

I don't remember the process. I watched it, and I drank it, and I was proud of my father for making it. He was an expert.

People would get together, stash the *rozhinkes* away, or we'd trade: one person said, you know, I'm making some wine, I'm going to give you two bars of candy and a can of peanut butter, two packs of cigarettes, and we would trade. We traded because the little pack of *rozhinkes* that you got

---

62 Passover

were not enough to make the wine. We needed a lot, and we saved them up for a long time.

For the seder we had the *rozhinkes* wine. Also for Shabbos, but for seder, we made it with special care, to guarantee that it would be kosher for Passover. And don't ask me whether it was "*shmira d'shmira*"[63]! We made it, and we drank it for Pesach.

Much, much later, the Vaad Hatzalah and the American soldiers' chaplains brought some wine. But in the first years, there was no wine except for what we made.

My father made enough wine for more than just our little family. Other people came to the seder. How did we make room for seder guests? We'd sit in the hallways, pull up a chair, and you'd have a seder.

MATZAS FROM AMERICA

The matzas came from the United States. The only matzas we knew that came in a box were the American Manischewitz brand. These were distributed as part of the food distribution process. As my father was one of the people in charge of the distribution of food, we had plenty of matza. For others, it was scarce, though. I remember people eating bread at Pesach in the camp—not everybody was able to observe the holiday the traditional way, and not everybody chose to.

MY AUNT AND THE UNDERCOVER TURKEY

I had this aunt, Brocha. She was a real trader. She could sneak anything under her big coat. She had no children of her own, so she treated my brother and me like we were her own.

It was *Erev*[64] *Pesach*. I remember it like it was yesterday: all the meat was "in 5 Block" (meaning not kosher). It looked as though there would be no meat for our seder.

But then, an hour or two before sundown, I saw my Aunt Brocha walking in, singing the Partisan Song, with a turkey's face sticking out of her coat!

She called the *schochet*. We had kosher meat for our seder: A *hindik*— a turkey!

---

63   A good-humored reference to extra-careful rabbinic supervision
64   The day before (Hebrew/Yiddish)

TISHA B'AV

This sad fast day in the heat of the summer had the potential to spark the deepest feelings of grief in the camps. Even now, it is always the most difficult day of the Jewish ritual year. It is a 24-hour fast, mourning the destructions of the two ancient Temples in Jerusalem, and other Jewish catastrophes like the Spanish Inquisition. But with what we had just been through, who would have cared to mourn something from so long ago? Another destruction? Big deal. Look what had happened to us two years ago, one year ago.

ROSH HASHANA & YOM KIPPUR[65]

The first time I heard a *shofar*,[66] was in the DP camp.

Although most of the people in the DP camp were not observant, when it came to Rosh Hashana and Yom Kippur, the synagogues would be filled to capacity. Especially on Rosh Hashana, during the blowing of the shofar, and on Yom Kippur, everybody came to recite the *Yizkor* (memorial service). During this service, there was a lot of emotion.

The number six million had by this time been accepted as the total number of Jews murdered by the Nazis. That number was engraved on everyone's mind. It was also made visible on memorial tablets we could see on the walls in public spaces throughout the camps.

A special prayer—an additional *Kel Malei Rachamim*[67] —was recited for the six million martyrs. People would cry as they recited, loudly, the names of their individual loved ones who had been so recently murdered. Even today, we do this, but in the DP camps, there was a real Godly type of *chazzanim* (cantors), who really belted out these *Kel Malei Rachamim*. People fell apart, weeping.

SUKKOS

Someone built a *sukkah*.[68] But there were many more shuls than there were *sukkahs*. There were one or two *esrogim* and *lulavim* In the whole camp,

---

65 Jewish New Year & Day of Atonement, part of a month of autumn holy days
66 ram's horn, traditionally blown on the Jewish New Year observances of Rosh Hashana and Yom Kippur
67 Lit., "God Full of Mercy," a memorial prayer honoring a loved one. On certain holy days, Jews share both communal and personal versions of this memorial prayer.
68 the temporary dwelling prescribed in Leviticus 23:42

there were only one or two esrogim and lulavim:[69] what was this all about?

Those two agricultural items—the *esrog*, a lemon-like fruit, and the *lulav*, a carefully tied bunch of branches—were brought in from Israel. They were passed around very, very carefully. The grownups taught us about guarding against breaking the *pitom*.[70] I wasn't allowed to hold the esrog myself. An adult's hands were around mine, because they didn't trust that I wouldn't drop it.

Since there were so many shuls in the DP camp, not every shul had a lulav and an esrog. They had to time the *Hallel* [71]services—I had no idea what the heck *Hallel* was—they had to time them in a way that would allow someone to run with the *esrog* and *lulav* from one little shul to another little shul, so everybody would share them. It was the older Chassidic boys who were the runners. I can still see them with their peyes flying, running from shul to shul. In Foehernwald, there must have been 20 different *shtieblach* (small synagogues).

MY BAR MITZVAH[72] IN NEU ULM, AT LUDENDORFF-KASERNE

The bar mitzvah was totally different than the bar mitzvahs we have now in the United States. Not only the parties, but even the preparation. There was no interest in teaching the kids to chant the Haftorah,[73] or to chant the Torah. At least not in the classes I was in, which were in the Galitzianer tradition.[74] In the Galitzianer shuls, the Haftorah was not read aloud. You mumbled it. You read the blessings before the Haftorah, and then you mumbled quietly, while everybody else read.

First time I heard the Haftorah being chanted out loud in a synagogue

---

69   Observance of the autumn holiday of *Sukkos/Sukkot/* "Feast of Tabernacles" requires the use of an *esrog* (citron) and *lulav* (palm branches) tied with other prescribed branches, during a section of the morning synagogue service called *Hallel*. The fruit and branches are carried in a procession, as psalms of praise are chanted. This festival of thanksgiving represents the culmination of the autumn season popularly known as the "High Holidays."

70   *Pitom,* the Hebrew word for the tiny stem remnant on this oval fruit. Snapping off the *pitom* renders the *esrog* unusable for ritual purposes.

71   Extra psalm service inserted into morning prayers on joyous festivals

72   Literally, "son of commandment." At the age of 13, a Jewish boy becomes obligated as an adult to perform the *mitzvahs,* or commandments, entitling him to be counted as an adult in any *minyan,* or quorum, required for the recitation of certain important prayers.

73   Weekly reading from Prophets

74   Vs. "Litvak, litvische" Distinct prewar Jewish communities, Galitzia and Lithuania, spoke with identifiably different Yiddish accents. Galitzianers, like the Gortlers, lived in western Ukraine and eastern Poland.

was when I came to the United States. My *davening*, until I came to Yeshiva University, was *Galitzianer*. Here's how it sounded: *"BOO-rich ah-TOO…"* *"MEY-lich haOY-lum," "asher BU-cher BOH-ni mi-KOHL ho-OH-mim, vNOO-san LOH-ni es h-TOO-roh…"*

That's how I read it. It was not *"Bar-OOKH…"* No! It was *"BOO-rikh!"* I kind of went through a "pronunciation conversion" process at YU, because when I read the Gemara, they looked at me like I was from the moon. They knew what my accent was, but YU is a *Litvische* yeshiva. And the pronunciations I used were those of a *Galitzianer*.

The bar mitzvah boy's job was just to make the two blessings for the reading of the Torah. You made the first one, then somebody else read from the Torah, and then you made the second blessing, after the reading. My bar mitzvah—like most of them—was not on Shabbos. Bar mitzvahs in the DP camp usually took place on Mondays or Thursdays or on *Rosh Chodesh*.[75] Mine was Rosh Chodesh Iyar 5709 (April 30, 1949). I was taught how to read and say the *brachas*, that's all. Somebody else read a portion of the Torah, and I did the *brachas*.

That was it for the bar mitzvah preparation. And the celebration afterward? My mother made a sponge cake (a *leikach*) and there was a *l'chaim* (a toast), with some schnapps—whatever was available at the time—and some herring. Right after that, you would put on *tefillin*,[76]and the bar mitzvah concluded with the l'chaim. Mazal tov, I'm now a man. So now I'm entitled to make a minyan. No big deal at all.

WEDDINGS AND GOOSE PIMPLES

In the camps, there were so many weddings, and so many births. They were constantly happening in the DP camp. It wasn't unusual to have weddings a couple times a week.

The Jews were multiplying, almost like the Jews in Egypt. In the Torah it says that Pharaoh wanted to kill the Jews because they were multiplying so fast. Now, in the DP camps, the Jews felt that they were liberated from

---

75 On Mondays and Thursdays, in addition to on the morning of the Sabbath, the Torah scroll is traditionally opened and read aloud in synagogue. This is also done on *Rosh Chodesh,* the day marking the New Moon, to start the new lunar/Jewish calendar month.

76 One of the adult obligations taken on by a *bar mitzvah* boy, *tefillin* combine small boxes containing certain Biblical words, with leather straps. Worn during most morning prayers on head and arm, in fulfillment of the commandment to attach those words to head and heart. Sometimes translated "Phylacteries."

slavery, just like the Jews of ancient Egypt. We knew that 6 million had been destroyed, and we had to reproduce a new generation of Jews.

When there was a wedding, you didn't get an invitation. An announcement would come over the camp loudspeakers: "ACHtung! ACHtung! *Sibn a nacht vil zien a chassene, alle menschen ken kummen!*" Attention, attention! At seven tonight, there will be a wedding! Everyone can come!

And everybody went! The food was—a piece of cake. There was no sit-down dinner. There was *challah*. Maybe some *leikach*—a sponge cake. And some schnapps. And some wine.

There were six white wedding dresses that were sewn by the women. One of the seamstresses was my mother. I'm not sure what the material was. Sheets that they found? Maybe they found satin from the Germans somewhere? These dresses belonged to the camp, so to speak, not to any individual person.

Each of these gowns was made in a different size. When the bride walked down the aisle, dressed in white, there were five other girls, or young women, walking behind her. Each of these girls was carrying one of the other five gowns. They were not wearing them. These five, with the bride, were representing the 6 million Jews that died.

I have goose pimples as I talk about it, because I see it in front of me so clearly. Some of the girls who married were able to walk with their parents down the aisle. Some were not.

THE CHALLAH DANCE

Then the wedding dancing began. The dancing I saw is an experience we don't see at a strictly Orthodox wedding in America, where the men surround the groom and the women surround the bride, sort of in the background. In the DP camp, everybody participated. It was coed.

And that challah!

For the wedding, the women would bake a challah. They made a big, big *challah*, a huge challah. After the wedding, the women would hold up this challah, and dance in front of the *chosson* and *kallah*.[77] And then we would eat it. I don't know what the symbolism is, maybe that we have bread, we have prosperity, but the challah was a very central part of the ceremony, the women dancing with the enormous challah.

---

77   Groom and bride

It reminds me of an important moment in the Torah, when we read the song of Miriam and the women (Exodus 15:17-21). The Jews have escaped from slavery in Egypt, the sea has miraculously split, and as they complete their safe passage, Miriam comes out, leading the women. You see her dance with the tambourine. And now, here in the DP camp, you had the women dancing with the challah.

You know, I've read so many books about the Holocaust, but I don't remember that imagery anywhere that I read. I saw that dancing every time somebody got married. It was a celebration for all of us.

MY FATHER, THE COMMUNITY MAN

My father (cigarette in hand) at a conference in Munich, (1949 or 1950), with representatives of all the DP camps.

This photo dates from while we were living in Föhrenwald. The meeting takes place at a fancy hotel in Munich. There's Manischewitz wine on the table. The job of the people at this conference was to express concerns, what's happening in the camps, set goals and policies. My father was in the distribution of the food, an elected role in the DP camp.

But what's interesting in this picture is that these all look like secular Jews. Yet my father, an observant Jew, was clearly very comfortable in this company. They're pretty nicely dressed already. We see the suits and ties. It's mostly men, but a couple of women in the background. And that was typical.

Note the background of the first-class hotel, as compared to my school in the camp. *Courtesy of the Joshua Gortler collection.*

MY MOTHER, THE COMMUNITY WOMAN

In the DP camp: my mother, standing, in the center, to the left of the tallest woman. My mother had the most gorgeous face you can find. A kind face. You can see, she does not cover her hair. Some of these women cover their hair with shmattes. She was a dressmaker. You can see from the cut of collar she is wearing that she knew how to dress. This was probably taken in Föhrenwald.

These women in the photo are the chesed group, so to speak. They were involved in two projects: They made dresses. And they helped plan celebrations. If, G-d forbid, somebody passed away, this was the Chevra Kadisha[78] too.

The seated lady in the middle of the photo was an American, either a social worker from the Va'ad Hatzlah, or from the Joint, or she was a Red Cross nurse. She would be either organizing or supporting this group when they needed something.

If there was a birth and the baby was a boy, these women would provide everything for the bris. For a bar mitzvah, these women helped organize for the bar mitzvah. They must have organized mine too. Well, there wasn't much to organize, because it was just a schnapps and a piece of herring. *Courtesy of the Joshua Gortler collection.*

---

78   Religious burial society

WOMAN AT DOORWAY: Estera Gortler, my mother, in front of our entry, No. 18 Wisconsin Strasse, Föhrenwald DP Camp, Germany, approx. 1949.

How appropriate that our home address was 18! The number 18 has immense significance in Jewish life. Written with Hebrew letters, "18" forms the word "chai," meaning life. Thus, "L'Chayim!" "To Life!"

There were two doors marked 18 on our house. Two different residences in the one building. *Photographer unknown. Courtesy of the Joshua Gortler collection.*

CHAPTER 13

My Camp Years End and
My Journey to America Begins
1950 - 1951

CAMP CHANGES: MY FRIENDS LEAVE

Once the Partition Plan for Palestine passed in 1947, and the State of Israel, *Medinat Yisrael* (its name in Hebrew), was established in 1948, about ninety percent of the people in the DP camps left for Israel. After all my education by the Zionist teachers in the DP camps, I really wanted to go there.

But making a home in the brand-new State of Israel at that time was a very hard life. My mother was very strong in insisting on not going there. She herself had developed many, many medical issues. And she felt that we had all suffered enough, running and barely surviving, from Siberia to Uzbekistan to Poland to Germany. She felt that if we went to the United States, the children would have an opportunity for a better life. And of course, a better life was the goal for her and her husband as well.

She also knew that her two teenage sons would immediately be called up to serve in the Israeli army, and we would be beyond her protection.

The culture and the atmosphere in our DP camp, Föhrenwald, had changed drastically by 1950. The first people who left, in really big groups, were the orphan children, the *yesomim*,[79] of about ten to twelve years old and up. These were the kids who went with the *shlichim*, the emissaries from Palestine ("the *Palestin'chiks*"). Those emissaries, members of the Palmach, the Haganah, B'nai Akiva, Hashomer Hatza'ir, had trained

---

79   Orphans (in Hebrew)

and recruited as many young working people as they could, to come to Israel to fight the Independence War of 1948, and to secure and populate the young country.

One group that really does not get the credit for the amount of support they gave to the DPs who left to settle in the new State of Israel was Breicha. Breicha was not a political group, but a logistics group. They were the people who would arrange for transportation and food for these immigrants to travel to Israel.

These were the people who were ready to go the minute the British mandate was lifted, allowing mass immigration. Before that, there was the blockade, the one that my cousins on the ship Exodus were caught up in.[80] Once the United Nations voted in favor of establishing two states, one for Palestinian Arabs, and one for Jews in Eretz Yisrael, the blockade was lifted.

I WAS SAD NOT TO FULFILL THE
DREAM I'D LEARNED TO LOVE

The Palestin'chiks didn't want anything to do with the people who were not going to Palestine. That made me feel like an outcast, a deserter. I wondered, "Why aren't I going there?"

I had totally absorbed that feeling. I thought of myself as a real Zionist. A real chalutznik.[81] We had marched every morning, and we had been taught how to defend ourselves with sticks. They had even taught us Judo, the Palestin'chiks.

I finally let that feeling go when I said goodbye to Europe in June of 1951, at the port of Bremerhaven. I didn't know where we were going, really, but I was looking forward to the next chapter of my life. It turned out that my mother, also, had expectations that would not be fulfilled. She thought we would be joining her brother in New York.

BY 1950, WHO WAS LEFT?

By 1950, Föhrenwald was a different camp: the school was different, the friends were different, the people were different. By 1950, all those people who wanted to go to Israel had emigrated there.

The schools changed. Where I had been in class with 20 kids, now

---

80   See "Yehuda's journey" in chapter 11.
81   Pioneer-type

there were 5 kids. Some of the teachers had left, too, for Israel. There were teachers who were so attached to some kids that they didn't want to let the kids go by themselves, so they accompanied them to Eretz Yisrael.

Who was left in the DP camp, besides us? The elderly, and people I would now call "the walking dead." People with many psychiatric problems. I don't think Israel really wanted them. Israel wanted the young people. The country wasn't equipped for people who would require so much health care. The DP camp, on the other hand, had an elaborate health care system, with doctors and a nearby hospital. A person's basic needs, like food and housing, were taken care of. No one needed to look for a job.

The other people left behind, like the Gortlers, were families who had made applications to resettle in different countries. We were all waiting for our visas.

The number one country, of course, was the United States. Number two was Canada, then Australia, New Zealand, England—basically, English-speaking countries. Some did go elsewhere, to South America or other places. Europe was definitely out. Burned out. Going to Belgium, or someplace else in Europe? In the 1950s, that did not look like an option. The option was to go abroad. Our choice was to go to America.

HAD WE GONE TO PALESTINE

With my drive, my perseverance, I probably would have become involved in the political arena in Israel. That would have been an opportunity I would have sought out. I don't think I would have been a laborer on kibbutz or anything like that. I doubt I would have made the same career as I did in the US. I imagined serving in the government, shaping it, through B'nai Akiva, or the Mizrachi movements. I believe I would have gravitated towards that.

But I moved on, once I was in the US. When I first came to New York as a student, I was involved tangentially in B'nai Akiva. I was always a Zionist, but not the kind who would give up what I had in the US.

I THREATEN TO SABOTAGE MY PARENTS' PLANS

I was very sad. I wanted to go to Israel. As a matter of fact, my mother said she would put a piece of tape on my mouth, because before we went for the interview, I told her that I was going to tell them I had a disease, and I that I could not go.

I was missing my friends. We had been encouraged to love Eretz Yisrael, to love the idea of a Jewish state. Why would I want to go to America, at my age? I was an idealistic fifteen year old. I wanted to be part of the creation of the new State. So, I threatened. But that's what you do when you're fifteen. I had a *chevra*, a group of friends. We would hang out, we'd talk about our life, and our dreams. Life in the DP camp, for a twelve to fifteen-year-old, meant freedom! We could do what we wanted, we could go into the orchards and pick apples, and throw rocks; we could bring home a cow or a chicken, or climb trees. I felt certain that my life would be like that in Israel.

But I did not spoil our plans. When the time arrived, the people from HIAS[82] picked us up in some German trucks and took us to the train station for our journey to Munich, to the American consulate. We began applying for our visas.

GOING TO AMERICA: *"THE GOLDENEH MEDINA"*

The only family we had in the States was my mother's brother Chaim Balsenbaum. He had come to New York as a refugee several months earlier. He was unemployed and therefore unable to sponsor us, since one of the requirements for a sponsor was to assure that the refugees would not become a burden on the United States social welfare system.[83] Therefore, we went through the very, very difficult application process, to find a sponsoring community in America.

FROM UNDOCUMENTED MIGRANTS
TO HOLDERS OF AMERICAN VISAS

We had to go through a very lengthy background check. A document that I later obtained from HIAS states that we had no criminal convictions. However, it also states that we had no documentation when we crossed the border from Stettin to Berlin in 1945.

My family and I had actually been "illegal, undocumented aliens" when we entered the US Zone in Berlin. But from 1946 to 1951, the DP camp years, we did have very detailed documentation.

---

82 Hebrew Immigrant Aid Society
83 When I arrived in New York to study at Yeshiva University, Uncle Chaim met me at the bus, and we occasionally saw each other during my years there. But he and my mother never saw each other again.

There was also a health certification. The US has a policy of not letting anyone in with a communicable disease. I have the paperwork that shows our immunization records. We were immunized against certain carrier diseases, whether we had them or not.

How did we get the opportunity to emigrate to this country we knew as the *goldeneh medina,* the golden land?

Since we did not have any relatives in the US who were capable of sponsoring us, we were put into a lottery. We needed a sponsor. New York, Chicago, Los Angeles, those communities were filled up already. HIAS now had to look for smaller communities to accept the refugees.

AMERICA'S QUOTA SYSTEM

To apply to come to the US was a very difficult and lengthy process. Other people got visas right away. Australia was easy. South America was open to refugees. Canada made it much easier to obtain a visa. But the US was very difficult.

It took about five years from the initial application date to when we actually left for the US. The US had a quota system: how many people, how many kinds of people, from where, even how many Jews they would allow in. That system gave priority for family unification, and then for certain trades. We didn't qualify for any of those.

The US had a limit on immigrants from Poland. And my official nationality was Polish. That was ironic. The whole reason we were in this position was that our Polish neighbors hadn't wanted to welcome us back home.

If we had waited to come in as Poles through the quota system, I would still be in the DP camp waiting.

But President Harry S. Truman issued an executive order in December 1945, announcing that the US would give priority to Displaced Persons from the war in Europe. On that basis, we qualified. By 1952, over 100,000 Jewish DPs—among them, me and my family—had settled in the United States.[84]

That's why, in the Bible provided by the Va'ad Hatzalah, there's a tribute to President Harry Truman, printed on a page with an American flag.

---

84   https://newspapers.ushmm.org/events/president-truman-orders-quota-preference-for-displaced-persons

Cover of Va'ad Hatzala "The Holy Bible" *Courtesy of the Joshua Gortler collection.*

Inside page of Va'ad Hatzalah Bible, with dedication printed over American flag, beginning "The remnants of Israel" *Courtesy of the Joshua Gortler collection.*

PROCESSING

Once we got our papers in Föhrenwald, we had to go to the American consulate in Muenchen (Munich), the headquarters of the DP camps in Bavaria, where my father had attended those regional camp representatives' meetings. It was about a two-hour schlep by train and by bus to Munich. There must have been two or three interviews. All four of us went for all of them. The medical exams were with German doctors, which was a little creepy.

Although the streets in Föhrenwald were named for US states (we lived on Wisconsin Street), I knew very little about the actual United States. Same with my parents. We had no idea where Arizona was, but that was the state that gave us our sponsorship.

As for cities, we knew three names: "*Nev York*," as we said it—we knew this was a place all Jews wanted to go to (we had no idea what it looked like, but we had heard of it). And we knew of "*TSCHI-kago*," (Chicago) and Los Angeles.

But *FAW-nix*? Which we learned much later was pronounced "FEE-nix?" That was never among these places. For all we knew, it could have been on the moon. As for the great distances between places in America, we had no idea. We would find out soon enough.

"Processing" Immunizations
Courtesy of the HIAS.

Criminal background check
No criminal record "decent,
honest-looking man"

May 9, 1950 USNA
[United Service for New
Americans] File #3339

Lists all 4 family
members

Lists Josef's birthplace
as "Krasnogrod" – worth
comparing "Krasnobrod"
and "Krasnogrod"

Moses listed as dental
technician

"Szija" as "student"

Also lists "none" under
"health problems" for all 4!

Note: "decent,"
"honest looking," and
"literate." *Courtesy of the
HIAS.*

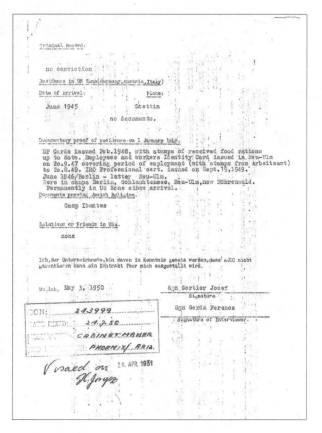

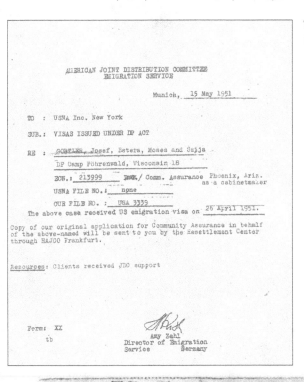

AMERICAN JOINT DISTRIBUTION COMMITTEE
EMIGRATION SERVICE

Munich, 15 May 1951

TO   : USNA Inc. New York

SUB.: VISAS ISSUED UNDER DP ACT

RE : GORTLER, Josef, Estera, Moses and Szija

DP Camp Föhrenwald, Wisconsin 18

ZON.: 213999   REG./ Comm. Assurance Phoenix, Ariz.
                                     as a cabinetmaker
USNA FILE NO.: none

OUR FILE NO. : USA 3339
The above case received US emigration visa on 26 April 1951.

Copy of our original application for Community Assurance in behalf
of the above-named will be sent to you by the Resettlement Center
through HAJCO Frankfurt.

Resources: Clients received JDC support

Form: XI
tb   Amy Zahl
                    Director of Emigration
                    Service   Germany

Visas Issued.
Courtesy of the HIAS.

Left for America.
Courtesy of the HIAS.

Left for U.S.A. 8 Mai 1951
INDEX CARD "A" J.D.C. EMIGRATION SERVICE MUNICH

Last Name GORTLER   File No. USA 3339
First Name Estera   Sex F   Opening 31 Oct 49
Address DPC Foehrenwald   Date
Birthdate 20/4/08 Birthplace Tomaszow In transit
                                     from:
Nationality:
  Present   Former   Accompanied by
                                       Josef, Moses, Szia
Occupation:
  Present Dressmaker Former
                                     Closing
Country of destination U S A   Date

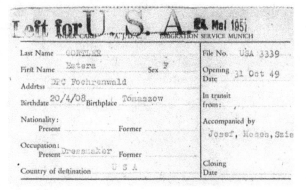

Left for U.S.A. 8 Mai 1951
INDEX CARD "A" J.D.C. EMIGRATION SERVICE MUNICH

Last Name GORTLER   File No. USA 3339
First Name Estera   Sex F   Opening 31 Oct 49
Address DPC Foehrenwald   Date
Birthdate 20/4/08 Birthplace Tomaszow In transit
                                     from:
Nationality:
  Present   Former   Accompanied by
                                       Josef, Moses, Szia
Occupation:
  Present Dressmaker Former
                                     Closing
Country of destination U S A   Date

CHAPTER 14

Goodbye, Europe
1951

I learned much later in my life that my parents had been expecting to go to New York, not Phoenix. My mother had had expected to rejoin her brother there. A trail of documents shows how much confusion swirled around our arrival, and how disappointed my parents were not to be sent to New York.

It was a full month after our arrival in Phoenix by the time my parents made their peace with settling there. During all their years in the United States, my mother and her brother never saw each other. They stayed in touch by writing letters. People didn't just call each other to chat on the phone, especially not long distance. It was very expensive.

In Munich, we had been entered into a lottery to find a sponsor. HIAS looked for smaller communities to accept the refugees. Phoenix, Arizona agreed to accept a small number of refugees, and that's why we ended up there. The Jewish Family Service and the Phoenix Jewish Federation were our sponsors.

There were no other families going to Phoenix when we did. Phoenix had maybe a dozen refugee families. We didn't know any of them when we arrived. There was nobody from Föhrenwald. I think there were one or two other refugee families who came to Phoenix after us. But that was it.

TRUCK, THEN TRAIN, THEN BOAT

A German truck took us from Föhrenwald to Munich.

I remember that truck ride very vividly. It was an open truck with a canvas cover over it. Four benches, with two on each side of the truck, and two in the middle. There was a very, very small aisle. Twenty people were put into this truck like sardines. Every space was occupied, and underneath the bench, or on our laps, we had our little suitcases.

When our truck got to Munich, we were put on a German train. We had what I would call third-class tickets, the cheapest of the cheap. We were on our way to Bremerhaven, where the Americans would give us a place to stay. It was to be our last stop in Europe.

A QUICK FAREWELL TO MUNICH

As soon as we arrived at the Munich station, we boarded the train to Bremerhaven. There was no overnight stay in Munich. We remained in the truck for what seemed like a few hours, before the train came. Some staff from HIAS finally escorted this truckload of people into the train, and off we went to Bremerhaven, the port of entry and port of departure for the American fleet.

When we arrived, different trucks were waiting for us. These were American Army trucks, *huge* trucks! For me, it looked like three times the size of the trucks we took from Föhrenwald to Munich. They were very high, and hard to climb up on. On each side of these green trucks, there was a white five-point star. There were two drivers in the front of each truck, all in American uniforms.

A STAY AT THE U.S. ARMY BASE IN BREMERHAVEN

We had no idea now where we were going. We knew we were going to the United States, but where were we going in this truck? We got in, and about half an hour later, we arrived at an American army base, in Bremerhaven.

THE MOST HORRIBLE EXPERIENCE
A 15-YEAR-OLD COULD HAVE

When we arrived at the Army base, after we were shown where to put our belongings, I had the most horrible experience that a fifteen year old could have. Even today, I feel invaded when I think about this.

They separated the men from the women, the boys from the girls. We were led into this huge bathroom that was used for the soldiers' showers. We were asked to disrobe. Some people panicked. They said, "It's a gas chamber."

Now, we had been disinfected a number of times, but this was different. Never before had we faced people in uniform with covered faces. For us, after the DP camps, this was terrifying, but the reactions of the people who had survived Auschwitz, or Buchenwald, were something else again.

The people who had been through the Nazi death camps knew about gas. For many of them, the loved ones they had arrived at the camp with had been murdered in gas chambers. They had seen and smelled the smoke from the ovens that burned their loved ones' asphyxiated bodies. The survivors of those camps knew all too well what a uniformed officer could do with gas. After we disrobed—until we were completely naked—a couple of soldiers came in, with their faces covered by a mask. They had what appeared to me to be a pump that must have been ten feet long, and they started spraying disinfectant.

The soldiers sprayed that stuff on the genitalia, in the front and in the back. Then we had to raise our hands, so they could spray under the arms. They sprayed every place where there was hair, to kill the lice. Even talking about this now is difficult. It's a miracle we kept our eyesight. It was a totally dehumanizing experience.

And we hadn't expected it. There was no warning. I had a feeling that some of these young soldiers even had a good time doing it.

When it was over, we got dressed again in the same clothes we were wearing when we arrived.

It's true that most of us refugees were covered with lice. Back in Munich, when we went through the medical exams, my mother insisted on making sure that we were free of lice. She knew what the examiners were looking for. So, before those exams, she made sure that we washed all our hair—our hair on the head, and our hair in the genital areas—with a mix of gasoline and water. It smelled terrible, and it hurt. But it killed the lice.

SETTLING IN AT THE ARMY BASE AT BREMERHAVEN

We spent about two weeks at the American army base. We were placed in barracks built for American soldiers. We ate with the soldiers at a buffet at their mess hall. There was no provision made for kosher. There were fruits and vegetables, and all kinds of *treifos* (non-kosher foods). All we could eat were hard boiled eggs and the fruit that was locally grown—some apples, pears, plums. Whatever was ripe in May. Mainly we ate hardboiled eggs, this weird bread, and the fresh vegetables and fruit. We were hungry.

BROWN STUFF IN A BOTTLE?
I KNEW BEER. THIS WAS NOT BEER.

I saw these little bottles which I had never seen before in my life. They looked kind of cute. Inside, there was some brown stuff. "Coca-Cola?" I'd never seen Coca-Cola. This was not something that the Germans had. In the DP camp, we drank beer. We drank a lot of beer. You know, beer, we got gratis there. They had this big pitcher, and we'd go to the bar, and they would *psssht!* fill it up with beer, and we'd take it home!

But at the army base, there was this stuff called Coca-Cola. I got a bottle of Coca-Cola. But I had no idea how to open that thing.

THE SOLDIERS MOCKED ME

With the bottle, this black thing, I tried to screw off the cap, remove it somehow, but it wouldn't work. I asked a soldier to open it, how to do it. He said, "with your teeth." I believed him, and I tried. I didn't break my tooth, but I couldn't open it.

So often they made fun of us, the soldiers. Another guy came over, and he gave me a bottle opener. Together, we opened the Coke.

That was the first time I tasted Coca-Cola. It was delicious! It was a terrific drink. I was hooked on Coke, rather than Pepsi. Pepsi was not available. Only Coca-Cola. "Koh-kah koh-lah!" I learned to say.

THIS WEIRD BREAD!

We saw some kind of a bread that we had not seen before in the mess hall. All the bread that we had in the DP camp came from local bakeries. In Neu Ulm, in Föhrenwald, there were bakeries. The bread was unbelievably delicious: hard rolls, good bread.

At the army base, they had this white stuff. My father called it cotton. The soldiers called it "Wonder Bread." (Was it kosher? Don't ask me, we didn't ask for *hashgacha*,[85] there was no OU.[86]) We were blown away by this stuff! We took it, and said, what's this? We tasted it, and hated it! There were hard rolls, too. But apparently the soldiers would not eat the hard rolls, they would not eat the local bread, they would eat only this Wonder Bread.

That's how the American military was made to feel at home. The Coca-Cola, the Wonder Bread, the peanut butter, all kinds of things that we knew nothing about.

TWO WEEKS ON THE BASE

At six o'clock every morning, a bugle would sound. I would look out from the barracks and see Army soldiers running, lining up by a pole, and raising an American flag. I rarely saw a soldier walk. It looked to me like they were always running.

What we didn't know at the time was that this base was a collection spot for people being resettled in the southern states and the west coast, but not the New York area. New Orleans turned out to be the entry point for us. We were all waiting for transportation to the United States.

While we waited for our ship to come in, other refugees arrived from other camps. There were not only Jews, but non-Jewish refugees, too, who were resettling in America from DP camps.

Did I talk to anybody from those other places? No, there was not a single child my age. I was very lonely. I did have my brother, but I had left behind all my good friends. Actually, they had left me and gone to Israel.

BECOMING AMERICAN: MOVIES

On the base, there was an YMCA (we pronounced it "IHM-kah"). HIAS sort of managed it. It was a mass introduction to America.

Here's what they did: they showed films. The films helped us answer questions like, what is life like in New York? What does New York look like? What does the South look like? Basically, they were geography-type films, with some kinds of propaganda films about America. They had

---

85 Trusted kosher certification
86 OU (Orthodox Union) is a trusted symbol of kosher certification

patriotic stuff – big, grand music, Fourth of July parades, circus scenes – whatever there was, they selected films to try to introduce us to America. These movies were not made for foreigners, they were made for Americans. There was a Chamber of Commerce produced movie about the spirits of the soldiers. A few were about industry: we would see how Boeing made airplanes, or how farmers made cheese.

I began to listen to English. Before that, I hadn't heard English. All the movies at the base were in English.

BECOMING AMERICAN: MAPS (PHOENIX? IT'S NEAR FLORIDA)

At the YMCA, they also had atlases. Maps. I had no idea where Phoenix was on the United States map. (I still called it FAW-nix, like my parents did).

Back in the DP camp, we had had no world atlas, or American atlas. But the library in the camp did have hundreds of maps; maps of Israel, of Palestine, but no maps of America. When people would ask me, where are you going? I would say, I'm going to FAW-nix, Arizona, and they said where is Fawnix? I would say, "Fawnix is near Florida." That's what I imagined; that's what I was told.

I always imagined that Arizona and Florida were next to each other. After all, I figured, they're both somewhere in the South. We looked very carefully at the maps at the YMCA, and we began to realize the distance. I took a piece of paper, and measured according to the scale on the map, to find how many kilometers there were from Florida to here, and how many kilometers from New Orleans to there, and I realized, oh my God! *America is* a big country! It's not like getting from Munich to Föhrenwald in an hour, or taking a train for two hours to get from Munich to Bremerhaven

Soon enough, we would travel across the Atlantic Ocean to New Orleans. From there, we would take a train to Phoenix. The train trip would last for days.

ALL THAT MAP STUDY, AND JUST TWO SANDWICHES?

A couple of years later, I would get on a bus from Phoenix to New York, to go to Yeshiva University. My mother would pack me just two sandwiches for the whole trip. I did not understand how far I was going, even then.

How could I not have realized how long that trip would take? How was it that I thought, "I'll get on this Greyhound bus and in a few hours, I will be—" I have no idea. Maybe I wiped that map out of my memory? Maybe I didn't want to think about it?

Was it because my mother, in particular, didn't do the map study? It was *shtetl* mentality: on a horse and buggy, you get from here to there. Two sandwiches should be plenty.

BECOMING AMERICAN: MAGAZINES

There were magazines at the YMCA—*Life, Saturday Evening Post*—so we started looking at pictures, to see what average Americans looked like. We couldn't read it. But just sitting there, going through magazines, this was how we spent our time. Watching films, looking at maps and magazines. No school.

SAYING GOOD-BYE TO EUROPE

We could leave the base as long as we got a pass. They had a guard post, so if you said you wanted to go out, they would give you a pass, and you could come and go anytime you wanted. It was not restricted. My brother and I would walk out, and we would sort of explore the territory outside of the installation, the Army base. We walked into the town of Bremerhaven. We walked to the water. The time we spent wandering around Bremerhaven was our farewell to Europe.

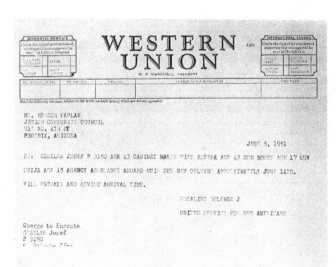

Western Union telegram to Phoenix. Gortlers are on the way. *Courtesy of the HIAS.*

WAS I STILL SAD?

I looked forward for the next chapter. I was very aware of not knowing where we were going. I think by then I pretty much had given up on being sad.

I had conversations with the soldiers, and that helped.

Despite some practical jokers, the soldiers were by and large quite friendly. We would hang out with them. They would shine their boots, and make fun, and we would help them shine their boots. They took us to their barracks, which was just like our barracks, except for them, everything had to be done a certain way.

There were a few Jewish soldiers. Some spoke Yiddish. We gravitated to them, and they to us. We knew who was Jewish and who was not. First of all, everybody had a dog tag, with their religion stamped on it. The Jewish soldiers' dog tags had an "H" for Hebrew. I don't recall a Jewish chaplain at the base.

We were ready to pack and move.

We were given one day's notice.

PART THREE

FINDING A PLACE IN AMERICA

CHAPTER 15

On the Boat and Beyond
June 5 – June 14, 1951

We boarded the USS Muir and traveled for about two weeks. We couldn't eat. Almost everybody on the ship was seasick. The weather was rough.

The accommodations were extremely poor. We were in a humongous long room, like an old-fashioned hospital ward. Men were in one part of the boat, women in another. The beds were army bunks, four to the stack, from floor to ceiling. The food was extremely marginal. There were hard boiled eggs, and more Wonder Bread! Our soup was hot water and some vegetables.

Everybody on the ship had to perform some kind of labor. Was it just to break the monotony? I don't know. We had hammers, we were knocking off paint, removing rust. The sailors were constantly painting, fixing up the ship.

I had heard some American music—was it jazz?—in Bremerhaven. The same music came blasting through the sailors' speakers. The sailors had better accommodations than we did. We kids would sometimes sneak into the sailors' area.

There were a lot of Jews on that ship, people going to the West Coast and to the South for resettlement. We had name tags pinned on us.

ARRIVAL IN NEW ORLEANS

When we arrived in New Orleans, we went down a long, long hallway to get off the boat, schlepping the few belongings we had. We were met by people I imagine were volunteers from the Jewish community of New

Orleans, part of the HIAS group. We went on a school bus to the Jewish Community Center. There, we were given a warm, welcoming reception.

There was lots of food! Nice, cooked kosher food—with meat! And chicken! It was all prepared by the volunteers. It was delicious.

This was the first time we ate bananas. I ate the peels and threw away the inside.

We slept in the gym of the JCC, on Army cots. Men and women together, families together.

The next day, we were taken by bus to a train, the Santa Fe railroad. It was June, so the weather was extremely hot, and extremely humid.

This train was more comfortable than the ones in Germany. They packed food for us. The refugees were in separate cars from the other passengers. That separation felt more like an accommodation to us, with friendly intent.

Port Reception notice, New Orleans.
All document images on pages 104-108 courtesy of the HIAS.

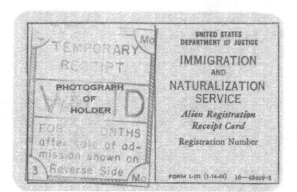

Green card for "Szyja" Gortler

June 20, 1951 telegram to Florence Frank, Phoenix, indicating Gortlers might go to NY. Describes possible trade of Gortlers for another family.

Please exchange 2 cases (Gortler - NY NYANA) [handwritten]

COMMUNITY SERVICE DEPARTMENT
JUN 21 1951 [stamp]

June 20, 1951

Miss Florence G. Frank
Executive Secretary
Jewish Social Service
702 East Adams Street
Phoenix, Arizona

Re: GORTLER; Joseph, Estera,
      Moses, Szia

Dear Miss Frank:

This is in reply to your telegram of June 19 regarding the Gortler
family's request to resettle to New York City. We have checked our
files and find that the brother, Chaim, whose name is Balsenbaum
and not Bakenbaum as indicated in your telegram, is active with
NYANA. This family consists of Mr. and Mrs. Balsenbaum and a child,
and has been active with us for about 8 months.

Our review of the record indicates that there is little help
that can be expected from the Balsenbaums. Obviously, since they
are receiving financial assistance from this agency they cannot be
of financial help. Also from our knowledge of the husband we can
see that he could be of little help to the family in helping them
with their adjustment, such as help in looking for work etc. We
had a good deal of difficulty, as a matter of fact, in getting
Mr. Balsenbaum to accept employment himself. They occupy a 4-room
apartment. Interestingly, they have never mentioned any relatives,
nor have they asked us to consider bringing his sister to New York
City. We are planning to discuss the situation with him to see if
they are interested in having the Gortler family join them in
New York and also to determine whether they can provide temporary
housing.

We have also discussed the situation with USNA. They have little
information in their records about the Gortler family. Again their
record does not indicate any relatives acknowledged by the Gortler
family prior to their arrival in this country. The record does
indicate that Mrs. Gortler's maiden name is also Balsenbaum, which
would seem to verify the relationship partially. We would appreciate
having more information, such as names of Mrs. Gortler's parents,
birth date, etc. so that we could verify the relationship.

Further, your telegram gives very little information regarding the
Gortler family. We are interested in knowing what kind of work
Mr. Gortler does, how employable he is and how employable the other

Miss Florence G. Frank   -2-   June 20, 1951

members of the family are. I think you should know that the labor market in
New York is very tight and that it is not easy to secure employment. Whatever
employment is available is generally as helpers in factories, doing shipping
clerk work, packing, etc. This family should understand this fact and th
will be expected, if they come to New York, to take whatever work is avail.
which may not necessarily be, as indicated, in their regular occupational f.old.
Housing is also difficult to obtain here, and the family may have to live in
furnished rooms for a while. I mention these facts since I am sure you will want
to discuss them with the family.

We have recently written to you regarding two single unattached men whom we are
interested in resettling to Phoenix. Their names are   r and
, If after your discussion with the family regarding the conditions in New York
they are still interested in coming here, we would be willing to consider them for
resettlement in New York if you would accept these two persons as an exchange.
This is, of course, subject to verification of the relationship and the interest
on the part of the brother in New York to have his sister and her family here.
We are proceeding to interview Mr.   in New York City pending receipt of
your reply. Will you please let us hear from you as soon as possible.

           Sincerely yours,

           Bernard Goldstein
           Executive Assistant

BG:rs

   c.c. (blind): A. Burstein, CRS
            B. Behrman, USNA

June 20, 1951 Two-page letter to Florence Frank, Phoenix, RE request to settle in NY.

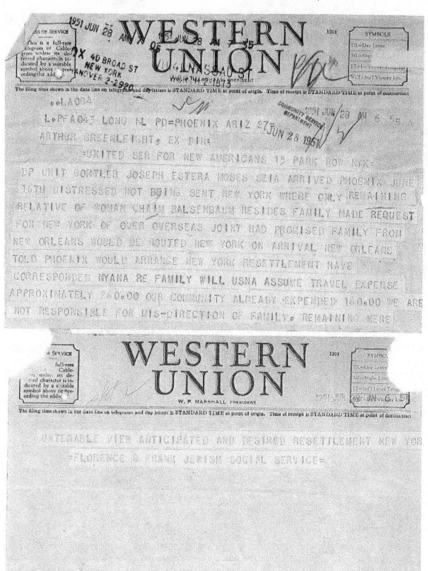

June 28, 1951 telegram from Frank, Phoenix, to United Fund, NY, describing "distressed at not being sent to NY...We are not responsible for mis-direction of family. Remaining here untenable [in] view [of] anticipated and desired resettlement [in] New York."

July 9, 1951 transcription of telegram to USNA from Frank, Phoenix: Gortlers decided to remain; community "not prepared to accept" other named person

July 10, 1951 forward of above telegram to NYANA [New York Association for New Americans]

CHAPTER 16

Arriving in America, Settling in Phoenix
1951-1952

We were on the train for about two days. We arrived in Phoenix at 4:20pm on June 16, 1951.

Three or four people met us at the station. One was the head of Jewish Family Service: Florence Frank, a social worker. And the sponsoring family met us: the Sheinfelds. The man's name was Harry, and his wife was a member of the National Council of Jewish Women. There was a translator, since neither the Sheinfelds nor Florence spoke much Yiddish. My father always, for the rest of his life, called it "Faw-nix." My mother, too.

THE SOCIAL WORKER GIVES ME A NEW NAME
Florence was the one who told us that we had to shed the shackles of Europe and become good Americans. She was the one who changed my name to James.

My father's name was Yosef, which of course became Joseph. My mother's name, Estera, became Esther. My brother's name, Moses, became Morris. My name, Szia, however, presented a problem. "With a name like Szia," Florence said, "you'll never make it in America."

In the 1950s, America was supposed to be a melting pot. The name "Szia" did not melt very well.

"We need to give you a very strong, non-Jewish American name," she said. Without hesitation, she came up with the name "James." And that's how

I came to be called James. She told me that my friends would call me Jimmy.

My parents called me Szia in the house, but at school I was James.

SETTLING IN TO A NEW HOME

The American Jewish novelist Herman Wouk, in his novel *Inside, Outside,*[87] explored the idea of a dual identity: Jewish inside the house, practicing Jewish rituals; but stepping out of the house, a Jew tried to fit into the general society. That idea is the one we were living out in those early days in Phoenix.

We were taken to a garden-type apartment that Jewish Family Service had rented for us, a one bedroom, with a "swamp cooler" in the living room window.

The weather was extremely hot. The "swamp cooler" was a fan in a box, with three panels. In front is a fan. Outside, there is a water hose, like a straw, dripping water into hay or straw. That cooled the air. It blew in cooler air with moisture. If you sat in front of it, you got sprayed with the cooler, moist air.

My parents slept in the bedroom, with Morris and I in the living room on couches. The place was not badly furnished. It was a palace to us, compared to the space we had in the DP camp. It had a kitchen, a table with chairs, couches, all donated by the Jewish Community of Phoenix. It was the first time that I could remember that we actually had a bathroom. Flushing water. A bathtub with a shower. All in the apartment. A private bathroom: what a novel idea.

We had no telephone. They told us the landlady had a phone. If we needed a phone, we were told, we should go to her and she could call for us. But we wondered, who would we call?

At that time, four or five families were resettled in Phoenix. All were housed within walking distance of each other, and we kept in contact with them. There were daily or every-other-day visits from Jewish Family Service, and by Mrs. Sheinfeld. She would sit and visit with us, and she tried to find employment for us.

She found a school for me. There was one other refugee child my age in the school—a guy whose last name was Toporek—in my grade. We were fifteen. I was never given classes in English. I was just dropped into high school.

---

87   Herman Wouk, *Inside, Outside*. Little, Brown, 1985.

THE SOCIAL WORKER'S IDEA OF A
GOOD EDUCATION FOR ME

Florence wanted to push us into trades. She enrolled me in Phoenix Technical School, one of the three public high schools in Phoenix at that time. Phoenix Tech was the closest high school to where I lived. It was within walking distance. I took up architectural drawing as my major during my one year there, when I was known as James Gortler.

Probably the reason I was enrolled in that school was because the social worker thought it would be an easier path for me. I think her mindset was, "Go to the school, get a vocation, get a job."

As it turned out, that schooling was useful. Years later, when I was Chief Executive Officer of Kline Galland, and it came time to design The Summit, or the extensions of the Kline Galland Home, I knew how to read blueprints, because I had learned drafting in that one year at Phoenix Technical School.

THAT FIRST SUMMER IN PHOENIX

When we arrived, it was summer, so school was not in session. I walked around in the Arizona heat, and hung out. For a summer job, I was introduced to a young man, Berkowitz, who had a car. He was two or three years older than I was. I was fifteen, so he was maybe seventeen. Florence's friend connected us.

I went with him in the morning to a farm, to pick cantaloupes in the fields. It was hot as could be! He then drove us to different neighborhoods to sell these cantaloupes. He would stay in the car, and I would go to the door. I would call, "Two for two bits!" The first customer gave me a 25-cent coin. I said, "Where's the other coin?" I had no idea what two bits meant. American English has changed quite a lot during my lifetime. In those days, a "bit" meant twelve and a half cents. Two bits meant a quarter. Berkowitz explained it to me.

When we were selling them, I got a kick out of it when I saw a mezuzah[88] on the door. We sold them in the more affluent neighborhoods, not the neighborhood where we lived

I wasn't allowed to keep the two bits. I was just picking and selling. Probably Berkowitz ripped me off. I never met the farmer. Was this another

---

88   Doorpost marker of a Jewish home: a small box with Torah passages inside

rip-off? I don't think we paid anything to the farmer. I had no idea. This farm was on the outskirts, not in Phoenix itself.

The first year in Phoenix, Morris worked as a janitor at the JCC, and then as a dental technician. He was the main financial supporter for the family. He did not go to high school as I did. The second year, when I left for New York, he enrolled at Phoenix High, and graduated with honors. He earned an AA degree at Phoenix Junior College and continued his studies at the University of Arizona school of pharmacy in Tucson.

Morris worked for several years as a pharmacist, then opened his own pharmacy, MG Pharmacy, in a Phoenix medical building. He married Marcelle Sebag, an Israeli woman originally from Morocco. His son David followed in his father's footsteps by going to the University of Arizona school of pharmacy. David taught at Yale and then worked for the FDA in Washington DC. His daughter Deborah graduated from the University of Pennsylvania and its dental school, becoming an endodontist. When Morris retired, his son David continued the Gortler tradition by becoming the owner of MG Pharmacy.

My father got a job as a cabinetmaker. He did not know how to use the equipment, so he didn't last too long. My mother took in ironing. She would iron shirts for people. Then my father got a job at the old age home, The Kivel Home, working in the kitchen, whatever was needed.

Certainly, working in an old age home myself wasn't my original ambition! I did want to work with people, but my early work was with youth. I kind of fell into the work with the elderly. Eventually, that became my life's work, a profession that has allowed me to leave a legacy that continues to serve my community.

THE LOCAL CONSERVATIVE[89] RABBI INTERVENES AND CHANGES MY LIFE

After my first year at Phoenix Technical School, a Conservative rabbi named Harry Schechtman influenced my next move and changed the course of my life. He was very nice and kind. We went to his shul,[90]

---

89 The "Conservative" movement liberalized certain longstanding Jewish traditional, or "Orthodox," practices around the turn of the 20th century. It was not uncommon for rabbis serving Conservative congregations in the mid-20th century to have received their rabbinical training in Orthodox yeshivas.

90 Yiddish for synagogue

the big shul, Beth El. I couldn't understand a word of his sermons in English. The davening was familiar—very little English, all in Hebrew—with familiar words, but Litvak pronunciation, not Galitzianer. The shul's *shammes* (sexton) was also a refugee.

Rabbi Schechtman despite the fact that he was a Conservative rabbi was a Yeshiva University graduate. At that time, many YU grads ended up in Conservative shuls.

Probably my father was the one who initiated the conversation with the rabbi about my education. I was fluent in Hebrew. Next to Yiddish, it was my best language. I wrote, read and spoke Modern Hebrew fluently, more than I do now. (My grandson and I speak Hebrew on the phone all the time.)

I had my Gemara from the DP camp (which I still have). The rabbi found an older man for me to study with, to prepare me for the entry exam to YU high school. It was obvious that my Jewish education was far superior to anything in Phoenix, so I would either stop going to school or go elsewhere for a Jewish education.

The rabbi wrote a letter of introduction to a Mr. Abrams, the registrar of Manhattan Talmudical Academy—Yeshiva University's high school—about this young man from Phoenix. I was accepted into the next year's class, to begin in September of 1952. And so, my next adventure began.

CHAPTER 17

The Bus Trip To New York:
I Learn I Am A "White Person"

September 1952

The bus ticket was $40 from Phoenix to New York. Jewish Family Service bought the ticket and gave me $20 for pocket money. At that time, a cup of coffee cost a nickel, and so did a candy bar; a pack of cigarettes was about 15 cents; a loaf of bread was a quarter. Life magazine cost 20 cents.

The trip lasted days and days. My mother had packed me, for my trip, two sandwiches and an apple, with a pear for my dessert. After the first day, we were still somewhere between Phoenix and St. Louis, and the sandwiches were gone. You know, when you sit on the bus and you look out through the picture windows, you need to do something. I consumed the sandwiches, and of course, the apple and the pear. I had the $20 in my pocket, so for the rest of the journey, about three more days, I lived on candy bars, which I purchased at the bus stations. There was no interstate highway system at the time, and no rest stops as we know them. The bus would normally stop in some small towns. The station was either a general store, or a pharmacy. They always had candy bars.

Some of the people on the bus were black. I didn't know that segregation was such that people of color – called "negroes" back then—couldn't sit just anywhere. I wanted to sit in the back, where there was more room. But the bus driver wouldn't let me. "White people don't sit there," he said. I'd never known of this separation. I'd never heard of myself as a "white person."

Interacting with black people was new to me. We had seen a few black soldiers, but we had no idea about the black people living in the US. One of the first TV shows I saw, on the first TV I ever saw in my life, at the JCC in Phoenix, was Amos 'n' Andy. That show stuck in my mind. I couldn't understand a lot of the stuff that was going on.

At one of the stops, I found a magazine, and brought it onto the bus. It was *Jet*. The white people on the bus couldn't figure out why this white boy was reading *Jet* magazine. Some middle-aged white men came over and asked, where did you get this? I found it, I said. They said "Put it away. White people don't read *Jet*." They actually took it away from me. I guess they thought they were taking care of me.

I would look at the pictures and figure out the story with the text. *Life* was a good magazine for me. The *Saturday Evening Post*, too. *Jet* was a good one: it was small and easy to hold, and it was also easy for me to read. Later on, when I was in high school in New York, I realized that the stories in Jet were written for especially easy reading. And I bought one. The cover price was fifteen.

The bus trip across America was an amazing experience. To see the country from a bus, traveling on two-lane roads, through little towns. I always chose a window seat. I saw America up close, on that bus trip.

Reading billboards was very exciting. The letters were very large, and the messages easy to read. "Cigarettes." "Mr. Clean." I looked out from my window seat, and I got to know America.

I improved my reading by looking at the billboards. I could understand English in a very rudimentary way. I could write, basically. Even today, many times I pronounce all the letters. I started out saying the "k" in "know" and "knee."

I managed to change buses in St. Louis without getting lost, but passing through Newark, New Jersey, I almost got off, because the name sounded like "New York."

Back in Phoenix, my mother was going absolutely crazy during my trip. She had no phone. I sent a telegram when I arrived, four or five days after I left. It was not even instantly delivered. She had to have my brother read it.

I was met at the Greyhound station by my Uncle Chaim Balsenbaum, my mother's brother, who lived in a rundown neighborhood of Brooklyn called Brownsville, where a lot of refugees lived. He took me by subway to Yeshiva University. I was amazed to find, at the subway station at 181st Street, a blue tile sign on the wall that read, "Yeshiva University." I realized how important Yeshiva University was, to be marked at the subway station.

Uncle Chaim dropped me off at the office of Mr. Abrams, the registrar. I became a member of Yeshiva University's Talmudical Academy High School Class of 1954. During my New York years, I occasionally saw Uncle Chaim. I even attended the weddings of his son and daughter.

CHAPTER 18
High School in New York
September 1952-June 1954

So here comes "James." My arrival was not exactly well coordinated. Rabbi Schechtman had communicated by mail with Mr. Abrams, but Abrams never connected with the people in the dormitory to expect me. Normally, people make the full formal applications, and deposits, and housing arrangements in advance. But housing was never part of the arrangements that were made for me. When I arrived and met Mr. Abrams, he said, "Where are you going to sleep tonight?"

I said, "I don't know." He asked if they had arranged for a dormitory. I didn't know.

It was my first day of high school in a city I didn't know, and I had no place to stay. The dorm was full. There were usually some dropouts, but that day, every room was taken in the high school dormitory. A note was sent around to the college dorms. But they were also full.

In the high school dorms, there were two guys to a room and two desks. The college dorms had bunk beds. They asked if anybody would like to put in another bunk bed in their room. You could put another bed on top of the beds there.

Two guys answered yes, they were willing to take in another temporary guy. These boys were both New Yorkers, and they would go home for the weekend. One of the boys was Marvin Blackman. The other, Nathan Lewin. He went to law school. I never had any further contact with him, but he became one of the most famous lawyers in the United States.

I moved into the college dormitory that first night. In those days, YU provided all the bedding, so I was all set for the night.

VAKE UP, AMERICA!

I was in a college dorm with the big guys, and I'm this young *pisher*, "James." They were kind of taken aback by the names James. James Gortler? What is this? But they were very nice and accepted me.[91]

Blackman would always remind me that I was the first to wake up, and while he and the other guy were still asleep, I would yell, "Vake up America!" He thought that was so funny. He would imitate me beautifully. I had learned some English, and I was waking them up to go daven. I was better than any alarm clock!

After about a week, a place opened up in the high school dormitory, and I was moved there. YU gave me a full tuition scholarship, and eight dollars a week for food.

Other than the DP camps, I had had basically no formal elementary education, so I came into high school with a big disadvantage. I was missing eight years of preparation. English? History? Sciences? I had learned very elementary science, but I had learned it in Hebrew.

It is very difficult to pick up eight years' worth of the kind of education that prepares you for high school. The difficulty was more intense because I was also getting acculturated to the American way of life. What English I knew, I had acquired during that one year in Phoenix: listening, driving around with the cantaloupe guy, doing what I could to use the language that surrounded me in my classes at Phoenix Technical High School.

THE ENTRANCE EXAM: "JIMMY" BECOMES JOSH

The next day, I came down to take my placement exam for the rabbinic studies program, known as RIETS (Rabbi Isaac Elchanan Theological Seminary). School had started already. I had arrived at YU late, a few days after the semester had begun, because of my bus ride. (I thought I would be there in one day; the trip took four.)

---

91   This guy Blackman had a sister who married someone from Denver, a fellow who funded the start of the Bais Yaakov school in Denver. Blackman would come to Denver to visit his sister, and he became eventually a teacher in Denver. So after I married Sarah, when I would come to Denver to visit her family, I would always hang out with Blackman. My relationship with him picked up again years later and we would reminisce.

From the DP camp, I had my Gemara and a Mishna. Those were what I had started learning from with the man in Phoenix. We had reviewed two or three chapters very thoroughly.

At the time, at YU, both for the high school and college levels, all the Yeshiva programs were taught in Yiddish by all European rabbis. Some were in the US prior to the war. Many teachers were from European yeshivas. I knew I would have my exam with Rabbi Mendel Zaks. He was the main examiner.

That first day, I came in to meet Rabbi Mendel Zaks in his office. I entered the office with trepidation. My entire body was shaking. I knew that Rabbi Mendel Zaks was the son-in-law to the Chofetz Chaim![92] That was enough *yichus*[93] to be plenty intimidating.

Rabbi Zaks was a man with a gray beard, who would smoke cigarettes continuously. Continuously! And how did he smoke? He held the cigarette in an unusual way, between his middle fingers, with the fire inside his cupped hand. We would all make fun of the way he smoked. In between puffs, he asked me questions.

As I entered the room, I said, in Yiddish:

"*Gut morgen.*" Good morning.

R. Zaks answered, "*Gut morgen. Voss is eihr nommen?*" What is your name?

"*Mein nommen,*" I answered proudly, "*is James.*" My name is James. "*Aber ihr kannnt mich riffen Jimmy.*" But you can call me Jimmy.

He puffed, and puffed, and puffed. "*Voss fahr a nommen? James?*" What kind of a name is James? Puff. Puff. Puff. "*Voss is ihr yiddisheh nommen?*" What is your Jewish name? He smoked, and smoked again.

I told him with a smile, "*Mein yiddisheh nommen is Szia, und mein Hebraische nommen is Yehoshua.*" My Yiddish name is Szia, and my Hebrew name is Yehoshua.

"*Ohhhh, Yehoshua! Deineh nommen in America vet zein* Joshua, *und deineh freunde vell dich riffen* Josh." Your name in America will be Joshua, and your friends will call you Josh.

He continued with questions. "*Vi bist ti geboren?*" Where were you born?

---

92 "The Chofetz Chaim," Rabbi Israel Meir Kagan, one of the most influential rabbinic figures of the late 19th and early 20th centuries, is known by the title of his 1873 book, *Chafetz Chaim* (The One Who Desires Life), an ethical guide to the perils and avoidance of gossip.
93 Impressive family history

"*Ich bin geboren in Poiland.*" I was born in Poland.

"*Fun vannt kummst di aheher?*" From where do you come now?

"*Ich kumm fun Faw-nix.*" (I still said "faw-nix.")

"*Voss teet a yid in Faw-nix?*" What's a Jew doing in Phoenix?

"*Mir zennen ungekummen fun der lagern.*" We came from the camps.

"*Und ver hot dich geschicht ahehr?*" And who sent you here?

"*Rav Harry Schachtman, der rov in Foh-nix.*" The rabbi in Phoenix.

"*Ohhhh. Ich gedenkt: Ehr ist geveyn a gutteh talmid.*" Oh, I remember him. He was a good student. "*Aber er iz ungenemmen a shtelle in a Conservativeh shul.*" But he accepted a position in a Conservative shul.

That was my introduction.

"*Und yetzt, zog mir voss vilst du lernen heint.*" And now, tell me what do you want to study with me today?

"*Ich hob mein Gemoreh fun dem lager.*" I have my own Gemara, from the camp.

It was *Baba Metzia*.[94]

"*Vellchen perek villst du lernen?*" What chapter do you want to study?

"*Dem ersten perek,*" I said. The first one. "*Shnei ochzim b'tallis…*" Two guys find a tallis…

Rabbi Zaks, after fifteen to twenty minutes of hearing me read the text, with Rashi and Tosafos,[95] commented that my depth of understanding of the Gemara was on a high level. He asked me where I studied Gemara. I answered that it was with several Lubavitcher rebbes in the DP camps. He told me that he was under the impression that the educational system in the DP camps was mainly secular. He was amazed.

I knew that it was thanks to my parents' decision that my DP camp education included both yeshiva learning and secular.

Rabbi Zaks placed me in fourth year Gemara, the senior class, in Rabbi Weiss' class. Here I was, a sophomore, this *greeneh*[96] kid from Arizona, still fresh from the DP camps in Europe. The rabbi didn't care that I was sixteen and the other guys in the class were eighteen. I was a good student.

Those two years at the YU high school, MTA, were very difficult for me, both with the English language itself and the subjects that I was confronted

---

94 Talmud chapters dealing with property rights
95 Two traditional commentators included in every Talmud
96 Literally "green," meaning inexperienced; a common Yiddish expression among recent immigrants for those even more recently arrived

JOSHUA GORTLER
This cowboy from Phoenix, Arizona, has been selected to the "elite" few to be a three year student at Talmudical. An editor of Hatchiyah, Josh hopes to establish a Hebrew language paper in the Far West to further the cause of Torah education among the Western correspondents.

Editor of Hatchiyah, S.O.Y. Representative, President of Chug Ivri Club.

"Joshua Gortler, the cowboy from Phoenix..." Courtesy of the Joshua Gortler collection. Yeshiva University yearbook, 1954

by. I would go into English class and try to sit in the back of the room, because the teacher would ask people to read sentences. I was embarrassed, that first year. I was known as "the cowboy," because I was from Phoenix.

I was actually going to three schools, because I wanted to graduate with my peers. (Although I entered as a sophomore, I was actually a year older than the other sophomores, because when I started high school in Phoenix I was fifteen. The normal age was fourteen.) I was in the YU yeshiva program—Judaics—in the morning. I was in the YU secular high school—math and science and the other subjects—in the afternoon. And I had to catch up with even more subjects just to qualify to take the New York State Regents exam, which was required for high school graduation.

My second year at MTA, I went to George Washington High School in Washington Heights in the evenings. I took World History and English 3 and 4. My classmates at GW were mainly adults, mostly immigrants, who worked in the daytime and were trying to get a high school diploma in the evening.

English 4 in GW was easier than English 3 at MTA. In English 3, I was competing with future doctors. In English 4, I was a star.

I did homework whenever I could fit it in. I had very little time to think, very little time to play. I just worked extremely hard to get my high school diploma.

CHAPTER 19
Yeshiva University
1954-1958

Most of the Holocaust survivor kids at Yeshiva University and the YU high school did not talk about our lives during and after the war. There were a few others there who had been in other DP camps. We were just too busy building an education for ourselves, building careers, building family life. As far as we were concerned, the war was just one stage of our lives, and then we had to move on.

There was nobody at Yeshiva University whom I knew from my earlier life. But I did find myself drawn to people with backgrounds like mine. Most of my college friends were the children of European parents, who had suffered their own losses during the war.

Was there any support for us there? Did we give each other support? Was there any support from the university? There was none. Today, you would think there would be a staff person for students like us, but that was not on YU's, or anyone else's, agenda. There was no one who handled "survivors," no one to help us cope with college and the issues that each one of us faced, physically, socially, and mentally. Did I notice this? Did it have anything to do with my choice of profession?

Probably. It's certainly true that when it came time for me to choose a career path, I turned to my experiences in the DP camps. Looking back, I see the influence of the DP years throughout my social work career.

COLLEGE AS A BRIEF VACATION

After all that work in high school, I started college with the attitude that I would be taking a vacation for the next four years. I worked as little as possible academically in college until my senior year, and then I said, oh my gosh, I have to do something with my life. Should I go to grad school? What *am* I going to do when I finish college? I began to buckle down, and I decided to go to grad school, where I worked extremely hard once again.

I DECIDE TO WORK AT REPAIRING
THE REMNANTS OF LIVES

I didn't decide that I was going to go into social work school until my last year in college. Most of my classmates already had a definite plan. As far as I could tell, most of the kids going to YU were either pre-med or pre-dental. If you couldn't make it in med school, you were going to dental school. A few would go to grad school in psychology. Business was not an option at that time; marketing, which is a big thing now, was not either. The sciences? I wasn't interested in medicine. I was never prepared in the science field.

I majored in psychology in college, and I heard about graduate school in social work. A light bulb lit up in my head. I remembered the social workers in the DP camps, who patched up the remnants of lives that had been torn apart.

I remembered my summer jobs as a camp counselor at the Phoenix Jewish Community Center. I knew that the top echelon of the Phoenix JCC—the executive director, the program director, and the youth director—were all social workers. I said to myself, hey, let me apply and see what this is all about. I can do it!

Will I get in? Will I not get in? I applied to three schools—to Yeshiva University, Hunter, and Columbia. I was accepted to all three. YU offered me the best financial deal, so I went to YU. It was very simple.

Somewhere between the first teacher in the DP camp who showed me how to make out letters, and the people who accepted me into graduate school at these three distinguished places, I had acquired a great many skills.

In the DP camp, I had worked extremely hard at my education. I knew that I was pushed by my parents to succeed and to take this learning business very seriously. But the hardest I ever worked in my education was in high school, during the one year at the school in Phoenix, and the two years at MTA.

MY MOTHER DESCRIBES MY CAREER CHOICE

My mother had a sister, Brocha. I could write a whole chapter about Brocha![97] She's the one who smuggled the live turkey into the DP camp on Erev Pesach. She settled in Munich after the war. After my mother came to the United States, there was a weekly letter exchange between my mother and my aunt.

When I started grad school to become a social worker, and my brother went to pharmacy school, I remember the letter my mother wrote to my Aunt Brocha: "*Mein teirisch schwester Brocha. Meine tzvei yingelach gehen en college—universitat.* (My dear sister Brocha, my two children are going to college—to university.) *Monyik* (Morris) *zien an apteker* (a pharmacist). *Szia* (me) *zein a social worker.*"

Letter comes back from my aunt: "*Mein teire schvester Ester: ich farshtei* (I understand) *vos Monyik lernent zol zein an apteker* (that Monyik is learning to be a pharmacist). *Aber vos lernnt Szia?* (But what is Szia learning?) *A social worker? Vos* (What) *ist a social worker?*"

Letter from my mother to my Aunt Brocha: "*Mein teire schvester Brocha: A social worker meind* (A 'social worker' means:) *er shpielstach mit meshiggener kinder.*" (He plays with crazy kids.) That was the definition of a social worker, according to my mother.

I myself had no real idea what a social worker was. Obviously, neither did my mother. But I knew what social workers did. As I understood it, they either played with "crazy" kids or worked with people who are "crazy"— people with torn-up lives—and they tried to put them back together.

Eventually, in my professional life as Chief Executive Officer of the Kline Galland Center and Affiliates, I would facilitate the work of a staff of hundreds of nurses, therapists, social workers, and others, to help them understand the dynamics of family relationships. I helped to provide them with the tools to assist not only the residents in our facilities, but also many dysfunctional families, to resolve issues that had been lingering for years. In short, to help stitch together the remnants of their lives.

---

97   "Aunt Brocha's Journey," Chapter 6, part 1

CHAPTER 20
Jobs During College
1953-1958

THE DISHWASHER, 1953

I went home to Phoenix after my first year at MTA in New York and got a job as a dishwasher at the VA hospital. I had to take two buses to work, but I always arrived on time.

By then, I was already pretty good at English. In this job, I was introduced to another new language, since most of the kitchen staff spoke Spanish. Boy, did I learn to curse! I had no idea what the swear words meant, but they taught me all the important ones. They realized that I was not American born, so they knew I wouldn't know. They enjoyed being on a higher *madrega*[98]—a higher social status. Here was somebody lower than them! (Those Spanish words turned out to be very useful later in New York.) I wore a white uniform, a white apron, and a paper kitchen hat. My job also included putting the trays together. And I washed dishes. I could load the dishwasher in no time at all.

Part of my job was to deliver food, in these huge containers, to the wards. These were very large rooms. The majority of the patients were men.

When I delivered the food, I connected with the people, even at my age. One of the older men was Jewish. We started talking. He asked me why my English was so poor. He was a veteran of the Second World War. He was bedridden, and I would take the tray to him. Once I got to know

---

98   Usually means a level of spirituality, but often used in fun, as here.

him, I would bring him his food and talk to him some more. I got bawled out more than once for doing this, because my job was not to talk to the patients, it was just to deliver the food and leave.

When I see the dishwashers at The Summit and at Kline Galland, I think: I was there. And along with the same feelings that a CEO has, and the same needs that the director of a department has, I've learned a lot of humility. These people are people. I thought, if I ever have a bigger job, I'd treat people well.

When I look at my Social Security history, I see the dishwasher job income. My cantaloupes, I didn't declare.

THE SUMMER CAMP COUNSELOR, 1954-56

I was very goal oriented. I wanted to make it in the United States. I always worked very hard to move up from one position to another.

After my experience as a dishwasher at the VA, when I came home for vacation, I found summer jobs in Phoenix at the Jewish Community Center. First year, I was a counselor. Second year, I was promoted to unit counselor. The third year, I made it to head counselor for the whole camp. This experience might have led me to my later work at the JCC in Englewood, New Jersey.

A SUMMER CHALLENGE: KEEPING KOSHER IN PHOENIX

I continued to live in a dual world: In New York, I felt very comfortable being Jewish. On the YU campus, I was connected. But when I came home to Phoenix, it was a different world. When I was a dishwasher I never mentioned that I was Jewish. I remembered the advice from Florence the social worker: keep your Jewishness as a low profile.

There was also antisemitism in Phoenix. I remember once, driving with Berkowitz, my cantaloupe partner, near the Phoenix Country Club. The club had a sign: No Jews. No Negroes.

In Phoenix, there was one kosher butcher, Katz's. There was a *schochet* (kosher slaughterer), but he only slaughtered chickens and turkeys. "Meat," meaning beef, came in from elsewhere.

I had a hard time with the workers at the VA, because we were supposed to eat the food that was served to the patients, and I only ate certain things—bread, or fruit—and I didn't want to discuss why. I was very uncomfortable about being an observant Jew.

I remember eating the Wonder Bread, which I still found funny. I also ate the cheese, as hard cheese was an item that kosher people ate. Was it really kosher? Let me put it this way. I finished high school in 1954. It wasn't until '55 or '56 that we started to look further into the *hashgacha* of cheeses.

This issue came up when I traveled. After my first trip to New York, I graduated from bus to going by train. In Chicago, I arrived at one station on the Santa Fe line, then took a bus to a different station to take a different line to New York. At the station, I ordered cheese sandwiches. I was a freshman in college when I learned that this cheese was not acceptable to a person who kept kosher.

At least I knew how long the trip was, now. I started bringing along more food. And I started looking for *hashgacha* (a reliable symbol of kosher certification). The whole concept of a kosher mark, and *mashgichim* (kosher supervisors) was becoming more widespread. At the time, in the 1950s, there were almost none of the *hashgacha* symbols that we take for granted today.

A WAITER IN "THE BORSCHT BELT" 1955-58[99]

Unlike my other American friends, I had no checkbook, and nobody was making sure that cash was available to me whenever I needed it. I had to fend for myself.

In New York, during my college years, I had a number of part-time jobs that helped me with my financial situation.

Orthodox Jews in the New York area, at that time, would spend Jewish holidays away from the city in various kosher hotels in the Catskill Mountains. Through an older classmate, I met a headwaiter from the Loch Sheldrake Hotel, one of the kosher Catskills hotels.

My classmate was working as a waiter there. He asked me if I would be interested in going up for Pesach to work as a busboy. I said, "Why not? But what is a busboy?" I'd never heard that term. I was informed that a busboy picks up the dirty dishes and helps the waiter serving the guests. I said, "I can do that."

---

99   Catskill Mountains resorts were popular among some American Jews from the 1920s through 1970s. The term "Borscht," a beet soup common among Jewish immigrants from Russia and Poland, indicated the patrons' tastes in both food and humor. The style of entertainment featured in these resorts—incubators for some of America's most celebrated comedians— came to be known as "Borscht Belt" humor.

My first day on the job, one of the guests asked me to bring him some matjes herring.[100] I marched into the kitchen, and I took some herring and some matzos. I'd never heard of "matjes herring!" I took the pickled herring and the matzos and brought them to the guest. He looked at me as if I'd just stepped off the moon. "What kind of idiot is this kid?" he told the headwaiter. "He doesn't know what matjes herring is!"

We didn't have matjes herring in the DP camps. How would I know?

I eventually graduated from being a busboy—or as I would call it, a "boybus." I moved on to be a waiter in the Pine View—a step up in the economic level of the guests—and then the Pioneer Country Club. Eventually, I worked at the crème de la crème of the borscht-belt hotels, Grossingers.

Grossingers was known for the best entertainers. Joey Bishop, Henny Youngman, Rodney Dangerfield, and Jack Benny, among many others, started their careers there.

In this hotel, I worked three jobs. I was a waiter. In between meals, I was a tea boy. In the evenings, after dinner, I worked in the bar. The bar at Grossingers was very unusual. The ceiling of the bar was the floor of the swimming pool. (The guys in the bar would watch to see whether swimmers' suits were staying on).

The waiters were served the leftovers from the day before. We soon figured out, why not order extra items on the menu, hide them in our waiter station, take them up to our dorm rooms—we slept five in a room—and have a great meal?

You know, just like in the DP camp, *a yid gefint zich an eitzeh*—we found a solution. We waiters ate well. I could write a whole chapter on my life as a waiter in the hotels. There was so much waste of food, it was a heartbreak, especially after what I had experienced in the DP camps.

FOOD JOBS AT COLLEGE

One of my jobs in college was working for Mr. Webber, the head of catering at YU. Mr. Webber also provided outside catering to *bar mitzvahs*, weddings, and other social events. We, the waiters, schlepped the food prepared in the cafeteria, served it at the event, then schlepped the leftovers back to the YU kitchen after the event.

---

100 Bits of herring prepared in a spicy wine sauce, a delicacy from "the old country"

In the catering jobs, there was never a *mashgiach*.[101] Things are totally different today. Every kosher event has to have a *mashgiach*.

I lived on eight dollars a week at YU. I got two cards, or stipends, to the cafeteria. There was more than once that I went hungry. I tried to stretch the food; five dollars, I used for the week. A dollar a day. And the other three dollars, I prepaid for Shabbos meals; a dollar fifty each, for dinner and lunch.

I got a job my third year of college—senior year—in the YU cafeteria. I worked on Shabbos, as a waiter. If you were a waiter, you got meals free, plus one or two dollars. On Friday night, Shabbos lunch, *Shalosh seudes*[102]—the third meal was free anyway, paid by the YU women's auxiliary. Lots of challah, tuna fish, some fruit, all family style. Shabbos lunch would be coleslaw, chopped liver, chicken and cholent. That lasted me until about Monday. I would take home leftovers from the *shalosh seudes*. About a dozen guys worked in the kitchen. You had to break into their club, so to speak, to work this job.

I became head waiter, head of the *sholosh seudes* committee.

Once again, I started at the bottom and moved up, from dishwasher to busboy to waiter to headwaiter.

There's a pattern here: I was always looking for opportunities to move up. I think I was born with certain leadership abilities, and with the drive to put myself into positions where I could be a leader.

---

101 Supervisor of kitchen to ensure that food meets kosher standards
102 Literally, "third meal," a supper late in the afternoon on Saturday, the third of three traditional festive Sabbath meals

CHAPTER 21
Social Life in College
1954-1958

In college, I certainly had friends. I was called "Arizona," or "Phoenix." We survivors, too, found each other. The American kids looked down on us.

I dated just one girl who was a Jewish refugee like myself, who was very "poor." She was at Brooklyn College, and had a brother and a mother, no father. Her name was Judy. She was the only immigrant I dated. I was seeking out American girls. I wanted to become much more American.

The first person who really extended a hand and invited me to his house for Shabbos was Israel Bick, who was a year behind me. His mother was a cook in one of the yeshivas in the Bronx. She would bring home food. There were three children that his mother supported. I was there for Shabbos a number of times. I would share a couch with him.

I was invited for Shabbos by Lenny Shapiro in Brooklyn (he signed my yearbook "to the cowboy"). He was "rich." So was Skippy Jotkowitz of Boro Park, who became a physician.

There were a few American-born guys I really connected with. Of the people in my graduating class, I'm still in touch with Lenny, now a retired ophthalmologist in Monsey, New York. And Israel Perlmutter, who became a psychologist in Israel. He was a grandson of the famous Rabbi Heller. Tsvi Nussbaum, a'h, was a friend. Also Anschel Schachter, in Teaneck, who became a dentist. Monis Dachman from DC was a great roommate. His mother would make delicious strudel, with nuts and raisins. I ate a lot of that strudel.

JOSHUA H. GORTLER
Phoenix, Ariz.   *Psychology*
Y.U. Drive, chairman; MASMID;
Hamelitz; Soccer; Psychology Club;
Sociology Club; Hebrew Club; Dean's
Reception

Joshua H. Gortler. Yearbook photo, undergraduate. *Courtesy of the Joshua Gortler collection. Yeshiva University yearbook, 1958*

CHAPTER 22
Becoming a U.S. Citizen
1957

In my junior year of college, I realized that I was eligible to apply for U.S. citizenship as a naturalized citizen. Unlike my immigration, when my parents did the paperwork for me, now I was on my own. Other family members were taking care of their own citizenship applications. I was an adult now, responsible for myself.

After all the paperwork was complete, and the required criminal background check showed that I was not a danger to the country, the last step would be for me to take a citizenship test.

I received a little booklet, similar to the kind you get for taking a driver's test. It covered the same basic material as a first-year high school social studies class. I remember putting on my Shabbos clothes—a white shirt and tie—and going to the immigration office in Manhattan. An intimidating-looking gentleman came out, sat opposite me, and fired off questions. The first question, which I still remember today, was: "Tell me," he said, "who was the first President of the United States, and who is the current President of the United States?"

I kind of smiled, and I said, "George Washington and Ike." His answer was "Wow. You call your President by his first name. And your English is pretty good. Let me ask another question. If you do well on this one I will not ask you any more questions. Tell me," he said, "how does a bill become law in the United States?"

Citizenship certificate. *Courtesy of the Joshua Gortler collection*

"Well," I said, "there are three branches to the government: legislative, executive, and judiciary. A bill needs to pass the two houses of Congress and be signed by the President."

"Mazal tov," this intimidating New York Irishman said. "You are a citizen now!" I had to attend a swearing-in ceremony, where I had to pledge my allegiance to the United States and swear that I would not bear arms against the United States. I also had to swear to give up my loyalty to any other country.

A few weeks later, I received by registered mail the certificate with my picture on it. It was a very proud moment in my lifetime.

PART FOUR

BUILDING AN AMERICAN LIFE

CHAPTER 23
Graduate School
1958-1960

After four years of relatively little work in college, graduate school became a new challenge. The social work school at Yeshiva University was relatively new, with few students, and a much more diverse population than the college. Of the 25 or so students in my class, most of them were not graduates of Yeshiva College, as I was. The grad school not only was coed, but also included some non-Jewish students. The school was located in midtown Manhattan, and it required a subway ride from the main campus in Washington Heights.

In my first year in grad school, I had a job as a dorm counselor. The compensation was a free dorm room. One of my tasks as a dorm counselor was to help new students, freshmen, adjust to New York life, and help them with other personal problems as well. Perfect training for a grad student in Social Work. My other job was to wake up the boys at 6:30 a.m. to go to minyan. I had to knock on every door, sometimes using my master pass key, to get them up. It was not a very pleasant task, and not everybody followed the orders. I took it with a grain of salt.

One of my big challenges in grad school was the requirement to write many papers. Since I did not have typing skill, I did my papers longhand. After I submitted two papers to my professors, I learned they had difficulty reading my writing. So I hired undergraduate students to type my papers. I paid them maybe seventy-five cents a page. I tried to keep my papers concise and short. That was not an expense that I had originally budgeted for!

In addition to classroom work, grad school required twenty hours a week of field placement, what is now called internship. My first placement was at the Bronx YMHA. I had an excellent supervisor, a graduate of University of Pennsylvania, a first-rate social work school. He was an excellent mentor. His approach to me was to ask the kinds of questions that would help me analyze my personal behavior, almost like a self-analysis. He helped me grow and understand myself, so that I could be nonjudgmental and focused on the clients.

I had three assignments. One to work with gangs in the Bronx, mainly Puerto Ricans. This was the time when the musical *West Side Story* came out. The kids I was working with were like the ones in that musical. The Y received a federal grant to work with this population.

My second assignment was to work with a group of young single adults who had emotional problems and were trying to adjust to the responsibilities of adulthood. I thought I had problems? After seeing what these kids had, I felt like a very well-adjusted individual.

My third assignment was with pre-teens in an after-school program. Parents would drop off their kids at the Y, or the kids would walk over from school, for recreational activities and basically to hang out until their parents came home from work.

That first year in grad school was very difficult for me but I felt I was making headway with my professional career.

The second year brought new challenges and a great deal of learning including my own behavior and myself. I spent a great deal of time in the New York Public Library, in the grand building on 42nd St. I always occupied the same chair in the research room and came to know all the librarians, who were extremely helpful.

My second-year field placement was at the Englewood Jewish Community Center. I would spend two more years there, after I received my MSW. My work assignment at the Englewood JCC was with a completely different population than the one at the Bronx Y. In the Bronx, I was dealing with kids in gangs, in an impoverished neighborhood. In Englewood, the kids were spoiled and overprivileged.

CHAPTER 24
Rabbinic Studies and *Semicha*[103]
1959-1962

While I was in graduate school, I had a conversation with Rabbi Dr. Moshe Tendler, an eminent teacher of Talmud and biology at YU. I expressed disappointment at the schedule conflict that prevented me from attending the advanced Talmud *shiur* (class) by the world-renowned Rabbi Joseph Soloveitchik. Rabbi Tendler suggested to me that I should try his father-in-law's yeshiva, MTJ—Mesivta Tiferes Yerushalayim—on the Lower East Side. Rabbi Tendler's father-in-law was none other than the most respected halachic (Jewish law) authority of our generation, HaGaon HaRav Moshe Feinstein.

Starting when I was single, I took two trains to the Lower East Side to learn at Rabbi Feinstein's yeshiva. After I got married and moved to Englewood, I would take a bus from Englewood to Washington Heights, along with two trains, to continue my studies with Rav Moshe.

Rav Moshe Feinstein gave his *shiur* in the morning. The schedule worked out well for me. The subject matter wasn't new to me: it was *Mesechta Kiddushin* (a part of the Talmud), something I had learned before, in my second or third year at YU.

Sitting in a classroom with Rav Moshe Feinstein was just an unbelievable experience. He was very soft spoken. He sat in the *beis medresh*,[104] in front

103 Rabbinic ordination
104 study hall

of the *aron kodesh,*[105] behind a little desk, wearing a big yarmulke. He spoke in Yiddish. He spoke very quietly.

When you looked at him, at his face, you felt that almost the *Shechina*[106] was right there.

I am not an emotional guy that gets excited by the mystical gurus or "rebbes." But with Rav Moshe, you felt that you were in a really holy place, that the *Shechina* was over him when he talked. He never got excited. It's now sixty years since I was in the class, and when I talk about it, I'm transformed into that young man sitting in that room, listening to him, and just seeing the *Shechina* on his face.

It was not a huge class. There were about thirty to forty students, including his two sons, Rabbi Dovid, who succeeded Rav Moshe as *rosh hayeshiva* (head rabbi of the yeshiva) at MTJ, and Rabbi Reuven, now the *rosh hayeshiva* of the Staten Island branch of MTJ. Rav Moshe knew each student by name, and he knew something about each one of us. He called me Szia. Not Joshua. Not "Mister."

After three years of studying at MTJ, I was honored to receive *semicha* from the *Gadol HaDor,*[107] Rabbi Moshe Feinstein.

I have never used the title "Rabbi" in my professional life. When I started my position at the Kline Galland Home in Seattle, some people assumed that I would serve as both Executive Director and rabbinic authority. I told them in no uncertain terms that I would not be their rabbi. I would be their Executive Director.

---

105 Holy ark, where the Torahs are kept
106 Spirit of God
107 Great Scholar of our generation (Hebrew)

CHAPTER 25

Josh and Sarah: First Date.
Marriage. Friends.
1959-1963

It was the beginning of my first year as a graduate student. Sarah Barash had just arrived in New York from Denver. She was enrolled in the women's college of YU, Stern College, as an undergraduate.[108]

There was a young lady from New York, Judy Leifer, who had spent some time in Denver because she had asthma. One of my closest friends, Matisyahu Weisenberg, had a date with her. She asked Matt if he knew anyone who'd be willing to take out this other young woman from Denver.

I said, sure, I'll go out with her. Another adventure.

I was very excited about this double date. Matt had a car. Getting out of the car, on the way to pick up our dates, I hit my forehead on a glass door, and I ended up in an emergency room. After a short examination, the doctors said not to worry, nothing serious, it was just a scratch on the forehead.

We were late to pick up Judy and Sarah, and told them of our adventure. At first, they didn't believe it, but the bandage on my forehead was proof enough.

We had tickets to a Yiddish play on the Lower East Side, "The Kosher *Almanah*"—the Kosher Widow—a story about a groom who dies under the *chuppa* (marriage canopy) during the marriage ceremony, so the bride's still a virgin, but she's also married. A kosher tragedy. Some first date.

---

108 In Sarah's family, there's a story that the name Barash is actually an acronym for "ben Rashi," indicating that the family is descended from the great 11th century Torah commentator known as Rashi, Rabbi Shlomo Yitzhaki.

We arrived at the theatre late, of course, and when we went to the balcony, we found our seats were taken. That began a whole drama, separate from what was going on, on stage. The usher told the people who were in our seats that they had to move. What followed was a very loud debate—in Yiddish, of course—about who had the right to those seats, the ones who were sitting there, or the people who had the tickets. In the row behind us, a man with a cane started knocking loudly on the floor to emphasize his point in the argument. He said, "They came late. They should go find other seats." This whole commotion became a second show in the balcony, until the actors on stage looked up, and yelled, "*Sha shtil*" (Shut up)! As they went on with the play, we were still standing in the aisle, waiting for our seats. Finally, the people who had the seats got up and left, and we sat down.

An older gentleman next to Sarah, asked her, "*Die redst Yiddish?*" (Do you speak Yiddish?) She said yes, but then he went on as though she had said no, and provided Sarah with a running translation of the play for the rest of the evening.

I already thought of myself as a big man on campus, there in New York. To me, Sarah was an "out of town" girl, from the little *shtetl* of Denver. I thought of her as a cute little country pumpkin. I was dating another girl at the time, also from Stern. Sarah gave me an ultimatum: dating both me and my classmate is making me uncomfortable. You need to decide who you want to date. I said okay, I want to date you.

Sarah is an amazing woman. I was smoking a lot then. If you want to date me, she said, you can't smoke. I quit cigarettes cold turkey for her. But I still was smoking a pipe. Later, when we lived in Teaneck and Englewood, and I was smoking cigars with my supervisors, I had to change clothes before I came home.

I was sure I was going to marry Sarah. She was not so sure.

It was touch and go; would we, or wouldn't we get engaged? Sarah was a very good student. I didn't come across as a very serious student in college. In high school, I had been a hard worker, but in college, I had been kind of like a wild teenager, a big joker, a storyteller. Now that I was in graduate school, I had to buckle down and get back to work.

Sarah's mother was not that enthusiastic about me, either. A future as a social worker? She wanted someone more established in a profession, or who at least showed more promise. She also wanted somebody who was not a refugee.

In the summer of 1960—the break between my first and second years in graduate school—I was in Phoenix. Sarah was in Denver. She invited me to come to Denver to meet her mother. Her father had passed away several years before.

Her mother served tomato soup. I hate tomato soup. But I told her I loved it. Her mother approved of me. I had already learned that if you want to get points with a girl, make her mom happy.

After meeting her mother, who finally approved of me, I asked Sarah to go steady. She said, "What is this 'steady' business? Either you're serious or you're not!" So I became serious.

Once I felt committed to marrying Sarah, I brought her to my *rebbe*, R. Moshe Feinstein. He spent some time talking to her, in Yiddish. He gave us a *bracha*, a blessing. I don't remember his exact words, but they were very meaningful. By then, I definitely knew that I had made my right choice. I had found my *zivug*, my perfect match.

When I asked Sarah to marry me. I think we were on the ferry boat to Staten Island. (The tickets cost a nickel. We were very frugal.) She said she needed to think about it. After a few long telephone conversations, and a couple of longer dates, she finally agreed to be my wife.

When Sarah and I got engaged, I knew that we were going to be getting married in Denver, so our New York friends would not be able to come. We had a big engagement party in a shul in the Bronx.

I was working for the caterer, Webber. That afternoon, there was a big *bar mitzvah*. Webber ordered a little more food for this *bar mitzvah*, and the tons and tons of leftovers became our engagement party. By the way, this is common at Jewish events: there's always way too much food and an embarrassing amount of leftovers. At least in our case, we made sure it went to another celebration.

Sarah and I got married in Denver on June 20, 1961. We moved that summer to Englewood, New Jersey, where I was working for the Jewish Community Center of Englewood, my first paid professional job. Sarah had just finished her certification as a teacher in the New York public school system. She was teaching third and fourth grade in the Breuer's Elementary School for Girls in Washington Heights, New York.

When Sarah was pregnant with Nina, in the fall of 1963, we went back to Yeshiva University to daven for the *yomim tovim* (Rosh Hashana and Yom Kippur, "the high holidays"). We stayed in the dormitory and ate in the

Wedding photo, from left: Morris Gortler, Josef and Estera Gortler, Josh, Sarah, Sarah's mother Dorothy Barash, Sarah's sisters Esther Barash, Rachel Barash. *Courtesy of the Josh and Sarah Gortler collection.*

dormitory. Why did we go back to YU for the Holidays? For inspiration. A man like me, I just wanted to have a *yeshivishe*[109] davening! I just couldn't see myself going into the *baalebatishche*[110] minyanim. When you are a yeshiva boy, you want a *yeshivishe* davening. The davening was led by one of my YU teachers, Rabbi Volk a'h[111]. He was just so concerned with Sarah being pregnant and fasting on Yom Kippur. He kept on coming over to Sarah during the breaks and saying, "You feel okay? Maybe you should drink something. You know, you don't have to fast. You shouldn't be fasting. If you need to drink something, just take one sip at a time." He was a very kind man.

The guy who introduced Sarah and me, Matt Weisenberg, didn't wind up marrying Judy, the gal from our double date to the Yiddish play.

---

109 Intense, like the prayers of committed rabbinical students
110 middle-class suburban men's
111 a"h = *alav hashalom* (peace be upon him/her), traditionally appended to the mention of the name of a deceased loved or respected person

Matt and I didn't cross paths much after that, but years later, much to my great pleasure, one of our friends from that time showed up in my life.

Four of us—Matt and I, Izzy Rivkin from Rochester and another guy, Shep Levine—had shared an apartment in Washington Heights. Shep, who was from Brooklyn, went to dental school at NYU. He stayed with us so he could walk to his classes on Shabbos.

Years later, Sarah and I were living in Seattle, and we had some people over, including Alan Genauer. When I showed an 8mm movie of our engagement party, Alan recognized Shep Levine. Shep, who was a dentist by then, had taken a Public Health job on an Indian Reservation in the Pacific Northwest, instead of going into the draft. He had gone to work at the VA in Seattle. He had given up *Yiddishkeit*.[112]

I connected with Shep Levine, and, I'm proud to say, I brought him back into the fold. Shep became a steady presence in our house. He started to come regularly to our shul, became a member, and bought a house within walking distance of the shul in our own Seward Park neighborhood.

---

112 Jewish observance

CHAPTER 26
Englewood. Teaneck. The Arrival of Nina.
1961-65

I was strapped for money during all of college. In addition to my food service jobs, I accepted a two-thousand-dollar scholarship from the Jewish Community Center in Englewood, New Jersey. The purpose of this scholarship was to recruit new YU graduates for entry level positions in social work. The condition for accepting the scholarship was that upon graduation, the recipient would have to give two years' employment at the JCC in Englewood. So, after I received my MSW,, I did a practicum—an internship, we would call it today—at the Englewood JCC.

I was offered a number of jobs right out of grad school. But I had this commitment to the Englewood JCC for two years. When I was employed there, in 1961, with a master's degree, my annual salary was $5,000. I was the highest-paid graduate social worker from my class.

The Jewish community of Englewood at that time was really divided between the haves and the have-nots. The people who made it big, economically, lived in big mansions; then there were the schleppers on the other side of the tracks. I liked working there, but not so much living there.

In Englewood, we lived on the other side of the tracks, in a one-bedroom garden apartment. There were a few other young people in that same development. One of them was my supervisor at the JCC—Irving Brickman, a very kind, gentle human being, and a great supervisor. (He actually had Seattle connections.) His title was Program Director. My title was Youth Activities Director.

Nina was born in Englewood on February 24, 1964. Sarah's mom came to visit from Denver.

It was Purim when Nina was born. Sarah's sister, the aptly named Esther (Esther Barash Abrams), had just come back from Israel, and she brought me an unbelievable, beautiful *Megillas Esther*.[113] This *megilla* is a very unusual *megilla*: it's the *"HaMelech" Megilla*. That means that the *sofer*, the scribe writing the *megilla*, had to figure out just how to put the word *HaMelech*—The King—on top of each column. It's very complicated; in some places, you can see how he had to stretch letters out to make it happen. These are very, very special *megillas*.

I read this *megilla* at Englewood Hospital for Sarah.

Nina brought great joy into our lives. Her Hebrew name is Henya, for Sarah's grandmother, her mother's mother, whose last name was Litvak. She had raised her family in Pueblo, Colorado. Her husband, Sarah's grandfather, came from Russia to Pueblo, and worked as a coal miner. After he survived a flood in a mine, he said he'd never again set foot in one. He bought a horse and buggy and became a peddler. He earned a little money, opened a furniture store, and brought over the rest of his family from Europe. He was a real pioneer.

We lived in Englewood for about two years. I liked the work there, but after those two years we moved to Teaneck, where we could live with more "my type" of people: less showy, less wealthy, more down-to-earth.

In Teaneck, we had a small apartment, with one actual bedroom and one closet-size bedroom for Nina. Teaneck at the time was a startup Orthodox community. Quite a few YU graduates would commute from New Jersey to New York for work. There were no kosher restaurants in Teaneck at that time. Teaneck had one small *shtiebel* (a very small synagogue), and a part-time rabbi. There were no services during the week. Even on Shabbos morning, we would sometimes daven up until *Borchu* (that is, we would pray up to a certain point in the prescribed order, at which point a quorum of ten men would be required to continue), and then we would have to wait for a *minyan* (quorum). After a few years, more people started moving in, and Teaneck became more and more a community where YU

---

113 Hand-scribed parchment scroll of the complete *Megillah* (Book) of Esther, traditionally used for the pubic reading of this megillah on Purim

people wanted to live. Of course, today Teaneck is one of the leading communities in the Orthodox Jewish world.

Teaneck was very warm and welcoming. The rabbi and his wife lived in the same garden apartments as we did. Very few families owned their own home. The only family that I remember that did own a home was the Manischewitz family, who were part of our shul—the same Manischewitz family whose name was on the matzas we had eaten in the DP camps.

I became very active in that little shul. For the three or so years we lived in Teaneck, before we moved to Bayside in Queens, New York, I was the *baal tokea*, the man who blew the *shofar* on the High Holidays.

Even today, I still blow a mean *shofar*. Every year, the week before Rosh Hashana, I blow *shofar* for the residents at The Summit. I don't do it in public for *shuls*. From the beginning of my position at Kline Galland, I wanted to make it clear that I was the CEO, not a rabbi, not a *chazzan*,[114] not a *baal koreh*,[115] not a *baal tokea*.[116] I was the CEO. I wanted to make the lines between administration and religious service provider very separate and clear. But I did blow as a demonstration, like I do at The Summit. It's not with a *bracha*, so it's not official. That is, it doesn't serve the purpose of fulfilling the *mitzvah,* the commandment to hear the sound of the *shofar*.

In Teaneck, we would get our meat from New York. It would be delivered by the butcher from Washington Heights. Sarah would get the meat, look it over, and say, "You know, this chopped meat has a lot of fat." Little Nina had a big *pisk*—a big mouth. The butcher would show up, and this little *pisher*, Nina, would say—and here's the voice she used— "My momma says the meat is no good, it has too much fat, and we are paying big dollars for the meat and you should improve delivering better meat!" She hardly could talk yet, but she could verbalize to the butcher that we're not so happy with the meat! And believe it or not, the meat improved. He listened to the little *pisher*! Nina always verbalized exactly what she heard. You had no secrets. We laughed so hard.

Nina grew up to earn a degree in nonprofit administration.

---

114 Skilled traditional singer who leads prayers
115 Torah reader, skilled in traditional chant
116 The one who blows the shofar

CHAPTER 27

Two Very Different Mentors
1960-1969

I tried to learn from the best and the worst of what I saw in my supervisors. I often asked myself, what would I make a part of me? What would I discard?

The Englewood JCC Executive Director was an exceptional person in developing budgets and making sure that the organization was on a good financial footing.

What he lacked, and I picked it up right away, was a feeling for people. He never trusted the people who worked under him. He was controlling. Here's an example: I was the youth director. One of my jobs was to take kids on trips during school breaks. He would come and personally count the kids to confirm my numbers.

I learned that when you hire people, you hopefully make a good decision in hiring. Then you trust them and let them work.

One of the trips I organized for the Englewood kids was to Washington, D.C. This must have been 1961. I took two or three busloads of teenagers. The other chaperone was the athletic director of the JCC, Gil Landau. I was in charge. At night Gil and I would take turns walking the hallways to ensure that the boys and girls didn't get into each other's rooms.

Englewood was a very snobby community. When we traveled with those kids, we stayed in four-star hotels—that gives you a picture of Englewood at the time. One of the kids in the Englewood JCC program was the son of a TV comedian who was famous at the time. He belonged to that JCC.

About a day or two after I returned from this trip, I got a registered letter from the hotel, with pictures: "Dear Mr. Gortler. On such a date, you occupied 50 rooms, paid in full. However, we have to share with you pictures of the rooms." The kids had taken cigarettes and engraved their initials in the carpets. How stupid could they be? They put their own names! They thought they were beyond punishment.

I thought of my own teenage years in the DP camps. We were a bunch of *vilde chayas,* like uncaged beasts. However, our activities and behavior were never destructive. We would play jokes on one another but we would never cause harm to one another or damage property.

I called the Executive Director and told him this behavior was not acceptable.

First, we called the kids and their parents to a meeting. We told the parents, "Your children were in this room, this is what they left, they engraved their names." I said the parents have a responsibility to reimburse the hotel for all expenses that will be incurred in regard to the trip. They readily agreed to pay for the repairs and the hotel's lost time, too.

Then we suspended the kids from any future trips with the JCC. There was a little pushback from the parents. They felt that the punishment was too severe. These were big donors. Big members. But I couldn't have cared less! I felt there needed to be recognition of what they did. And I prevailed.

When I finished my commitment in Englewood, I said to the Executive Director, "I would like to open up my profile," which meant my resume, to the Jewish Welfare Board, a sort of clearing agency for jobs. I had been promoted from Youth Director to Program Director, number two in the JCC hierarchy. I had been there three years. I had more than paid my scholarship commitment.

The boss gave me two weeks. He said, "Decide if you're staying, and if not, I'll make your job available."

That wasn't right.

I talked to Sarah. I said, "I don't think I'll stay." That took a lot of guts. Nina was a baby. It was scary to have a new baby and no commitment to know where my next dollar was coming from. I was paid very little – five to six thousand dollars, with more than half going towards rent.

I took a chance. I told the boss it was over.

By chance, one of the people who looked at my profile was Larry Matloff, the Executive Director of the YMHA, the Young Men's Hebrew Association, in Flushing, New York.

Larry was a visionary. My current boss was compartmentalized; Larry was free-spirited, always thinking out of the box. He was always two steps ahead of everyone else. I just fell in love with the guy. I said, "When do you want me?" He said, "Yesterday!"

A lot of my innovations in Seattle are due to my mentoring with Larry.

He was building a new YMHA in Flushing. He said he wanted to do a YMHA different from any that had been there before. Larry saw an opportunity in a vacant lot near the Y. He met with an organization called United Help—an organization in the New York area that got millions of dollars from the German government to develop programs and housing for Holocaust survivors. Larry envisioned a building attached to the YMHA, with the Y as a recreational center for the building's residents, who would be elderly Holocaust survivors. He envisioned the Y as a gathering place, providing cultural, social and recreational activities integrating youth with these elders.

He asked me to be the director of this new center. What an opportunity! I just fell in love with the possibilities. He told me, "Any programs you want to do, you are the boss." I *grabbed* the offer.

I said to Sarah, "*Hashem*[117] really directed me to a certain road. Here I am, stifled by this Englewood job, and now I'm offered this."

I went to my boss and gave my notice. I told him it was final. He offered more salary, but I told him he had actually cut me loose himself. When I had first indicated that I wanted to look around at other jobs, he hadn't made any effort to offer more salary or convince me to stay. He had lost me.

Larry would sit in a chair, smoking a cigar, and say, "Josh, what else could we do?" (At one point, he said, "Josh, you need to smoke cigars." Larry introduced me to Cuban cigars. Now, one of the conditions to marry Sarah was that I stopped smoking. Sarah allowed smoking with Larry, but in our tiny apartment in Bayside, New York, I had to change my clothes when I came home.)

Larry was the innovator. But he would often ask, "Josh, what else could we do?" Thanks to his encouragement, I developed programs for the elderly that had never at the time been done. They included home health, a kosher cafeteria, tutors for citizenship applicants, and recreational activities that brought the elderly and youth together.

---

117 *Hashem* (Hebrew) literally, "the name," a word observant Jews use to avoid any use of an actual name of God in non-prayer environments

We developed the home health idea as we started to create housing, when we realized that people needed health help, too.

We developed a kosher cafeteria in the Day Center, since we realized people might not be able to cook.

We integrated youngsters from the recreational YMHA programs to help the elders. We had them tutor the elderly on US citizenship applications.

This was the first concept of intergenerational programming. The elderly were even integrated with younger people in physical exercise programs.

We created a library. Some of the residents in the survivors' home were retired librarians. Some were teachers. We used their skills in tutoring the teenagers in our youth program at the Y.

Programs like these were unheard of in 1962.

We brought in graduate students, and I became a field instructor, called a "preceptor." Grad students would be placed under the supervision of a preceptor. I became an affiliate faculty member of the YU graduate school of social work, and of Hunter College in the Bronx.

Everybody wanted to work for Larry. We attracted the best graduate students in the city of New York. The reputation of the Flushing YMHA/United Health project influenced the agendas of YMHAs all over the country. Budget was not an issue, because there was reparation money coming from Germany.

These two mentors of mine were so different, and I learned from each of them. From my boss in Englewood, I learned what not to do, but I also learned how to do budgets. From Larry, I learned to hire the best employees, ask for their ideas, and let them do their work.

Larry said, "I surround myself with people who are smarter than I am. I let them know they're smart. I always hire the best people and give them the best salary. I don't micromanage." As opposed to the executive director in Englewood, who would always bring up what you did wrong, Larry would always ask, "How can you move to the next level?"

These were my two guiding forces. I thought, "If I will ever be in a position to be the executive director of an agency, I will use the lessons from my first boss, but most of all I want to be the best of Larry."

CHAPTER 28

The Arrival of Shlomo
1966

From Teaneck, we had moved to Bayside, New York, to the least expensive housing with an Orthodox community available. It was a great community. A lot of young people our age were living there. Rabbi Louis Bernstein, a teacher at YU, was rabbi of our shul, the Young Israel of Bayside; it was a weekend job for him. We rented a two-bedroom garden apartment about a block away from the shul. The night Shlomo was born, there were three *shalom zachors*.[118] People were shuttling from one house to another, sharing celebrations.

Shlomo was born August 21, 1966. Two weeks after we brought him home, he started projectile vomiting. I read Dr. Spock—that was the textbook for all parents—and I diagnosed Shlomo with pyloric stenosis. *Erev*[119] Rosh Hashana, we went to the pediatrician, and the doctor immediately admitted him for surgery.

What a scary situation for a young couple! Nina was two and a half, and then Shlomo came down with this. The surgery took place on the first day of Rosh Hashana at Booth Memorial Hospital in Queens. That was the nearest hospital where we could get in right away. The second day of Rosh Hashana I walked from Bayside, which must have been at least five miles

---

118 *Shalom zachor* (Hebrew for "greetings, boy"), a Sabbath night open house to welcome home a newborn boy
119 *erev* (Hebrew/Yiddish for "the eve of") is used to mean "the day before,"especially before a holiday or the Sabbath ("*erev Shabbos*") This was the day before Rosh Hashana.

each way, to visit Shlomo and talk to the nurses. There were three other kids in the same room, in cribs, and they all had pyloric stenosis. It was a Rosh Hashana I'll never forget. I stayed there until Rosh Hashana ended.

I called the hospital the next day, and they wouldn't put my call back to the nurses. I called back and said, "This is Dr. Gortler," and they put me back. Then they started to recognize my voice, and said, "What kind of doctor are you?" I said, "Doctor of Divinity." They said, "That doesn't count."

After a few days, we brought Shlomo home. He had a scar, but he was okay.

Apparently, this condition runs in families. I was talking to my mother—she was alive then—and asking about our family history. On my mother's side, there are a whole bunch of sisters, but only one brother that survived, my Uncle Chaim (the one who was an actor, who did Yiddish plays in the DP camp, who came to America and met me at the bus in New York). My mother told me there were a number of other boys, siblings, but they didn't survive past about one month. This is why, when my Uncle Chaim was born, he wasn't named after anyone. He was named to be alive—*chaim* is Hebrew for "life"—after all those losses. The research shows that this runs in families, and primarily affects the males in the families. Shlomo got the gene, and he also got the blessing of being born when medical science could take care of him.

Shlomo developed into a very mischievous kid (a bit like his father). He taught himself to read; he was very bright from the beginning. He grew up to become a professor of computer science at Harvard. Like his father, he is a problem solver.

In my profession, I have solved many different kinds of problems. Whether it's a building construction issue, or staff conflicts that require negotiation, there's a step by step approach in my mind. I'll always try to find a solution.

PART FIVE

SEATTLE:
THE KLINE GALLAND YEARS

CHAPTER 29

Why Seattle?
1967-1968

While I was working for Larry Matloff, I gave a paper at a national conference in D.C. I presented what YMHA and United Health were doing.

I spoke about our integrated approach.

There was a guy at the conference from United Way in Seattle. He told me, "We are building this great agency called Senior Services of King County." They were building Jefferson Terrace. Then a lay leader of Seattle United Way, an executive of Boeing, approached me.

I met with Larry, and told him, "I've been here three, four years. I met this guy. They invited me to come out to Seattle." I had no idea where that was.

Larry had seen the paper I had presented. He said, "Josh, you're right for the position. Go for it. No timetable, but if this is the right time for you and your family, go for it." What a difference there was between my Englewood boss and my Flushing boss.

When I arrived in Seattle, I was met at the airport with a chauffeur and a car. I was told that this service would be available to me the whole time. They put me up in the most expensive place in town, the Olympic Hotel. They said, "Whatever you want, charge to the room. The bar, anything."

They had a very detailed schedule for who I was meeting with, including names, positions, and connections. Most were United Way bigshots: movers and shakers in the philanthropic community of Seattle. Among the people on the schedule was a professional whose reputation I was familiar with: the Director of the School of Social Work at the University of Washington, Arthur Farber. I knew of him as a pioneer in the field of social work and aging. He was serving as a consultant to United Way, in initiating services to the aging in King County. In the 1950s, he had been executive director of Jewish Family Service in Seattle, and he had actually served as Executive Director of the Kline Galland Home, before being recruited as faculty by the University of Washington.

I had a wonderful time. They offered me the job: United Way Director of Senior Services. It was a new agency, just being formed!

Here I am, a young guy, thirty-one years old, with all these bigshots. I had so much confidence. Guts. I informed them that they really didn't know what they wanted. Each one was going in a different direction. The agency is a great idea, but the director will be pulled in too many directions. I told them their director wouldn't last more than six months.

I turned the job down. I called Sarah. I decided to stay in Flushing.

A year later, I got a different call from Seattle. It was from Sol Esfeld, a *macher* in the Seattle Jewish community. He was coming to New York. The local Jewish home for the aged, Kline Galland, had just built a new building, moved out of their old house, when their director left them all of a sudden. They were looking for a new director. Would I be interested in meeting? He had gotten my name from Ludwig "Lutz" Loeb, a partner in the Jewish accounting firm Friedman, Loeb and Block—the three big *machers* in the accounting field in the Seattle Jewish community.

Ludwig "Lutz" Loeb was on the board of United Way. He was one of the people who had interviewed me for the United Way job. He had mentioned me to Bob Block, another big *macher* in the Jewish community of Seattle, who was active on the Kline Galland advisory board and in the Jewish Federation. Bob Block passed along my name to Sol Esfeld, and suggested he call me while he was in New York on business.

Sol was staying in the Statler Hilton on 33rd Street in New York. I had a great interview with Sol. Then he asked, "How did you get to the hotel?" I took the subway, I told him. He handed me two quarters for the subway fare.

Here were two approaches: United Way with the chauffeur, the expensive hotel, hundreds of dollars, and then this guy, who gave me subway fare.

When Sol Esfeld interviewed me in New York in November of 1968, we spoke for just thirty seconds about being an executive of a nursing home, because I didn't have anything more to say about that. I had never done that. As I told Adina Russak, in an interview[120] for the UW oral history project, "I had always worked well with the "well" aged, who did not present physical problems....I didn't know a registered nurse from a licensed practical nurse, but I had the ability to work with people, and [I had] experience managing budgets and running agencies."

United Way called me back not long after my interview with Sol. They said, "You were right, we've gone through three directors like you predicted. We're ready for you. Please come."

I told them I'd just had an interview with Sol. And I said, "If that doesn't work, I might talk to you."

Sol invited me to fly out to Seattle and meet with the Kline Galland advisory board. I came out in December of 1968 and had the interview. Things were going well.

The Kline Galland interview touched my deepest feelings for the Jewish people. I thought, I have a choice: how do I want to spend my career? Even though at the time, I didn't think this decision would determine my entire career, I said to myself, don't I want to enter a position where I could make an impact on my own people? Here I am, trained in a yeshiva. My two previous paid positions were in Jewish settings. I thought I'd be more comfortable in a Jewish setting. United Way was huge, and it encompassed many communities. I knew I could make a bigger impact at a smaller organization. It was basically a commitment to my own people.

In the evening, I found that my hosts had put me up in a motel on Empire Way (now Martin Luther King Way), The Empire Motel. It was the kind of motel that rented out rooms by the hour. Seriously. It certainly wasn't the Olympic Hotel!

But my decision was made. I didn't go to any more interviews with United Way. I took the Kline Galland job.

---

120 October 9, 1985 interview transcript, p.14. WA State Jewish Historical Society archives.

CHAPTER 30

Starting in Seattle:
I Meant to Stay for Just Two Years
February 1969

MY APPROACH TO LEADERSHIP:
MAKE HARD DECISIONS, WITH DIGNITY IN MIND

Making hard decisions is what people with a certain level of responsibility have to do. You make these decisions on budgets, on staff. Sometimes the staff is not cut out for a particular job, and you have to part ways.

Parting ways, for me, whether it was with a graduate student or an employee that I had hired and had to let go, was something I always did with a great deal of dignity and understanding, so it was not "You're fired!"

Unfortunately, not all of my colleagues are like this when they let somebody go. Unless it has to do with terrible mismanagement, or a person committing sexual improprieties, or someone who puts their hand in the till, you have to leave people with dignity, rather than just cutting them off, and saying this is your last day, you've got two hours to clean out your desk. You cannot leave a person in such a stage, psychologically, that their life is destroyed. Unfortunately, in many cases, that's what happens when people let individuals go.

It was the middle of the academic year when I started the Kline Galland job. I had been supervising graduate students from YU and Hunter College. I passed them on to other staff at the YMHA so they could complete their year of training.

I did recommend that one student from Yeshiva University not continue in social work. He was not cut out for it. That was difficult.

THE COMMUNITY WE FOUND WHEN WE ARRIVED

I agreed to come to Seattle for a maximum of two years. I really had no intention of staying outside of New York. To move to a place like Seattle was to leave the center of the Jewish world. We were surrounded by many, many close friends that we had a lot in common with—many were graduates of YU—and most of my close friends were in the medical field, with PhDs or MDs. Living in New York, we were very, very busy, with the kids, with our professional lives. We didn't have family there, so our friends were our family.

When we came to Seattle, there was just a handful of people our age in the Orthodox community. Even though my friendships extend way beyond the Orthodox community, and always have, there's something meaningful about the Friday night table. In Seattle, we found just about five families we could share that Shabbos table experience with. We said okay, we're going to give it a try for two years, and then move—whether it's going to be to New York, or Chicago—to some much larger Jewish community. Our thinking was based on a combination of the children's education, our contemporaries, and professional growth.

Also, Seattle did not have a good reputation in my field.

CHAPTER 31
Kline Galland: Creating a Mission-Driven Organization
1969 – 1974

The Kline Galland Home had a brand-new facility, just a year old, but it had many, many serious issues with growth. The most challenging issue was that, unlike other social service/nonprofit organizations, where a strong board of directors guides the leadership, this organization was led by a bank.

Caroline Kline Galland, when she passed away, left a will in which she bequeathed her wealth to a bank, Seattle Savings and Trust. She appointed four people to advise the bank on how the facility should be run. But the bank, basically, was in charge. It was the owner of the facility. A banker made the management decisions about the organization.

When I came out to Seattle, I was met at the airport by Arva Gray. As a former president of Jewish Family Service, she was one of the people who would interview me. I was interviewed not by any board of directors, but by an advisory committee.

There was no board of directors. Sol Esfeld, who first interviewed me in New York, was just a member of the advisory board to the bank. The will specifically stated that, when there is a dispute between the advisory board and the bank, the bank prevails.

At that time, Kline Galland was not even a legal entity. Not only was there no board of directors, but Kline Galland did not even have a bank account. This meant that, when I started as director, every Friday I would gather up the bills from that week, give them my okay, and take them to the bank. Then the bank would pay the bills. This was my bookkeeping routine.

A vice president of the bank—the guy's name was Kincaid—was the man in charge of Kline Galland. During the interview visit, I had been taken to his office for an interview with him. The advisory committee had interviewed me, yes, but the final decision to hire me was made by the banker.

Before 1967, the Kline Galland Home was just a house, a residential building in the same location it occupies today, on Seward Park Avenue. The house was a fire trap. A community study determined that a new facility was essential to keep up with the trends around the country in servicing the aged population. Sol Esfeld chaired the capital campaign. Donors' checks were not made to Kline Galland, but were made out to Seattle Savings and Trust Bank, trustee for the Kline Galland Home.

MY INSTITUTIONAL GOALS

My goal was to eventually separate the operation from the bank. I wanted to give the power of ownership to the Jewish community, rather than the bank.

I felt very strongly that the owner of the Jewish nursing home should be the Jewish community itself. When I arrived, the home's advisory board was advising the bank, but the bank had the purse.

My goal was for the home to become an independent, nonprofit Jewish community organization. It didn't take too long for us to accomplish the nonprofit part—name a board, raise some money—but it would be another ten years before the goal of independence would become a reality.

In 1973, Kline Galland officially became a 501(c)(3) organization, raising enough money that, three years later, we were able to double the capacity of the home.

AFTER TWO YEARS, I DECIDE TO STAY

In 1971, after my two years were up, I felt that the advisory board members were very thirsty for the kind of leadership I could provide. I could tell that they were hopeful that I was guiding them towards a very professional institution. And after two years, it felt as though we'd just scratched the surface. I decided to keep going. Challenges were there, but I was feeling fulfilled enough to continue. They were exciting challenges, and the board's response to me was very good, very accepting.

I didn't want a contract. I said, if you think I'm not doing the job, I'll get another job. I was offered jobs like crazy, some of which were in Seattle. At that time, the business of for-profit nursing homes was booming.

At Kline Galland, I saw a great community and great challenges.

ON A MISSION: MY TWO-PART VISION FOR KLINE GALLAND

First, we would build a not-for-profit institution from the ground up, with a good financial base.

Second, we would build a reputation for excellent care of the elderly, which Kline Galland did not have when I arrived. The way things were when I arrived, if a person of considerable means needed care, Kline Galland was the last place they would consider.

In a for-profit nursing home, the management's priority is the bottom-line, the profit. These are businesses that, all too often, cut corners on care in order to save money. But the not-for-profit home is about care with compassion. The priority in this kind of home, our home, is appropriate service in line with the mission of the organization, which in our case was a faithfulness to Jewish values, and putting the interests of the residents and their families first.

The advisory board had been guided on how to manage a nursing home by two people who were, at that time, investors in private, for-profit nursing homes. What I had to do, very quickly, was to help the advisory board understand the differences between a not-for-profit service-oriented organization and a for-profit nursing home.

To accomplish that second vision, I would have to build a capable staff.

HIRING THE BEST AND THE BRIGHTEST

I learned a lesson from Larry Matloff, my boss in Flushing: hire the smartest, best people in their respective fields. Provide them with an above-competitive salary. Give them a sense of partnership. And do not micromanage.

That's how we built the best team in long-term care in the Pacific Northwest.

Larry Matloff and I kept in close touch throughout my career. I even gave him advice after a while!

MY APPROACH TO CARE WAS DIFFERENT

The old Kline Galland model of service had been based on a medical approach to care. My approach was based on a psycho-social model, providing not only a medical component, but also considering the total person, the total *gestalt*. I wanted this to be a place that taught the staff to understand care as more than just treating a wound, or a broken hip, or dementia. I wanted them to look at the whole human being. The resident's background. The extended family.

That's why I started to bring in social workers who understood the holistic approach. They became a very important part of training everyone—nurses, physical therapists, and occupational therapists, as well as ancillary staff such as housekeepers, dietary, and maintenance staff. To me, everyone from the nurse to the janitor has to have a solid understanding of why they are there.

BUILDING A STAFF: SOCIAL WORKERS

When I arrived, there was one social worker, and she ran the show. She and I didn't see eye to eye. Every time I would meet with her, she would threaten to quit if she didn't get her way. One day, she made that threat, and I said, "You're quitting now."

Then,I hired an excellent social worker, Naomi Levine, a real star. She was not very Jewishly affiliated, but she was Jewish, and very active in the social work field. She was a great writer. She would go with her husband to their cabin on Hood Canal every weekend. I was heartbroken when both Naomi and her husband were killed in a head-on collision on one of those trips.

Next came Margaret Reed. She was the most unique human being I'd ever met. Margaret was an extremely proper lady. She showed up to the interview wearing white gloves. Margaret was fantastic at her job. She had been a successful psychiatric social worker in the Chicago area.

We had a great interview. She asked me, "Why do you want to hire a non-Jewish social worker?" since social work was often something a lot of Jewish women go into. I said, "Margaret, we'll make one deal. While you're at work, you will not convert anyone Jewish to Christianity, and I promise I won't try to convert you to Judaism. But I have one question for you. You have some black stuff on your forehead...." And that's how I learned about Ash Wednesday. This was one of the first of many opportunities that the Kline

Galland position has given me to encounter religious practices very different from my own. Margaret worked for Kline Galland for over twenty years.

As we expanded the home's capacity, we were able to add another social worker. It was our good fortune be able to bring in Dan Ozog. We knew Dan's abilities from his student service with us, when he was on a grant from the University of Washington. By 1973, we were already training geriatric social workers through a cooperative program with Kline Galland, through the University of Washington and Mt. St. Vincent, a Catholic facility.

Prior to his enrollment in the School of Social Work, Dan had been studying for priesthood in a Catholic seminary; he left that, got married, and served in the Peace Corps. He was with us at Kline Galland his first year of graduate school, and at Mt. St. Vincent his second year. When we interviewed him for the job, Mt. St. Vincent had also made him an offer. I remember Dan's reaction was, "I spent a year in a Jewish facility and a year in a Catholic facility. I choose the Jewish facility." He liked our philosophy.

We always competed with Mt. St. Vincent! I used to have great discussions with the Executive Director.

Dan spent his entire career with Kline Galland and retired in 2017. Dan's unforgettable personality brought an element of fun and surprise, as well as a deep sensitivity, to his work with residents, their families, our staff, and our volunteers.[121]

By the time I retired from the CEO position, the staff had grown to include four social workers at the Kline Galland Home, plus one at The Summit.

BUILDING A STAFF: NURSES

When I arrived, I knew that the current director of nursing services would not be able to continue in that role. I met with her, and developed a very appropriate new role for her, under a new director of nursing. The director of nursing services is one of the most essential positions in a long-term care facility. She sets standards, attracts appropriate staff, and oversees the majority of the staff, including registered nurses, LPNs, and nursing assistants, as well as ancillary service positions such as physical, occupational, and speech therapists. She is the person who sets the tone for the health care component of the organization.

---

121 See Dan's comments, "On Doing Social Work the Josh Gortler Way," Appendix.

Betty Finocchio was the top director of nursing services in the state of Washington. She was on the faculty of the University of Washington, and she was director of nursing services for another nonprofit nursing home. I knew Betty through my involvement with the Washington State Association for Aging Services. I met with her several times to try to entice her to join our staff. Betty was a former military nurse, who had seen firsthand the liberation of concentration camps in Europe at the end of World War II. Once Betty understood that some of the residents in our facility were Holocaust survivors, she joined our team. She was a tough nurse with a heart of gold.

BUILDING A STAFF: THE HANDS-ON CAREGIVERS

Many staff people started to leave when I arrived, because I insisted on rules and accountability. I did a lot of interviews. I placed ads and enticed people from other organizations. If you look at the ads we placed, they said, "We pay more, with great benefits." And people came.

When we got connected to the Asian community, particularly the Filipino community, that was a real gem. We hired a couple of Filipino people who just happened to come in for job interviews. I asked them to tell their friends about us, because I liked the way they were working. Kline Galland's work force became 50 to 60 percent Filipino. The cultures of honoring elders, including the Samoans, and more recently, the Ethiopian immigrants, made a good match with the values of our home.

BUILDING A STAFF: ADMINISTRATIVE ASSISTANT

In 1981, I was looking for a new administrative assistant. Mardell Krommer came to us with an exceptional background in nonprofit organizations. She had worked for the Lutheran church in several capacities. She was a very well organized, meticulous, capable person. She kept me on track in so many ways, whether she was acting as a press contact, newsletter editor, or as support for my meeting preparations.

Mardell served as campaign coordinator for our million-dollar campaign. When I transitioned to President of the Kline Galland Foundation, Mardell moved on with me, and continued to provide her excellent support. The beautiful albums of photographs and press clippings from my many years at Kline Galland were prepared with great care by Mardell's hand.

BUILDING A STAFF: KOSHER SUPERVISION

I looked at Kline Galland as a mission,-driven organization, built on Jewish values. It did not demonstrate those values when I arrived. The home provided kosher food, for example, but there was no official *kashrus*[122] supervision, besides volunteers.

When the board hired me they said, "Oh, great! Now we'll have a rabbi on staff, and we'll be supervised." And I said "Wait a minute. Either you hire a rabbi, or you hire an administrative social worker to run this place. I will not perform rabbinical functions."

At that time, there was no community *va'ad* [123] but we hired a *mashgiach*,[124] an independent *mashgiach*, Rev. Morton Solney. He was a *schochet*. He was welcomed in. He was a Holocaust survivor, a very gentle human being, a *talmid chocham*,[125] who would sit and learn while he was supervising the preparation of food in the kitchen. He also conducted Shabbos services at Kline Galland.

BUILDING A BOARD

It was essential for me to develop a very strong and involved Board of Directors. Since Kline Galland serves the total elderly Jewish population, it was essential for me that the Board of Directors reflect the diversity of the Seattle-area Jewish community.

Seattle is a unique Jewish community. It is the third largest Sephardic community in the United States. One of my goals was for the Board of Directors to reflect our resident population and the community.

Many Jewish organizations have a prerequisite of a minimum donation from those who would want to serve on a Board. I, however, felt that this requirement would eliminate some very capable people who would make good Board members. Therefore, I made sure that there was no such prerequisite at Kline Galland.

In her last will and testament, Caroline Kline Galland specified that the original board consist of four people: the president and secretary of Temple de Hirsch, and the president and secretary of the Ladies' Benevolent Society, which eventually became Jewish Family Service.

---

122 Traditional rabbinic adherence to Jewish dietary laws
123 local organization of rabbinic supervision
124 In-house kosher supervisor
125 Learned man, schooled in Jewish religious laws

The past president of Temple de Hirsch would automatically become the president of the Kline Galland advisory board. Eventually, the Jewish Federation appointed three more board members.

Around 1965 or so, when a modern building was being constructed, the advisory board was expanded to sixteen members, appointed by the Jewish Federation of Greater Seattle, to include representatives of the various synagogues as a better reflection of the composition of the community. Individual synagogues would each choose a representative to serve on this board.

When we became a 501(c)(3) organization in 1973, our advisory board had to become a Board of Directors, according to the laws that govern not-for-profit organizations. We developed broad bylaws, which included the election of Board members by Kline Galland's members. Anyone who contributed would become a member of Kline Galland.

Now we had the power to choose the Board members. The will, written in 1905, was a very antiquated approach to community service.

The existing advisory board became our first Board of Directors. Under the new bylaws, we expanded the board to 27 people. We carefully searched for leadership that would reflect the Seattle-area Jewish community. We identified the top leaders at the time and attracted them to serve on the board.

I developed a manual for new board members. I also developed a training and orientation process, in order to make sure the board members understood our philosophy, our needs, where we were going, and how important our service was to the community. They needed to understand what their own service to the community was all about.

It took about a year or two to build up to a 27-member board. We found our members this way: I would call the Federation and other Jewish organizations and get a list of their leadership. I would discuss this list with a nominating committee of our board, and identify certain people as candidates. Sometimes I would make the call, and sometimes one of the board members would. We would personally meet with the candidate. The meeting would include a board member who was acquainted with the candidate. That board member would issue the invitation to join the Kline Galland board.

I always took a potential board member on a tour of the facility, for them to see first-hand who we were serving. I remember distinctly how, after this orientation and tour, one potential board member felt uncomfortable enough, seeing the population of infirm elderly, that he told me that he could not serve on our board. He wrote us a big check, though! He could support it financially, but not emotionally. This was the only instance of someone who got that far in the process and then turned us down.

We developed a file of dozens of potential board members. There was so much talent, we couldn't possibly select all of them at once. We always had a long list of potential board members. Sometimes, we would invite people to serve on committees prior to joining the Board.

I GET AN OFFER, AND MAKE A BETTER ONE IN RETURN

Sometime during the 1980s, I received a call from Ray Galante, the president of the Jewish Federation of Greater Seattle, and past president of Temple de Hirsch. Ray was known as the best fundraiser in Seattle, with connections everywhere. He invited me for lunch. The Jewish Federation at the time was searching for a new executive director. Ray said, "We know your reputation, and I was authorized by the Federation to recruit you to become the Executive Director of Federation."

I told Ray I was very flattered by the offer. However, I told him that my commitment was to direct service. I also told him that I was extremely happy with my current position.

But then I turned the tables on him. I told Ray I was looking for a chairman for the new fundraising committee, to initiate the largest fundraising campaign in the history of Seattle: $25 million to build an addition to Kline Galland, and to develop a retirement community. I said, "Ray, you're the man for the job."

It took two more lunches to convince Ray to join the Kline Galland board, and to accept the position as chairman. This turned out to be the most successful capital campaign ever initiated in the history of the Seattle Jewish Community.

I TURN DOWN A TEMPTING OFFER

A Jewish real estate developer, in 1972-73, once said to me, I like what you're doing at Kline Galland. What I'd like to do is bring you onto my team. You'll run my places. I don't know how much money you're making, but we'll double your salary. In addition to your salary, you would look at how my organization is doing financially, and you would be profit-sharing in the organization.

I was very tempted, of course. I had a young family, and money was important. But there's more to life than money. I turned the offer down. I did tell tell the board about the offer. For the length of my tenure, they were always very generous to me.

Josh Gortler with Kline Galland Charge Nurse Linda Patterson, RN 1972.

The Social Work "Dream Team" 1988. Each one devoted an entire professional career to Kline Galland. Combined service to Kline Galland: over 120 years. From left: Josh; Lucy Spring, director of volunteers; Laurie Garber, director of activities; Karin Pollock, assistant director of social services; Dan Ozog, director of social services.

The Nursing Staff "Dream Team" celebrating Purim, 1993. From left: Mary Jane Colby, RN, MS Asst director of nursing; Linda Simmons, RN, MS, Director of Education; Mary Shelgren, RN, PhD, Director of Nursing; Joshua Gortler, MSW, CEO. *All photos this page courtesy of the Joshua Gortler collection*

CHAPTER 32
Kline Galland "Divorces" the Bank[126]
1973-1980

Caroline Kline Galland's 1905 will designated the bulk of her estate—totaling one and a half million dollars—to create a home that, in the words of her will, "shall be known as the Caroline Kline Galland Home for Aged and Feeble Poor...to serve all aged and feeble Jewish men and women," and "men and women members of and in accord with the belief recognized by the Society of Universal Religion...to have those occupy the Home who are in harmony upon religious creeds."[127] She appointed Seattle Savings and Trust as the Trustee.

From 1914, when a house in the Seward Park area was purchased by the Bank, until 1973, the Bank managed the Trust, and the home, with an iron fist, as if this were their own money and their own facility.

In 1973, when the new Board of Directors (in line with the 501(c)(3) status) was planning to double the capacity of Kline Galland, the Bank was not in favor. The first real schism between the Trustee and the Board became clear. The Board threatened a lawsuit for mismanaging of the funds through the years. They had good reason: the Trust had two million dollars in 1905, and less than two million dollars in 1973.

---

126 For the fascinating details of the saga of our "divorce" from the Bank, see UW Archives: my interviews with Adina Russak, Joseph Adatto, and the interview Mike Cohen and I did together, with Howard Droker.

127 University of Washington Archives https://digitalcollections.lib.washington.edu/digital/collection/pioneerlife/id/28983

There was never a lawsuit. The Board prevailed. The funds were transferred to the new nonprofit entity, Kline Galland Home. However, the property was still owned by the Bank. Kline Galland was now leasing the property from the Bank, a 99-year lease at $1 a year.

A LONG PROCESS, THIS "DIVORCE"

The new, independent Board initiated a capital campaign. The goal for the campaign was to raise approximately $3 million, enough to double the Home's capacity.

This was the first phase of the "divorce" of Kline Galland from the Bank. It took until 1980 for the second phase to be completed. At that point, the Bank released the ownership of the property as well.

By the time Kline Galland became totally independent, it was the major institution in the Seattle Jewish Community. We had the largest operating budget of any Jewish agency. Kline Galland did not receive any subsidies from the Jewish Federation of Greater Seattle. It became a model geriatric service organization, not only locally, but nationally.

I HADN'T MEANT TO STAY IN SEATTLE, BUT HOW COULD I LEAVE?

I was excited: this job was so challenging! How could I leave this place? I could see the accomplishment. I could see the institution being accepted. People were literally buying into the system.

This home was now owned by the Jewish community. Members of the community became stakeholders; when you gave even just a dollar, you became a member, and the place was yours. This was the whole idea, for people to have the feeling that it was theirs.

We did it all with no outside consultants. Members of the Jewish community provided the legal, financial, and public relations advice pro bono. I served as the enabler who attracted these talents.[128]

---

128 UW archive, Adina Russak interview with Josh, pp. 15ff

CHAPTER 33

Innovative Programs at Kline Galland
1973 onward

KLINE GALLAND BECOMES A TEACHING INSTITUTION

Three years after I arrived in Seattle, I connected with the various schools of the University of Washington. I was most comfortable with the School of Social Work. I established Kline Galland as an affiliate, and I was appointed as an auxiliary faculty member of the school. Our Director of Social Services, Margaret Reed, became a field instructor for graduate students.

Next, I reached out to the School of Nursing. After some negotiations about the value of training their students in geriatric care, the school agreed to establish Kline Galland as a training facility for RN students. They placed a faculty member at Kline Galland to supervise these students, and they appointed me as auxiliary faculty to the school.

A new Dean had just arrived at the School of Psychiatry and Behavioral Sciences, Dr. Carl Eisdorffer, a "guru" in geriatric psychiatry. I knew his reputation, so I reached out to Dr. Eisdorffer, and invited him for lunch at Kline Galland. Dr. Eisdorffer was impressed with us and agreed to place two fellows in psychiatry at Kline Galland.

These same two fellows also worked at the VA Hospital. While at the VA, they had developed a protocol for using a certain medication—one that had been around for a long time—that lowered blood pressure, and was used for post-traumatic stress disorder in veterans. Dr. Eisdorffer expressed a desire to use the same protocol for Holocaust survivors at

Kline Galland. After some discussion, this program was initiated on a limited basis. It was acknowledged among professionals as a great success.

In the mid-80s, the University of Washington established a new institute for geriatric research, which combined training for nurses, social workers, MDs, and pharmacologists. I was asked to serve on the board of this institute. They placed students in hospitals, and at only two nursing homes in the state of Washington: Kline Galland and Mt. St. Vincent.

After establishing a good working relationship with the University of Washington, I reached out to the Seattle University School of Nursing. Kline Galland became a training facility for their students, as well. This Jesuit school appointed me as an auxiliary faculty member as well, and I taught a seminar in sensitivity to Jewish patients from cradle to grave.

Kline Galland also became a field placement for the two-year program in nursing at Seattle Central Community College. For Green River Community College, we became a field placement for both their two-year RN degree students, and students in PTA, physical therapy assistants. Many of the students, after receiving their degrees, found employment at Kline Galland.

I always found that students challenge the employees and thus improve the total level of patient care. They also increase the morale of our employees, who know that in addition to providing a service to the residents, they are role models for future health care workers.

THE KLINE GALLAND MENAGERIE

My entire concept of long-term care was to create the atmosphere of a home. Instead of sterile white walls and white uniforms, I set about to create a living environment, not a place where people felt they were just coming to die. Even though they came with their ailments, their issues, I wanted to explore how we could make it as humane as possible.

There was some literature around this time, in the early to mid 1980s, that pet therapy was effective in helping the elderly with anxiety and depression. So once a month, somebody from the Humane Society would visit Kline Galland with animals in crates, and show off, say, a rabbit, or a dog.

Since it popped up in the literature, we talked about it in a meeting. One of the nurses spoke up and said she had found a really friendly dog at the shelter, and asked if she could bring it to work. Another person, a social worker, piped up and offered to bring a dog. Of course, the answer was yes to both. Now we had two staff people with dogs at work. Finally, someone said, "Why doesn't this dog stay overnight and see how it works out?"

One thing led to another, and an Irish setter named Erin, a former shelter dog, took up residence at Kline Galland, and became a member of the family. It didn't last very long. We had an inspection of the facility and the inspectors were going crazy! They said this dog could bring all kinds of disease and everything. But we took Erin to a veterinarian and got him certified as a therapy dog, all cleared by the health department.

He lived in the Alzheimer unit. He was so great that if a person became very agitated, Erin would come over and just sit there. The dog had a tremendous calming effect. Erin was gaining weight, too, because the residents were feeding him. He had the freedom to roam the facility, so he would show up in the dining hall.

At the time, Sarah and I would walk around Seward Park five days a week at six in the morning. I would go first to Kline Galland, take Erin in my car, then pick up Sarah and we would walk around the park with Erin to get some exercise.

Erin passed away. He came down with cancer. We spent a lot of money on him. Erin earned a mention in Seth Goldsmith's book *Choosing a Nursing Home.*[129]

Besides a dog, we also thought it would be nice to have some of those pygmy goats in the courtyard. We brought in two goats. Within a week, they had finished off all of the vegetation in the courtyard, and that was the end of the goats.

Next we had rabbits in the courtyard. They started multiplying. Maybe that's why there are rabbits in Seward Park.

One day, on the west side of Kline Galland, two ducks flew into the courtyard and laid their eggs. All of a sudden, we had a bunch of ducklings in the courtyard. So, we got a children's swimming pool and put it in the courtyard for the ducklings. When they got bigger, we gathered them all up and set them free at Lake Washington.

The janitors hated my guts, because ducks do a lot of damage, and three or four times a day they had to wash that stuff off the sidewalks.

---

129 Seth B. Goldsmith: Choosing a Nursing Home. ©1999 Prentice-Hall, p. 9

ADULT DAY CENTER

I understood that in addition to serving the elderly population of Seattle in institutional settings, like that of the Kline Galland Home (and in the future, at a retirement and assisted-living facility), there was a need to create services that would allow people to remain in their own homes. This would be a program where the elderly could utilize the existing services of the facility on an outpatient basis.

Around 1980, I met with Morris Polack, a great supporter of the Home, and a major philanthropist in the Jewish community. I asked him for a donation of $25,000 to engage two employees who would create this day center. The day center would provide transportation to Kline Galland, as well as social activities, nutritious meals, nursing monitoring, and physical and occupational therapies as needed. Morris, of course, gladly wrote the first check. We hired the two new staff members.

We began this program with five participants. It grew to fifteen participants, and then to twenty, in just one year. I again met with Morris and asked him to double his original donation. Again, he gladly wrote a check.

We hired additional staff. Shortly after the second donation, I received a call from Morris, who asked me to meet him in his office. In that meeting he said, "I will not live forever, and I don't know whether my family will support this type of program. What will it take to establish a fund that will perpetually support your vision?"

I pulled out a number: one million dollars. Without any hesitation, Morris said, "Can I do it in installments over two years?" I almost fell off the chair. I didn't expect such instant generosity at this level.

Hence, we created the Polack Adult Day Center. We created a new endowment program, where the income of the million dollars would be utilized to support this ongoing outpatient program at the Kline Galland Home. We purchased a bus, and named it the "MOJACK," for Morris Polack and his brother Jack.

NUTRITION PROGRAM

I met with the executive director of the Seattle Senior Services Program, which provided nutritious meals for Seattle-area seniors. The program took advantage of public school lunchrooms, inviting seniors who needed meals to eat lunch in the schools. It also provided meals to homebound elderly, through the federally subsidized Meals-on-Wheels program. I explained to their leadership that there were elderly people in the Jewish community who required kosher meals. The need for those meals was currently not being met through their program.

I explained to them that such meals would cost a little more, and I would be willing to raise the funds to subsidize the additional costs to make them available. They took my suggestion seriously and asked me to present a written proposal to their board of directors, which I did. After several more meetings, they agreed that such a program was within their overall mission of serving all elderly in the community who require special diets. They requested that we purchase special freezers to be housed in their senior nutritional warehouse. Kline Galland would package the meals in its kitchen, and deliver them to that warehouse. Meals-on-Wheels would then deliver those meals to the people who needed them.

They also agreed to provide transportation to bring these seniors to Kline Galland for a weekly nutritious lunch. During these lunch times, Jewish Family Service provided a social worker to assess other needs that these seniors might have. This program became a model for other Jewish communities around the country.

EXPANDING COMMUNITY-BASED SERVICES

Under the leadership of Jeff Cohen, my successor as the CEO of Kline Galland, the community-based programs today include Medicare-licensed home health. This division offers physical, occupational and speech therapies, as well as nursing, palliative care, hospice care, and care by CNA-certified nursing assistants, all for homebound patients. The offices of Kline Galland Community-Based Programs (CBP) are located in the Georgetown neighborhood of Seattle. Today, they are the largest home health and home care agency in the State of Washington.

CHAPTER 34

The Social Worker Becomes a Fundraiser

MY FINANCIAL HONESTY IS TESTED

In graduate school, I was exposed to many areas that prepared me as a social worker and as an administrator. However, at Wurzweiler, the YU School of Social Work, there was not a single course in fundraising, or, as it's called, "development."

I became a fundraiser by necessity.

I had two great mentors in Seattle: Sol Esfeld—the gentleman who was my first contact in New York for the position in Seattle—and Ray Galante, the longtime president of the Jewish Federation of Greater Seattle.

During my career as CEO, and subsequently as president of the Kline Galland Foundation, I raised close to $100 million for capital development as well as for endowments.

I RETURN THE FIRST BIG DONATION THAT COMES IN WITHOUT MY SOLICITING

On a Friday afternoon, not long after I arrived, a gentleman walked into my office. He said, "I'm here to give you a donation." This was in the early stages of my first capital campaign.

He said, "I would like to make a large donation. Would you like to come with me to the bank? I'll get you the cash."

I said, "Sure." We went to the bank. I sat in the car. He came back, gave me an envelope and said to me, "This is my donation of ten thousand dollars."

I didn't open the envelope. I didn't look in the envelope. I came back to the office. I gave the envelope to Raye Caraco, my secretary, and I said, "Raye, write a receipt for ten thousand dollars, and I'll sign it."

Raye wrote a receipt for ten thousand dollars, and I signed it. We gave the receipt to this gentleman. Before she put the money in the safe, she came in, her face was red, and she said, "It's only five thousand dollars, not ten. And we gave a letter of receipt for ten thousand dollars."

I called the man immediately, and I said, "You gave me five thousand dollars, not ten thousand." And he says, "Well, that's how we do business. I give you five thousand, and you give me a receipt for ten thousand. That's how all the Jewish organizations in town do business. In cash."

I said, "Well, maybe other organizations do it that way. But Kline Galland does not." It was my first big donation.

He said, "Too bad. I have the receipt, and I can say that I gave you ten and you kept five thousand dollars for yourself and you gave five thousand dollars to the organization."

I said, "I have witnesses in the office that can say I never opened the envelope. There are two other people I gave the envelope to. It was opened by my secretary, but there were other people watching when the envelope was opened."

And he said, "Yeah, that's fine, but I can say ten."

And I said, "You have one hour to come back and we'll give the envelope back to you, and we'll tear up the original receipt."

And he said, "What happens if I don't do it?"

I said, "I will call the IRS and I will tell them the kind of business you are doing."

I immediately called the chairman of the board. I shared this information with him. The chairman of the board called this man back too, and said, "If you're not here within—whenever sundown was, it was Friday afternoon—we are calling the police and the IRS. We know the bank you went into. We have the record of the bank, and how much you withdrew, because you came out of the bank with an envelope," so there was a record that he only withdrew five thousand.

The man came back. I gave him the five thousand dollars. He gave me the receipt. I did not tear up the receipt. I asked him to write, "The receipt is hereby returned to Joshua Gortler," and I put a copy of the receipt in our locked safe at the office. That way, we had a written record. And I had people there co-signing that this is a copy of the original letter of receipt that came back.

He said, "Give me a letter for five." I didn't want to take the five thousand.

I said, "I don't want any of your money."

This, I realized, was a test. Sometimes in life you are given a situation that puts you to the test, to find out whether you are really the person you say you are. I felt that I passed that test.

AN EARLIER FINANCIAL TEST THAT ALMOST GOT ME KICKED OUT OF COLLEGE

Back in my college days, I had many small jobs. One was working in the cafeteria. On weekends, I was a busboy or waiter. During the week, after hours, I would fill in at the cafeteria as a cashier.

One weekday, a guy came in to order dinner—it was maybe five, six dollars, very inexpensive—and he said, "I don't have cash. Can I give you a check?"

I said, "Sure, give me a check." He wrote a check, I took the check and threw it into the cash register.

My supervisor, in the evening, looked over the check, and noticed that it was made out to Joshua Gortler, instead of to Yeshiva University. He said to me, sign the check, "Pay to the order of Yeshiva University." So I did.

Six weeks later, I got a call from the Dean. He said the student made a complaint against me, saying that I stole money from the cafeteria. I said, "What are you talking about?"

"Yes," he said, "he gave you a check of five dollars" or six or whatever it was, "and you took the money for yourself instead of putting it into the cafeteria."

I said, "Let me see the check."

The Dean showed me the check, made out to me. On the back I had written, "Pay to the order of Yeshiva University Cafeteria," and I had signed it. So they did an investigation, because there was a record of how much money came in, and the till showed check number so-and-so, and the total was there, but this guy claimed that I took this check for myself.

This guy was angry at me, I forgot what for. We were kids! I was first year in college. I can't even remember his name. But I remember the incident. He wanted to get me in trouble. Who knows why?

I passed both those tests. On each one, I could have gotten into serious trouble. Could have lost my job. My life could have had a very different outcome.

CHAPTER 35
Kline Galland: Some Major Donor Stories

Some of the major Jewish philanthropists in Seattle played pivotal roles at Kline Galland because of the relationships I had built with them. These included Jack and Becky Benaroya; Edith and Morris Polack; Sam and Althea Stroum; and Stuart Sloan, each of whom donated over a million dollars to Kline Galland.

But there are less-familiar names, unknown as contributors to the Seattle Jewish community, who made their most important gifts to Kline Galland. These gifts resulted from my relationships with them, from the trust I was able to build with them.

THE LITVIN DONATION, 1990
I received a call from a Mr. David Litvin, who had made an appointment to meet with me at Kline Galland. I had no idea what this meeting was about. Usually, these types of appointments dealt with admitting a resident to the Kline Galland Home, or with some other personal need. I had never met him before. His name was not in any donor list in the city of Seattle (I always checked).

He was a man probably in his 70s. He arrived at Kline Galland in an older car, modestly dressed. At our meeting, he shared with me that he was meeting with his attorneys and was exploring charities where he could make an impact with his donation.

During our discussion, he told me that his personal physician was suggesting that he consider a gift to the University of Washington School of Medicine. His attorney was suggesting Swedish Hospital. And he shared with me that he also had heard, through an acquaintance of his, about Kline Galland. He said he came to explore with me what Kline Galland was, and what we were doing.

I had no idea the size of the estate this gentleman was talking about. I had experience, by now, with donors. Some talked about major gifts, meaning $1000-$5000. However, after some discussion, I had a feeling that this gentleman was talking about a larger number.

I shared with him the philosophy of Kline Galland: who we are serving, and the impact we make in the lives of the thousands of people who come through the doors of the Home. I shared with him the story of our original philanthropist, Caroline Kline Galland, and the impact she made on the Seattle community.

The University of Washington and Swedish Hospital, I said, are excellent institutions, and meet a great need. Kline Galland is not in that league. We are small. We serve a unique part of the community. But our impact on individuals is great.

For donations made to the University of Washington, and to Swedish Medical Center, both billion-dollar operations with very large endowments, a small donation of a million plus would be a drop in the ocean. However, to a small Jewish organization, a donation of a million dollars would have a huge impact now and for generations to come.

After a two-hour meeting, we said goodbye. I had no idea what his thinking was. Several months later, I followed up with a phone call. I asked him whether he needed any additional information, or whether he had made a decision. He told me he was impressed with what we were doing, but would not share with me what his plan was.

A year later, I received a call from his attorney, who informed me that Mr. Litvin had passed away. The attorney requested a meeting. When I arrived at his very plush office, he explained to me that he didn't understand what I had done with Mr. Litvin, but he had bequeathed his entire estate—with the exception of his fifteen-year-old car, left to his son—worth five million dollars, to Kline Galland.

I almost fell off my chair. This was, to date, the largest single donation any Jewish institution in Seattle had ever received.

In his honor, we built a new pavilion onto Kline Galland, and named it The David and Jennie Litvin Pavilion.

THE ZAFRAN DONATION, 2001

A woman called Kline Galland, insisting she had to talk to me, but refused to give her name. Mardell asked to take a message, but the caller repeated that she would talk only to me. After several calls like this, Mardell finally put her through to me. She told me her name, Anna Zafran. She insisted that I come to see her. She had read an article in the local Jewish paper about my arrival at Kline Galland. Something about her voice told me I should not refuse.

I had the address—an exclusive neighborhood north of Ballard, a gorgeous home overlooking Puget Sound—and I brought with me the social worker Karin Pollock, from Kline Galland. The interior of the house was in terrible condition, with an awful smell. Mrs. Zafran's adult son had died, and she had kept the body in the home for weeks. She sent Karin out of the room, and would only talk to me. She was a Holocaust survivor, a widow, a German refugee. Her son had been a brilliant mathematician. She couldn't bear to make the arrangements herself. She was in a dire situation—not a lack of money, but an abundance of grief and need.

I made the arrangements to ship the son's remains to California, where her husband was buried. I made arrangements for Mrs. Zafran's home to be cleaned.

After that, I visited Mrs. Zafran and brought her food every week. There I was, a CEO, running an institution without any assistant directors or associate directors, or a chief operating officer. But I made the time once a week to go and visit Mrs. Zafran. I brought her chicken soup, and food for the rest of the week. And we would talk.

Mrs. Zafran's will is an amazing will. She asked me to be executor of her estate. At first, I didn't want to accept it. But Mike Cohen urged me to do so.

Mike, a brilliant Seattle attorney on the Kline Galland board, whose father had been a Kline Galland resident, eventually came with me to Mrs. Zafran's home and wrote her will with her.

What we did there, it shows our approach to community. She wanted to give absolutely everything to Kline Galland. But we didn't want to take it all for ourselves. Mike talked to her to find out what other charities she wanted to give to.

First, to memorialize her son in Israel, we helped her set up a Mischa Zafran scholarship program at Hebrew University, and an international conference program bearing his name, at Rambam Hospital.

She was not religious, but she said, "I would like to have my *yahrzeit*[130] remembered." So, we set up an arrangement with Temple de Hirsch, where her yahrzeit is remembered every year.

We talked about education for children. I told her there was a Jewish school in town; she was not aware of that. She showed an interest in helping children to get a Jewish education. So she included Seattle Hebrew Academy in her will.

I asked if she knew about Jewish Family Service, and she said, "I heard of it through reading the paper"—*The Jewish Transcript*— "but I know nothing about it." So I explained what JFS does, with children, with abused women, with counseling, with the elderly, and she said, "What happens to an older person who comes to Jewish Family Service who doesn't have any clothes?"

I said JFS would give a voucher to the person to buy some: fifty dollars to go to Macy's to buy a dress, some shoes for the children. A person says they don't have a place to sleep tonight, JFS gives them a voucher to go to an inexpensive motel.

So she set up a fund for Jewish Family Service to help the needy, primarily the elderly, on welfare, who need clothes, transportation, glasses, medication. She understood their needs, because she had been in that position at one time. As a refugee from Germany, she came here penniless.

When Mrs. Zafran herself died, I made all the arrangements with the Jewish Chapel in Seattle, to send her remains to California.

Kline Galland received about one million dollars out of Mrs. Zafran's will. Part of her donation was in land: four or five parcels of land in California.

THE KOSHER BROTHERS' DONATION, 2004

The Kosher brothers—Max and Bill Kosher— were two attorneys living in Everett, Washington, not at all connected to any Jewish community. These gentlemen were in their upper 70s to early 80s. They had a distant

130 From the Yiddish, meaning "year-time," the anniversary of one's death, observed with certain rituals

cousin, a man who never married, living at Kline Galland Home. These brothers were also single.

On one of their visits to this cousin, I spent some time talking to them about Everett, a community I knew nothing about. We talked about philanthropy, and how philanthropy changes lives and communities. They indicated to me that they were very interested in services for children and were involved with the Shriners Hospital on a national level. They shared with me that their estate would be used to help children in need.

I was very supportive of their idea. But somehow, I snuck in the term "elderly" into the conversation, and the impact that Kline Galland has on people who have no means. How Kline Galland gives priority to people who have no financial resources, such as their own cousin, who was receiving excellent care, supported by the Jewish community. They had not been aware of their cousin's dependence on community financial support.

When these two men died within months of each other, I attended both of their burials. There was no minyan for either one.

It turned out that they had left 50% of their joint estate to a national charity, a Shriner's Hospital, and 50% to Kline Galland. In their memories, we have a plaque at the Summit at First Hill, which reads, "The Kosher Kitchen at the Summit at First Hill, donated by the Kosher Brothers." Our share of that estate was worth over two million dollars.

THE HEINZ SCHWARTZ DONATION, 2008

Mr. Heinz Schwartz, a single man, spent his adult life taking care of his ill mother. Born in Germany, they were Holocaust survivors. He did not want to place her in any institution, but insisted on singlehandedly caring for his mother for the long term. He was an accountant who was very much involved in serving the refugee German Jewish community in Seattle.

When he passed on in the 1990s, he did not have a written will. However, he met several times with his attorney and had written on a sheet of paper, from a yellow legal pad, a note about how he would like his estate to be distributed. He hadn't signed it. Charities included in that note were Kline Galland, Jewish Family Service, the Holocaust Educational Center (as it was called at the time), and The Jewish Club, which was an organization of German Jews who would meet periodically to serve as a mutual aid society.

Of course, when there is no will and no immediate family, the estate normally goes to the State of Washington. His attorney was an extremely dedicated person and wanted to ensure that Mr. Schwartz's financial intentions would be followed. The director of Jewish Family Service and I met with this attorney several times. We went to Olympia to meet with the relevant State of Washington department and shared our concerns about how we could honor Mr. Schwartz's intentions without the written will.

The person we met in Olympia was very sympathetic to our cause. However, he felt that the determination needed to be made by the court. We got our and Mr. Schwartz's attorneys to do an international search for relatives. After an exhaustive search, no living relatives were found.

We went to court in King County. As a Holocaust survivor, I testified, for the record, to what happened to the Jews in Germany. The judge was very sympathetic, and ruled in favor of the funds being used for Mr. Schwartz's intended purposes, even without a written will.

When The Jewish Club was dissolved, Walter Oppenheimer made the decision to give its share of the Schwartz estate to Kline Galland.

THE PATSY BULLITT COLLINS DONATION, late 1980s

After some analysis of where a new campus should be, we set about to build a high-rise facility to serve independent and assisted-living needs of the Jewish community. The First Hill area was our goal.

The Maynard Hospital—which was no longer functioning as a hospital—was an ideal place for our new project. The property, located on University Street at Summit Avenue, was owned by Patsy Bullitt Collins. Ms. Colllins was known for her civic generosity, as an heir to an old Seattle family known for its wealth and generous philanthropy.

We met with Ms. Collins in the Green Mansion, across the street from the hospital, on University and Minor. In several face to face meetings, we shared with her our aspirations and philosophy of care. I invited Patsy for lunch at Kline Galland. I introduced her to some key staff and board members. She quickly understood what Kline Galland's services were, and she expressed a strong desire to help us build the retirement facility on the property she owned.

We agreed on a price, which was the same price she had paid for the building several years earlier. She agreed to carry the mortgage at an interest rate 1% below prime.

As payments on pledges became available to us, I would personally meet with Patsy at the Green Mansion and present a check to her each month. She insisted that I occupy the chair at the head of the table marked "JG." I was honored, even though these were not the initials for Josh Gortler, but for Joshua Green, founder of Peoples National Bank.

Through our conversations, I shared with Patsy our philosophy and the services that we would be providing in the new facility. I also expressed to her that once the facility was completed, we would initiate a campaign to develop an endowment to support individuals who would reside there even after their personal funds were depleted. She was very impressed by our approach to providing dignity and care for people in their declining years.

When we were ready to make the last payment, $800,000, I presented the check to her. She told me to tear up the check and said, "This is my donation to help people in need." I tore up the check in front of her, and transferred $800,000 from our capital campaign account to our newly formed Kline Galland Foundation. Hers was our first major endowment gift.

When I stepped down as president of the Foundation, we had over $70 million in investments. Today, the Kline Galland Foundation is the second largest foundation among all the Jewish long-term care facilities in the United States.

Groundbreaking for The Summit at First Hill
July 14, 1999

Board of Directors and Major Donors,
including JG (center left, with tie and white
hat, no shovel); Patsy Bullitt Collins (white
dress with shovel, right of Josh); Seattle
Mayor Paul Schell (hat in hand, shovel)
Courtesy of the Joshua Gortler collection.

CHAPTER 36
Kline Galland: Building Facilities for People

THE ESFELD WING, 1976

Just as my training as a social worker did not prepare me to be a fundraiser, neither did it prepare me for becoming a land developer and construction superintendent. After several community population studies, we noticed two things: the local Seattle Jewish population was aging, and new people in need of elder care were moving in, to join their younger families who had moved to the area. This created a very large waiting list and demand for services at the Kline Galland Home. We determined in 1973 that the existing facility, which was adequate for only 70 residents, would need to double in capacity.

The process began with a community campaign with a target of $2 million (which we surpassed), and with the selection of an architectural firm to design the expansion. We very carefully interviewed the most progressive architectural firms in Seattle. Our plan was not to do a typical nursing home facility, but to create an environment that would serve as a true home for the residents. We were looking for sensitivities from the architect, to design the building for the people, rather than creating a Taj Mahal.

The firm we selected was Joyce, Copeland, Vaughan & Nordfors. Lee Copeland served as lead architect. He was great with us, a good listener who understood our unique needs; comfortable and progressive, and faithful to the current research on enhancing quality of life for those living there currently, as well as in the future.

He created for us a facility with warm colors and textures. It allows in a lot of direct sunlight, since Seattle tends to be on the gray side, which can create depression. Lee eventually became Dean of the School of Architecture at the University of Washington.

The project was completed in 1976. Within two months, we were able to fully staff it. We were 100% occupied within three months of opening the addition.

We instituted a policy of only admitting two residents per day. We wanted to be sure that each new resident received appropriate personal attention, so that they could adjust to their new home.

While this policy created some early financial losses, our philosophy has always been that the services and the needs of the residents came first. By the end of the first fiscal year, we were financially on target once again.

THE LITVIN PAVILION, 1996

With a lead gift by David and Jennie Litvin, we initiated a major capital campaign to expand, once again, the Kline Galland campus. Our goal was to serve residents, as well as to open a new campus for independent and assisted living.

The State of Washington, trying to curtail the growth of nursing homes in the state, initiated a requirement for a certificate of need. The State was making an effort to determine in what locations these kinds of facilities would be needed. So that was an obstacle. Another obstacle was zoning. The neighbors surrounding the Seward Park campus were very vocal in opposition to any expansion.

We methodically met with the neighbors. We met with State officials. We spent close to a year on these negotiations. Kline Galland wound up buying four houses adjacent to our property.

I was on the go twenty-four hours a day. There were no administrators besides myself. No consultants, no COO. We were working on ten different fronts: raising money, working with neighbors' objections, negotiating with the State. Meanwhile, I had 145 residents, their families, and a staff, whose top priorities, like mine, were the quality of care.

We prevailed on all fronts. The Litvin Pavilion became a reality. The capital campaign was ahead of schedule, and we began efforts to acquire the property on University Street, and to develop my third construction project, The Summit at First Hill. My story of acquiring the land for The Summit from Patsy Bullitt Collins is told in chapter 35.

CHAPTER 37

Kline Galland: The Summit at First Hill
1990s

"THE SUMMIT" WAS NOT THE ORIGINAL PLAN

Originally, when we purchased the properties—Maynard Hospital, with its adjacent parking lot, and a small three-story apartment building, The Wallace—the address was on Summit Avenue. Rather than going west to east on University Avenue, as it now does, the building was supposed to go north and south on Summit. It was originally designed as an 80-unit facility. We planned to build it after demolition of the hospital and the apartments.

On the west side of our property was an alley, which belonged to the city. West of the alley was an empty lot, which was owned by a Canadian company that wanted to build a high rise of about twenty floors or so. This would have been on the west side of the alley.

We talked to the Canadian company. They were having difficulty finding finances at the time. Construction loans were expensive, and they couldn't get the financial backing. They had the architectural drawings but no money to make them a reality. We approached them, and they said they would sell us the property; however, they had invested x amount of dollars into architectural plans, and they wanted us to pay for them. At that point we told them, go fly a kite. We are proceeding with our program; we'll be happy to buy the property from you, whatever you paid for it, the assessed value, however we are not going to pay for architectural plans to cut your losses. That's not our problem.

It took about six months before they came back to us. They had mortgaged the property, they had high payments to make and no financial backing for the apartment building. So we said okay, we'll buy this lot on the condition that we can vacate the alley, because if we can't do that it's useless to us. (What were we going to do? Have two buildings with an alley between them?) So that was a bargaining point, because we already had in mind that if the city would not give us the alley, we would build a bridge at the height that's allowable, like the Macy's in downtown Seattle.

We had hired a very sharp attorney, John Philip, who had worked at one time for the city, in the zoning and building division. He was our conduit to the city. First it went to the planning commission, then to the city council. Council decided to approve vacating the alley on the condition that Kline Galland would compensate the city for the value of the vacated land.

When we finally had the opportunity to buy the land, we had Jack Benaroya to consult with us. He said, whatever you do, buy the land. It is valuable to the organization, even if you can't build on it.

So we negotiated. The city's agreement to sell us the property and vacate the alley included a couple of stipulations. One was that the construction contractor would have to hire a certain number of minority people on the job. We were in a certain neighborhood, and they wanted people from the neighborhood to have jobs. That made sense.

The other stipulation was that a certain number of apartments be set aside for people of low income. That was our philosophy anyway! But we didn't say yes right away. We made it hard for the city, and said we had to go back to our board to have two or three meetings. We were negotiating. Finally, we were successful.

All of a sudden, our architects said wait a minute, now we can build a bigger building, going west and east on University. We can eliminate the parking lot from the footprint of the building. And now we don't have to take down the Wallace apartments, which we had paid a million dollars for.

As it turns out, the Wallace apartments were probably the best investment we ever made! In 2018, we were offered nine million dollars for that property! So glad we kept it. We were getting about 500 dollars a month for an apartment when we first bought them; nowadays those apartments go for $1200 to $1500 a month. It's the location. Young people want studios and one-bedroom apartments. The income from the Wallace apartments helps to subsidize the rent for residents of The Summit who cannot afford to pay full cost.

So now we have an entrance on University Street, instead of a Summit Avenue address. We couldn't call it University House; there was already one of those. Maybe "The Kline Galland on University?"

And then somebody on the board said, "Why not combine the name of the neighborhood with the name of the street?"

And that's how the name The Summit at First Hill came about.

After an exhaustive search for architects with experience in both retirement facilities and high-rise buildings, we engaged the Mithun firm. The lead architect was a woman named Leslie Moldow.

DALE CHIHULY AND THE SUMMIT

David Benoliel, a real estate developer and manager, served as chairman of development for The Summit. He oversaw the construction, representing the Kline Galland board. David was a close friend of the legendary artist Dale Chihuly.

When Chihuly was first starting his career, David had provided him studio space for his glass-working team free of charge.

While The Summit was under construction, David introduced me to Dale. I had heard the name. We reviewed the architectural plans, and toured the construction site. Dale became very interested in what we were doing, and we expressed our desire to have some of his work displayed in the new facility.

Without any hesitation, Dale expressed his strong desire to enhance the new facility with his work. He personally selected the areas where his work would be displayed. In all, the Chihulys at the Summit at First Hill represent one of the largest privately-owned collections of his work in the Seattle metropolitan area.

It was our intention to create a place of beauty, and we succeeded. I have enjoyed sitting in a corner of the elegant lobby, watching residents come down for dinner, dressed as though they were going to a nice restaurant. I think about what dinner might have been like for some of these people if they had been living alone, eating a hard boiled egg or cereal in front of the television.

People from all over the world—from Japan, the Netherlands, and all over the United States—have come to see The Summit as they planned such buildings for their communities. The Summit at First Hill has come to represent an example of care and dignity in a beautiful environment.

CHAPTER 38
An Unfortunate Responsibilty

Funerals are not a very pleasant subject to talk about, but working in long term care, the unfortunate reality is that residents pass on.

From day one as Executive Director, I made a practice of three things.

One, that I would attend every funeral where there's no family. We had a lot of people who had no connections, family, friends. Kline Galland was their life.

Two, I arranged with the Bikur Cholim Synagogue *Chevra Kadisha* [131] to provide the burial for people whose families couldn't afford it. If necessary, I would try to raise money for the burial. I felt that these people should get a traditional Jewish funeral. I worked with the Federation and individual people, and with the Samis Foundation, to make sure that we had some money available.

Three, I always attended the funerals of people I knew on a personal level, and people who were *machers*—movers and shakers in the community—because I thought it was important that Kline Galland was visible at those events.

Of course, if the deceased had made plans for a non-traditional funeral, that was their choice.

The first nontraditional funeral I attended, a few months after I came to Kline Galland, was quite a shock. There I was, from a yeshiva background,

---

131 Burial society (literally, "sacred fellowship"), a group of people who prepare the body and escort the deceased to burial, according to Jewish law

Orthodox, never having been to a nontraditional funeral in my life, and I had to confront an experience completely at odds with my background.

The funeral took place in a mausoleum. There were ashes instead of a body. The ashes were put into a vault. That flipped me out.

I was so distressed. It made me think about the conversations I had had in the DP camps with some of the kids who had survived the death camps, whose parents' lives had ended in the gas chambers, their bodies disposed of in the crematoriums. I wondered how you could take the remains of a human being, and remove them from the earth. These should go back to the earth. This was a difficult experience for me.

Another time, we had a truly bizarre farewell. A woman came to live at Kline Galland. Her adult son would come and sleep outside the mother's door, on the floor in the hallway. The staff was going crazy. This was not normal. We would occasionally permit one or two nights of a person staying over, on a cot in the room, to ease someone's transition, but not on an ongoing basis.

One day, this son took the mother out for lunch. He left her in the car, with the engine running, on a hill, while he went inside to pay the restaurant check. The car started to roll, and hit another car. Unfortunately, the mother passed away. It was a very traumatic experience.

After this happened, I received an invitation from the woman's son to attend what was called a "celebration of life with Mother." I came in, and I was completely floored! They had an unbelievable smorgasbord of foods that his mother had liked. It was not kosher, of course. There was cabbage with corned beef, salads, pastries, you name it, a great buffet. A string quartet was playing her favorite songs, and a videographer and photographer were recording the event.

In the center of this smorgasbord was an urn with the ashes of the mother! Now, the son took this urn and carried it around from guest to guest, collecting comments, with the videotape rolling. Soon it was my turn. "Now, Josh Gortler, what do you have to say to Mother?"

In college, in my homiletics class, we were taught: *Acharei Mos-Kedoshim*[132] (After a death, you have to say something nice, because the dead are holy). So, I found something nice to say.

---

132 A Hebrew Biblical pun. Literally meaning "after death, Holy ones," *Acharei Mos-Kedoshim* combines the titles of two adjacent passages from the Book of Numbers, frequently read together in the synagogue: *Acharei Mos* (After the death [of the sons of Aaron]), and *Kedoshim* (holy [you shall be]). The titles of these two, when combined and taken out of context, yield the homiletic lesson.

This was my second encounter with cremation. I talked to the Reform rabbis about how to handle it. I did not ask a *psak din* (Orthodox rabbinic legal ruling) because I might have been told not to go. But I felt it was necessary for my job that I attend.

I was not the director for the Orthodox community. I was the director for the Kline Galland home, and I had to accommodate all proceedings whether I approved or not.

Then there was the funeral where the hearse ran out of gas on the highway. A huge, huge crowd was waiting at the Herzl cemetery. There were no cell phones in those days, so nobody knew what was going on. I only had an idea because I had noticed the hearse on the side of the road on my way there. The rabbi filled the time by asking different people to tell stories about the deceased, so I spoke for five minutes, doing my part.

People come to funerals and sometimes express their emotions in the strangest ways. This brings back *Acharei Mos-Kedoshim*. You're supposed to ask for *mechila*, forgiveness. Whatever happened, happened. But some people have to finish things their way. In one instance, a person actually spat into a grave.

I spoke at a number of funerals. But I never served as rabbi. I gave eulogies in a number of places, including, for Jack Benaroya's funeral, in the Taper Auditorium at Benaroya Hall.

I think the most meaningful eulogy I ever gave was at a Catholic church, at Margaret Reed's funeral. Her service was at the Catholic church on 19th Avenue in Seattle, St. Joseph's Parish. It is a huge sanctuary with a capacity of hundreds, and it was filled to capacity. This was a full Mass, which I had never seen before. There were three priests who spoke, and I spoke. It was about a month after I'd had knee surgery. I was walking with a cane, and I had difficulty getting up on the stage. If I had asked for a rabbinic *responsa*,[133] I would not have been allowed to go there. But I felt it was important for both myself and the Jewish community to be present and to pay our respects for an individual who gave so much in her lifetime to our community. Surely, she was an *ohev Yisrael*, a lover of our people.

---

133 Same as *psak din:* official order by a rabbi based on Jewish law

PART SIX

A SEATTLE FAMILY

CHAPTER 39
Sarah Goes Back to School
1979-1982

In 1979, when Nina and Shlomo were settled into their teenage years, and doing well in school, Sarah and I decided that it was a good time for her to do what she had always wanted to do: earn a graduate degree and become a social worker.

She didn't want to disrupt the family life, so she decided that Seattle University's flexible program in counseling fit her schedule best. She could be home when Nina and Shlomo arrived from school, she could have dinner prepared, and in general take care of all the responsibilities she managed for our family. The program allowed a student to take up to five years to complete their master's, but Sarah did it in three, with minimal impact on our family life. When she would go to evening classes, I could be home. We did not want to leave our teenagers home alone.

In addition to her coursework, Sarah completed her internships in non-Jewish settings. She was awarded her master's degree in counseling in June of 1982.

By now, the name Gortler was synonymous with Seattle Jewish community social work, specifically elder care. We didn't want to have two Gortlers creating confusion in the same line of work. Sarah used her maiden name and became, professionally, Sarah Barash.

Shortly after her graduation, Jewish Family Service offered Sarah a position. She was soon recognized on her own merit as an excellent clinician, a respected leader, and a great advocate for her clients. She began her career at JFS in support services, and was then promoted to senior case manager and director of the senior services program.

At community functions in the 1980s, leaders were usually introduced by name. I remember our first Federation dinner after Sarah began her new professional role. We stood up and were recognized as Josh Gortler and Sarah Barash. When we sat down, one of the women at our table commented, "You know, you are a credit to this community. Even though you are now divorced, when it comes to the community, you sit together." That's a true story. This was in the early 1980s. Women of that generation were still being referred to as, say, "Mrs. Joshua Gortler." Sarah was a trailblazer, using her own name and professional identity in a way that has become the norm today.

Sarah has a natural gift for establishing excellent relationships with her clients, especially Holocaust survivors, who needed a sympathetic ear and a warm presence. As a professional she herself has stitched together the remnants of many lives. During her 30-year career, she made a difference in the lives of hundreds of people in this community. Even in retirement, she keeps in close touch with her former clients and their families.

CHAPTER 40
Travels With Sarah

You would think that, after all the displacements in my life, I would want to just stay close to home. But Sarah and I have found that traveling together to different parts of the world gives us much pleasure.

Whether we fly or take a cruise or a chartered bus, we have been privileged to discover something new everywhere. Of course, visiting our families has required a fair amount of travel, to Memphis or Boston or Phoenix or Denver. But here is a short list of some of the places we have visited as tourists:

South America: Argentina, Uruguay, Chile, Peru
Asia, twice: Hong Kong, Japan, Thailand, China
Australia, New Zealand
Eastern Europe*: Czech Republic, Hungary, Austria (Vienna)
Israel, at least 3 or 4 times
Canada, a couple of times to the Canadian Rockies
Alaska
Norway
Sweden
The Netherlands
Italy

*So far, we have avoided traveling to Poland, Germany, or Russia. We talked about it, but I never had any interest. Even when we change planes, I try to avoid German airports.

In all our travels, we always tried to connect with the Jewish communities. This provided us with many memorable connections. Here's one:

On our trip to Sydney, Australia, we spent a *Shabbos* in the Jewish neighborhood known as Bondi Beach. We researched the kosher takeout catering services as well as the synagogues. On Friday, I took a taxi to pick up our kosher provisions. We had decided that we would go to *Shabbos* services at the Mizrachi *shul,* which was Modern Orthodox. It was exactly what we thought we needed. On our way to *shul,* we encountered a young family who were also going to synagogue. We asked them the way to the Mizrachi shul. He quickly answered, "You do not want to go to the Mizrachi *shul.* The rabbi is a crook. You have to come with me. We are a breakaway *minyan.* And besides, we have the best *kiddush* in Sydney."

Now, here we are, "down under," on the opposite side of the world from our home, and we run into the old familiar Jewish politics. He insisted that we go to the breakaway *shul,* which we did. We enjoyed a very warm welcome with our brethren. Whatever issues their community was dealing with mattered less to us than the welcome we received.

CHAPTER 41
Why My Parents are Buried in Seattle
1978

MY FATHER, SUMMER OF 1978

My father was not feeling well. He called from Phoenix and said, "We want to come to Seattle to visit." When he arrived, I saw that things didn't look very good. I took him to my doctor—the head of the Kline Galland medical team, Dr. Ericson, who sent him to the hospital. They did a workup and found that he had the end stages of liver and pancreatic cancer. Saul Rivkin (the noted Seattle oncologist) was called in, and he was just amazing with my father. He tried just absolutely everything that was available at that time.

My father stayed in the hospital for about ten days before he died there. Rabbi Greenberg of Congregation Ezra Bessaroth came to visit him. They knew each other from Phoenix.

My mother was staying with us. Toward the end, my brother and my sister-in-law came to Seattle. On *Tisha b'Av*[134]—August 12, 1978—I was in the hospital with him. Three days later, the twelfth of Av, he died.

MY MOTHER, AUTUMN OF 1978

My father was buried in Seattle. My mother went back to Phoenix to stay with my brother. But right after the Holidays[135]—two months later—

---

134 For a religious Jew, the ninth day (*Tisha*, Hebrew for 9) of the Hebrew month of Av is a day of deepest sorrow. Rabbinic tradition established this as a day to mourn the loss of Jerusalem's holiest Jewish sites, the Temples, both destroyed on the 9th of Av, in 423 BCE and 70 CE.
135 *Rosh Hashana, Yom Kippur,* and *Sukkos*

she died. As I was still saying Kaddish[136] for my father, my mother passed away. Her remains were shipped from Phoenix to Seattle. My brother came with the casket, and she was buried next to my father. They were both sixty-eight years old when they died.

At the end of his life, in Seattle, a place surrounded by dense forests, my father felt at home. His life had begun near the forests of Poland. He loved the trees and knew many of them by name.

Of all places to resettle such an immigrant to the United States, he was brought to Arizona. In more ways than one—in terms of landscape, in terms of Jewish life—Phoenix was a desert for him. My mother, before the war, had never traveled more than a few miles from home. For both my parents, coming to Seattle was the first traveling they had done since their resettlement in Phoenix in 1951. Before the events that led to her exile from Tomaszów, my mother had traveled, by horse and buggy, no farther than the distance from Seward Park to downtown Seattle.

---

136 During the first year after the death of a parent, an observant Jew is required to say *Kaddish,* or have it said it on his or her behalf, at every daily prayer service, in memory of this loved one. *Kaddish* makes no mention of death but is often referred to as a "prayer for the dead."

CHAPTER 42
Aunt Brocha's Journey to Burial in Seattle
February 1981

After the war, we were in three different DP camps.

Somehow, I have no idea how, my Aunt Brocha—my mother's sister—and her husband Wolf ended up in Föhrenwald with us. Their last name is Uncyk. Their journey is similar to ours: Siberia, Uzbekistan, Germany. They never had any children, so my brother Morris and I were kind of like adopted kids to them. We were their closest relatives. In the DP camp, they always spent the holidays with my parents. Aunt Brocha was the one who smuggled a turkey into the camp under her coat, just in time for Pesach.

They never left Germany after the war. After the DP camps were closed, they settled in Munich, and opened up a bar.

My Uncle Wolf never had a job, like my father did, in the DP camp. My father worked for the UN, UNRRA—he was a *magaziner*, a stock-room manager, it says on the documentation from HIAS, my father's labor card. He was employed in various capacities in the DP camp, and he was a representative to the council of DP camps that met in Munich.

My uncle and aunt, though, were really dealing mainly in the black market. They would smuggle stuff in and out from Switzerland, because Munich wasn't very far from the border with Switzerland. He dealt a lot on the black market in currency exchange, which was not allowed, and in goods that he somehow got from the Germans and resold on the black market. This bar that they opened in Munich, in addition to serving drinks, I think it was pretty much an exchange for black market stuff.

When they became elderly, my brother from Phoenix would go visit them three, four times a year in Munich and help out with whatever they needed. They were okay financially, but he would hire someone to clean the house, to make sure that things were going well.

One day, Morris got a call from my aunt, saying that my uncle had died, and his remains had been shipped to Israel. Uncle Wolf Uncyk is now buried there.

She also told Morris that she would prefer to be buried next to my mother, in Seattle. My mother—who was still alive at the time, and regularly corresponded with Aunt Brocha—had let her know that she planned to be buried in Seattle.

My parents died first, both of them. Knowing that the wish of my aunt was to be buried next to my mother, I made sure that there was an extra grave next to my mother's side for Brocha.

When she died on February 21, 1981, my brother got a call from the *chevra kadisha* in Munich. They had his contact as surviving relative. My brother called me, and said, "Brocha just died, and they want $5,000 from us to ship her remains to Seattle. What do we do?" I said, "We're in." He said, "They don't want any cash, they want money wired to a bank." So, I said, "Okay, I'm wiring $2,500 to you, and you wire five thousand dollars to the *chevra kadisha*." It's done, I thought.

Two days later, he got another call: "The costs are higher now. It's another five thousand." So my brother called me. "What do we do?" I say, "We're in already for five; we're in for ten. I'm sending you another $2,500." So, he sent another five thousand. Now we were ten thousand dollars in for "costs," whatever that meant, to ship her remains to Seattle.

The *chevra kadisha* in Munich at that time was run by a group of real mafioso-type Israelis. They contacted me and asked where to ship the body. I met with Mr. Etkin of the Seattle *chevra kadisha* and got everything ready to have her remains come here.

Then came another call. It was Morris. "They want another ten thousand dollars." I said no. This is it. Tell them they can keep her in Germany. We're not taking her.

But that wasn't the end of the story.

I happened to know a Chaplain Dana of the United States Army. I had taken the pictures—the 8mm movies—of his wedding, when he married a daughter of the Pearl family of West Seattle. [137]

At the time the Aunt Brocha fiasco was happening, Chaplain Dana was stationed in Munich.

I called Chaplain Dana. He said he'd see what he could do and then told me to contact Scoop Jackson (Washington's legendary, influential US Senator Henry M. Jackson). The senator could then send a little note to the consul in Munich.

Within hours, my brother got a call. They were releasing Aunt Brocha.

Morris gave me a flight number for the casket coming into Seattle, on Northwest Airlines. I called up Mr. Etkin, *a'h*, and asked him to get ready for a funeral, my aunt was finally coming. I went to SeaTac Airport with Mr. Etkin, with a hearse, to meet her remains and transport them to the Jewish chapel, because overseas caskets are sealed metal containers. We would need to open it up, identify her, and put her in a wooden casket, as Jewish tradition requires, for the burial.

The flight arrived. No Aunt Brocha! I had ten people waiting for a funeral!

Somehow, the casket went to Miami. The guy screwed up one of the flight numbers, the connecting flight from New York.

It took us another day with Northwest Airlines before her remains arrived in Seattle. Mr. Etkin and I went back to the airport, picked up the casket, brought it to the Jewish chapel, opened it up, and confirmed it was Aunt Brocha. She had had a *tahara*[138] already there, but I think Rabbi Londinsky in Seattle had said (I forget why) that we should do the *tahara* again because of all that happened. We did that. Again, I brought a *minyan*, I said a few words, and we buried her next to my mother.

---

137 That's a story in itself: a Jewish family that arrived in Seattle around a hundred fifty, two hundred years ago. Their family story is on one of those telescope installations on the beach in West Seattle, overlooking the Sound.

138 ritual washing of the body, required for a Jewish religious burial

JCC Memorial with Balsenbaum and Gortler Names. *Courtesy of the Holocaust Center for Humanity, Seattle.*

CHAPTER 43
Remembrance

At the front of the Jewish Community Center of Seattle, on Mercer Island, there's a wide plaza where children play and wait for their rides. Parents make small talk over coffee and share cell phone photos.

At the back of that plaza there's a wall of names, and in the center of the plaza, a twenty-foot sculpture of the Hebrew letter Lamed. At the base of the Lamed are inscribed the names of Nazi death camps. On the wall are the names of murdered family members of Seattle-area survivors from the time we now call The Holocaust. I am one of those survivors. The names of some of my Balsenbaum and Gortler family members are inscribed on that wall.

The height of the Lamed, and its shape, and its gray color, might suggest the worst of the imagery of the Holocaust: the chimneys, from which arose the smoke from the crematoria, where millions of my people were murdered.

The Hebrew letter *Lamed* could stand for the word *lo,* meaning "do not." It was one of the first words I learned to read, in the DP camps: *lo tishkach,* "do not forget."

Lamed also could stand for the word *lomed,* meaning "learn." The way we Jews have managed to survive for all these thousands of years is by learning, and by passing on our tradition of learning to the generations that follow us.

PART SEVEN

FROM SILENCE TO SPEECH

CHAPTER 44
I Finally Become
A "Holocaust Survivor Speaker"
2002 and onward

For many years, the reliving and the telling of my personal story was on the back burner. During my college years, I was too busy with my schoolwork, papers, and social life. While some of my close friends at Yeshiva University were Holocaust survivors, too, this was never a topic that we dwelled on or spoke about.

After grad school, I was too busy with getting married, raising a family, and developing a career. It was Laurie Cohen of the Holocaust Center for Humanity, an education center in Seattle, who encouraged me to share my story with others. I knew Laurie because her husband, Mike, was on the Kline Galland board. She had been teaching at Seattle University, and had invited me to talk to her class about the Holocaust. But first, I spoke in a Seattle Public School.

FIRST TIME: RAINIER BEACH HIGH SCHOOL, SEATTLE
My first presentation was at Rainier Beach High School. It is an inner-city school in Seattle, with students from various parts of the city. It is a school that is more sports-oriented than academic. When I received the first call to do a presentation there, the teacher/coordinator informed me that the last Holocaust-related speaker had had a terrible experience. The group had been unruly, disrespectful, and not attentive to the materials presented.

In preparation for this presentation, I had brought a half-dozen slides and a projector. When I entered the auditorium, it was totally unprepared for the presentation: there was no screen. They didn't even have an extension cord for the projector. Someone found us a screen and an extension cord. I took a few minutes to organize my material, and then my presentation began.

I began to speak from the podium, but I soon left the podium and joined the audience. I walked around among the students. I got their attention, and I felt that they began to listen. They began to take part in the presentation.

After about 45 minutes, I asked the audience whether I should continue. There was a unanimous shout, "Go man. Go man. We want to hear more about it."

Towards the end of my presentation, I asked the audience to pledge "Never again," without realizing that this was the name of a song they knew. The entire 100+ students began to shout, or sing, "Never again, never again" to the tune of that song.[139]

I knew at that time that I had had an impact on those students, and they could relate to my presentation.

---

139 by Wu Tang Clan

CHAPTER 45
A Remnant Speaks at the Northwest School
DECEMBER 2017

A few years later, I was addressing a high school class, as I often do, telling stories of my childhood escape. I showed the maps of my family's travels on the run, and described our arrival in the United States, and my adjustment as an immigrant.

I showed them a document that my grandson Yosef found in the archives at the US Holocaust Memorial Museum in Washington, DC. The document confirms that I, a three-year-old refugee from Poland, entered a border town called Rava-Ruska, in Soviet-held territory, with "amnesty" for a limited time. It shows my birth year as 1934, two years earlier than the truth, probably to entitle my parents to receive a bit more food on my behalf. With the expiration of the "amnesty," my family was shipped off to a labor camp in Siberia.

The document demonstrates how narrowly my family and I escaped being murdered. When we compared this document (see chapter 2) with other historical evidence, we figured out that just 19 days after this "amnesty" expired, the Nazis came back to Rava-Ruska, and murdered all the Jews remaining there.

At the top of the document, it says my name, Szia Gortler. Of course, I was introduced to the class as "Joshua Gortler." A student asked me, "What does this Szia Gortler have to do with Joshua? Why haven't you taken back the name Szia again?"

I said, "Why do you ask that question?"

"Well," he said, "Joshua is more of an American name. Szia is definitely not an American name. Did you want a more American name to assimilate into the country?"

I said, "No, no, I tried to assimilate under the name Jimmy." Which I had never spoken about in any of my school talks. The question had never come up.

So, this kid brought it up. Then the next kid had another question: "Whatever you've gone through, I see you wear a *kippah*."[140] The kid knew what a *kippah* was. And all of a sudden, the conversation changes: "Why do you still believe in a God? After this happened?"

It was an amazing discussion. From there, we zipped into talking about the survivors in the DP camps, because that was my comfort level. I was there.

We talked about how there were two types of school there, the religious school and the secular school, and I said, frankly, that the majority of the Jews in the in the DP camps gave up every form of religion. Because the idea was that, if there was a God, why did this happen?

It was a discussion about assimilation, and the larger community, and why I would keep the faith after I'd seen what had happened? I got to talk to them about how it is not for us to judge, only history later on will judge what happened at that particular period. I mentioned the Harold Kushner book *When Bad Things Happen to Good People*.[141] I mentioned the Biblical story of Job.

I think Harold Kushner's book is definitely relevant to my story. I read it as support for my perspective. I think, as of now, good things have happened to me. Bad things happened there, but now, looking back on my total life, I see very positive things.

I'm coming now towards the end of my life, and I've asked myself, would I want to change anything? I say no. I know I went through a very difficult period, but since that period has ended, I've had a very, very fine life. When I came to the United States, we were very poor. We had nothing. But now, financially, I'm very comfortable. Socially, I'm acceptable. Religiously, I'm very comfortable with the level my family and I are at. So, I have nothing to regret. I think good things happen to good people.

140 Also called *yarmulke*, skullcap worn by observant Jews
141 Kushner, *When Bad Things Happen to Good People*. Random House, 1981.

I followed my parents' and grandparents' footsteps, and I found comfort. I cannot question that period of time, or ask, "Where was God?"

I look back, to what the she'arit hapleita[142] did in the United States, the survivors, the surviving remnant, the leftovers. It's a Biblical term, she'arit hapleita, for the Jewish people who survived the exile to Babylonia and came back home to the land of Israel.

I have been re-reading the 1950s sociologist Marshall Sklare's studies on American Jewish life,[143] where he claims that Orthodox Judaism in the United States would disappear. He predicted that Reform, and the big movement at the time, of course, the Conservative movement, those were going to be the big panacea for American Jewry. Orthodoxy was going to disappear.

But just the opposite has happened.

The she'arit hapleita, the Jews who came into the United States after the war, totally changed the tone of American Jewry. They themselves, my generation and the older generations, may not have been the "frummies,"[144] the people who took up all the Orthodox practices, but the next generation is the "frummies." They have revived Orthodox Jewish life.

If you look at most of the leaders of Orthodox Jewry in America today, you'll find that they are children or grandchildren of these remnants. Anywhere you look, people are saying, "My grandfather was a survivor." There was really an injection in Jewish learning, and Jewish scholarship, and Jewish commitment with the Jews who came over from Europe.

Was it because there was awareness that so much learning was lost, with the murder of so many scholars, so many brilliant, educated teachers of rabbinic tradition? I don't know. I cannot judge the reason. But the fact is, in American Jewry and Israeli Jewry today, there's more scholarship coming out in the Orthodox world than during the "golden era" of Spain, when there was a lot of scholarship about the high point of Jewish history.

We're not just living in a golden era. It's above golden. Lots of scholarship.

Who would have predicted that Torah learning would have such success, after we lost that generation, that people are hungry enough to

---

142 surviving remnant (Sephardic pronunciation), a Biblical phrase
143 *The Jews: Social Patterns of an American Group.* The Free Press, 1958.
144 A flip, sometimes pejorative term based on Yiddish *frum*, meaning one who is punctilious about observance of Jewish law. *Frummies* suggests observant Jews whose dress and speech make obvious the extent of their religious practices.

learn that they seek out the Sages' words, even in translation? When I was a student at Yeshiva University, if you had a translation of a volume of the Talmud, you had to hide it! A student had shame in using a translation. It was published under a pseudonym, "Barbara." Today, you can find the Talmud in all kinds of translations, available everywhere, in books and on the Internet.

A MAN, A CLASS, A PURPOSE

Back to that classroom at the Northwest School. In that school, you had these sixteen- or seventeen-year-olds who are being educated to become leaders in the political and business and intellectual worlds.

I feel I have a purpose and a commitment in doing what I'm doing with them, and in all the other classes I speak to—whether in prisons or juvenile detention centers, or adult community service groups—because these kids had never been exposed to this kind of conversation in history class, or in humanities class. These children had never met a person whose childhood was spent in a Displaced Persons camp. The very existence of the DP camps was news to them! They'd heard the term refugee camp, but not DP. I used the term "DP," and one of the teachers said, they have no idea what you're talking about. So I circled back, and told them about the DPs, and what my early teenage years were like, in that place.

And that's what I want to emphasize in telling my story in this book. I became who I am in the DP camps.

CHAPTER 46
Why I Keep Speaking

לַכָּל זְמָן וְעֵת... עֵת לַחֲשׁוֹת וְעֵת לְדַבֵּר (קהלת ג:א,ז)

There is a time for everything...a time to be silent and
a time to speak (Ecclesiastes 3:1,7)

As the older generations take leave of this world, I find that the child survivors of the Holocaust, like myself, have a responsibility and a gift that they need to share with others—high school students, college students, prisoners, fraternal groups, a wide variety of audiences. As of December 2019, I currently speak about a dozen times a year.

I spoke to juvenile detention centers in both the Kitsap and King counties of Washington State. I shared with them what it felt like for me as a teenager—a fifteen-year-old kid—to have been deprived of food, shelter, and freedom during his formative years.

An inmate once asked me if I had any anger against the Germans who had caused so much pain to the Jewish people, and to me personally. My answer was simply, "One could spend the rest of their life dwelling on that anger and stopping from doing anything positive. Or one can channel that energy towards creative and productive areas." This particular young man, who hadn't said anything during my presentation, all of a sudden became very verbal, and said, "You know, my life will change after this presentation. In the past, I would have grabbed a gun to settle a score. But after listening to you, I'll find other ways to handle my anger." I truly hope that is what he did.

Today, my presentations are far more high-tech than that first slide show at Rainier Beach High. On my Power Point presentations, I have maps, photos, graphs, charts, and photocopies of documents that help me tell my story. I show the Bible that was published in Munich in 1947[145] and dedicated "to Harry Truman, President of the United States." That dedication is a gesture of gratitude for the man who eased the American quota system to allow survivors like me to enter the US legally. He also played a key role in making sure the US voted in the United Nations to support the partition of Palestine, which led to the creation of the State of Israel.

After speaking to audiences who have never heard about the Holocaust, or have never even met a Jewish person before, I feel that my words have had an impact on their lives. I share with them the fact that the Holocaust story is not an invention to be argued about by deniers. As a survivor, I am a witness to this history, which I share with them, and which they, in turn, will be able to share with future generations, because they heard it from me.

Unfortunately, I see this history repeating in our times. The venom of antisemitism is spreading again in Europe and in the United States. Here is evidence from an April 27, 2017, Seattle Times article[146] about one of my talks ("Holocaust Survivor With Words For Today"):

Gortler reminded his audience of a piece of graffiti scrawled just last month at Temple De Hirsch Sinai in Seattle's Capitol Hill neighborhood. The graffiti read: "The Holocaust is Fake History."

Two years after that article ran, antisemitic graffiti was scrawled next to the photo of a child that appears in the window of the Holocaust Center for Humanity in downtown Seattle.[147] That child was me. That photo appears on the cover of this book.

---

145 Photo in this book
146 Reprinted in full in the Appendix of this book
147 https://www.kiro7.com/news/local/anti-semitic-graffiti-scrawled-on-holocaust-center-in-seattle/1001684382/

APPENDIX

A LEGACY OF CARE: MY MESSAGE ON RETIREMENT

AN INTERVIEW PUBLISHED IN
THE KLINE GALLAND NEWSLETTER
CHAILITES Vol. 103, no. 2
Summer 2017/5777[148]

INTRODUCTION

By Dick Rosenthal, *ChaiLites* editor, interviewer

February 28, 1969: We look back on that single day nearly five decades ago and can realize just how far we've come in literally a blink of an eye. History tells us:

- Presidents Nixon and de Gaulle met privately at the Elysée Palace
- The Dow-Jones industrial plummeted by 35 points, closing at 917
- Gas hovered around 30¢ a gallon; apples, 20¢ a pound
- The Pilots prepared for their only season at Sick's Seattle Stadium
-

A 32-year-old young man – a student of psychology, a social worker, a rabbi, a visionary named Joshua H. Gortler began day one of a 48-year journey at Kline Galland – first as CEO, now wrapping-up as Foundation President

We recently sat down with Josh. He looked back, looked around, looked ahead. He observed, "The incredible success of Kline Galland is not the success of Josh Gortler, it is the success of those around me – the community, its leaders, the Board, senior management and, oh my gosh, the caregivers and volunteers. Kline Galland takes care of people better than anyone else. Residents and patients come first – always have and always will."

---

148 Text ©2017 Kline Galland Center

TO MAKE A LONG STORY SHORT…

JG: In the mid-60's, I was selected to head the program side of an emerging joint venture between the YMHA of Flushing NY (Young Men's Hebrew Assn.) and United Help. We developed housing for elderly Holocaust survivors in the NY area. It was very interesting, challenging and unique. I presented a paper on my work at a conference in Washington, D.C. exploring the variety of emerging services for seniors – services combining housing, recreation, health monitoring and disease prevention. Someone from United Way of King County was in the audience and, apparently, was impressed. In 1968, as Kline Galland was searching for a new Executive Director, it was suggested they contact "this young man in New York with great ideas." They did. One thing led to another. To make a long story short, I was hired and here I am—48 years later.

DREAMERS, DOERS & NO RED INK.

JG: So what motivated Sarah and me to move cross country with our two young children? Let me tell you. I saw potential—lots and lots of potential. But it was the lay leadership that really impressed me. They were leaders, they were the heart and soul of the Jewish community, they were open to new ideas – always wanting to do their utmost to provide the best in senior care. They were dreamers. More importantly, they were doers and responsible stewards of the community's resources. I remember Bob Block and Sol Esfeld saying they would work with me and be directly involved so long as they did not see any red ink on the reports. They were quite clear, "no deficits." The budget at the time was $250,000 – 25% of which came from Federation. After five years, we'd become so self-sufficient that Federation began sending us just a buck a year.

A BLUEPRINT TO THE FUTURE.

JG: In 1972, I developed a blueprint for the Board. It was a vision looking towards what, in reality, is today. It put forth the rationale for Kline Galland going beyond serving just the 70 people we did at the time at the Home in Seward Park … for developing an outpatient program like a day center where people could arrive in the morning and go home at night … for providing short-term care – respite care as I call it … for post-hospital care, care for Alzheimer's patients, elegant independent and assisted living; community based services; the plan went on and on. It called for Kline Galland to be at the very forefront of training and become affiliated with the U.W. School of Social Work, Nursing, Occupational Therapy, Psychiatry and Physical Therapy. (By the way, we developed a very unique relationship with the most prominent geriatric psychiatrists in the region.) It was all there, in black and white, a blueprint for the future—for the 21st Century. Keep in mind, this was over four decades ago. It was unheard of at the time, yet the Board bought in. They worked with me hand-in-hand, step-by-step, making the blueprint a reality—so long as we didn't run a deficit. We didn't, and we haven't.

THE WINDS OF CHANGE.

JG: In the late 1970s and 80s, Seattle was growing. Kline Galland was too. We were the initial nursing home in the area to develop the psycho-social approach to geriatric care—looking at the total person instead of merely dispensing pills. With remodeling and expansion, we made it a priority to provide the maximum number of private rooms—creating an atmosphere of home in every way we could, including use of colors and natural light. We saw that "the needs" model was changing—evolving if you will. There was a shift from just helping and comforting the needy to more fully serving all those with a variety of needs—medical needs, care needs, socialization and the like. People wanted care, people required care, people were willing to pay for care. Our response? Simple. Kline Galland would continue on the path of providing the highest degree of excellence in everything we do.

We knew that the Jewish community would not come to us just because we were Jewish; we had to be the best. We were and we are.

PEOPLE WITH COMPASSION, PEOPLE WITH HEART.

JG: We had good policies. More significantly, we had good people—great people. Early on I learned that if you want a compassionate staff, you must be compassionate to your staff. If you want employees who care for residents, you must care for your employees. That being said, I am proud that Kline Galland was the very first in Seattle's senior care community to start a retirement program for each and every employee, regardless of status. We also developed a very strong volunteer core. I am so thankful we were able to engage people like Carolyn Danz and Lucy Spring, who initiated a superb volunteer program that continues today.

Alyssa Bobman and her crew. The best volunteers who are the frontline. The goal of our volunteers, as is the goal for all of us, is to meet the needs of the residents the best we can each and every day.

A GOOD STORY TO TELL.

JG: Kline Galland has a proven track record like no other. We've always had waiting lists. We're described as an innovator—"an organization definitely NOT in stagnation." We've had the support of giants in the community – people who believed in our mission, people who, thankfully, believed in me. Those giants I was lucky enough to work with represent a commitment of time and energy and compassion that set the standard for the rest of us to follow. People like Hank Wolf, Morris Polack, Barry Schneiderman, Paul Jassny, Arva Gray, Ray Galante, Sam Stroum, Jack & Becky Benaroya, Sol Esfeld as I mentioned before—they are among the "who's who" in service to community. The list goes on and on—and continues to build to this day. Thank you one and all.

SENIOR CARE WITH & WITHOUT WALLS

JG: Our Community Based Services are here to stay. They are growing and will continue to do so. We need to have different strokes for different folks. Some require services in a 24-hour setting within the physical environment of The Summit or Kline Galland Home. Others prefer to age in place, to stay at home and have Kline Galland come to them.

TAKING CARE TO TAKE CARE.

JG: As CEO, and this past decade with the Kline Galland Foundation, I have seen the community support Kline Galland because of the support Kline Galland provides to the community. An organization must move and grow and be up-to-date—actually more than up-to-date, up-to-tomorrow. You need a vision for the future. It's not about buildings, budgets or glorification. It is, however, about taking care of people. That's the one thing Kline Galland does—and we do it better than anyone else.

On Doing Social Work The Josh Gortler Way
By Dan Ozog, MSW

Josh Gortler influenced my work before I even met him. It was Josh who mentored the social worker I wanted to work with at the Catholic Home in West Seattle.

I grew up in a small town in Pennsylvania, in a big extended Catholic family. I had originally intended to be a priest and serve on missions in Africa. Then I left the seminary, got married, and served in the Peace Corps in Tonga.

I knew I wanted to work with the elderly. From my home in California, I came to the University of Washington School of Social Work in 1974, where my first-year placement in the program for my master's was at Kline Galland.

My second year, I worked at Mt. St. Vincent's, where my supervisor was a great admirer of Josh Gortler. At the end of that year, Josh hired me. I started as activity director, working with residents, guiding bus trips and so forth.

You know why people call Josh a visionary? As a student, I watched Josh's interactions with staff. We were a giant family! He really pushed the idea that we were not "social services," "dietary," "laundry," but we were the Kline Galland family staff. We interacted and our roles crossed. If there was a CNA (certified nursing assistant) who had a close relationship with a resident and the resident was dying, or they lost a child, or some other crisis, the CNA would be right there giving lots of support, not the social worker.

If a physical therapist noticed that a resident was depressed, and they came to one of our psych conferences, we didn't feel threatened. We all realized that they had a different relationship. They were there walking with somebody for half an hour, three times a week. They have that close, intimate contact, where there might be more sharing. Territory was not an issue. It was accepting, as in, "Great, you have that rapport, let's use that."

Josh had meetings often. He let everybody express themselves. In the end, whatever decision was made, we knew we'd all had input, and jumped on the bandwagon. He always had a focus, knew what he wanted. But he knew how to get everybody to converse and come together. We had some strong personalities! We could really clash! But we came together for the sake of the residents.

Josh always started a meeting with the question, "What's the right thing to do?" He wouldn't say that in so many words, but that's where he took the conversation: what is the humane thing to do? He brought out the goodness in people.

We would cry together when we lost someone.

I always told staff—nursing assistants, everybody—that when the families come in, don't refer to them as "Sarah's son," or "Sarah's daughter," but by name: "Hello, Mary, how are you today? Your mother's in the dining room," or "Your mother wasn't feeling well today, she missed her breakfast." Always identify every family member by name. Learn their names. You want them to know your name. And relationships did soften. There's nothing sweeter to a person than their own name.

Most of the residents wanted to be called by their first names. In other homes, it was always Mr. or Mrs. We would ask people what they wanted to be called. Some of our German residents preferred the more formal Mr. or Mrs. When the State licensing people came to check on us one time, they criticized us for calling one resident "Coco." They said we were being inappropriate by calling her by this cutesy nickname. But that's what she wanted! We said, "Go ask her." She said, "That's all I've ever been called!"

Josh was never threatened by staff relationships with board members. The board came out to visit; a lot of them were volunteers. Some had parents at the home. So we interacted. We were on committees together. They were part of the family, too. Josh fostered that relationship. We celebrated together. There were parades, potlucks, mazal tovs.

Josh allowed us to express our differences. I noticed that no matter what religious tradition we came from, Josh hired people with a strong belief in the goodness of people, and the ability to believe in an afterlife.

AN EXECUTIVE'S UNTOLD STORY
By Mardell Kromer
Executive Assistant to Josh Gortler
Kline Galland, 1984-2017

Early on, Josh didn't talk much about his past. I don't know at what point he did start talking about it more.

I still don't know why in the world he dictated that reminiscence to me. He spent a couple of days, and just kind of went through his whole story. It was hours we spent doing this. Whether that was in preparation, when he started doing the Holocaust talks, maybe? I just can't remember why we did that, nor whatever happened to the papers.

I don't even know how I came to know, early on, what his history was. Usually, when I would ask him something about it, he would say, "Oh, we'll talk about it over a cup of coffee sometime." For a long time, it was very upsetting for him.

One of the residents told me, "When we came out of those concentration camps, we were just animals." Then this man said to Josh, "How in the world can you do these talks? How can you do it?"

I asked Josh a different question: "You went through all this, how did you possibly put it from your mind and just go on with another life?" I guess there was a time early on when he maybe lost his faith a little bit? And he did have a struggle. I asked him, "How did you overcome that to be the person you are now?"

He said his teachers and rabbis in college, in yeshiva, helped him through all that.

He once walked out of a city planning meeting that was critical to one of our projects, in spite of the fact that he hadn't had his turn to speak, because it was running late on a winter Friday afternoon. He had to get home for Shabbat. Whatever we needed from the meeting, turned out ok.

He said that the point of view of this book, this memoir, is that you CAN undergo all that adversity, and all that trauma, terrible crimes against humanity, and you can still go on and make a vital difference in the lives of people.

Mardell Kromer
Executive Assistant to Josh Gortler, 1984-2017
Seattle, Washington

CLOSE ENCOUNTERS OF THE JEWISH KIND
By Mike Cohen
Board Chair, Kline Galland, 1989-1992

I am honored to add my words to the life story of Josh Gortler, who, to my surprise, became one of the most important men in my life.

I call my relationship with Josh "A Close Encounter of the Jewish Kind." After all, what were the odds that a fellow like me, Jewish by birth but raised in a small town in the hinters of the American Midwest, far from the centers of Jewish communal life, a lawyer of the baby-boom generation, would gravitate to such a mentor? To a remnant of the Holocaust, a social worker, a yeshiva-trained Orthodox rabbi? To a complex master of the tricks of head and heart required to grow a Jewish community? To a man committed to creating a Jewish home with world-class care for the least capable and most vulnerable, the ailing elderly?

Yet this is the man who led me, and hundreds of others, over his forty-plus-year career, teaching by example how best to care for our precious elders.

When my family relocated to Seattle, the one person left in Minnesota was my aging grandmother, my mother's mother, an immigrant from Germany. In 1970, she was ninety, blind from glaucoma, suffering from dementia and a tumor that would take her life. My mother brought her to Seattle, assuming that the care here would be available and better than in her home. But the undersized Kline Galland nursing home of those days had no capacity for her and sadly, there was no other place at the end of her life that could meet our standards of loving care.

I vowed that this would never happen to my family again. To that end, I sought the opportunity to get involved as a volunteer in the delivery of services to the Jewish elderly, and to study and learn the policy behind that delivery.

My good fortune was to be introduced to Josh Gortler, the head of the Kline Galland Home, by my professional mentor, the late Barry Schneiderman. He whispered to me that Josh was unique, the smartest person in the room, already, in his early 40s, a luminary in the world of services to the elderly. Josh had just spearheaded the doubling of the Kline Galland home from the size it had been when my grandmother was in need ten years earlier.

I was awestruck: in less than a decade after his arrival in Seattle, this man had managed to the raise the funds for the project, secure agreements from the State of Washington to approve an expansion that could just as easily have been disapproved, find banks to lend construction funds, and induce the trustees of the Galland estate to go along with this expensive but vital Jewish community project.

I knew that mustering this level of support was no small thing. After I was nominated to the Board of The Kline Galland Home, I paid close attention to how Josh, this mobilizer of the Jewish community, did seemingly magical work.

Why magical? Because who could imagine such a man? What is the likelihood that the savviest healthcare professional in the Pacific Northwest would be someone who:

-   was uprooted, homeless, on the run and unschooled until he was 10 years old?

-   had never set foot in the US until he was 15?

-   had never lived in Seattle or the Northwest until he was in his mid-thirties?

-   was educated in New York's Orthodox Jewish environment?

Wouldn't such a man struggle with community leadership in the Pacific Northwest's diverse Jewish world? How could he set up an appropriate support system for Jewish elders here?

Yet Josh did exactly that. Over three and one-half decades he led the entire Seattle community with humility and craft, ensuring care for all.

Josh understood that if the skyrocketing costs of first-rate elder care were to be managed, there could only be one Jewish community voice speaking up in public forums like the State Legislature, in support of the care of the elderly.

Josh became that voice. He built bridges between Jewish clergy and lay leaders who had had little experience working together. Josh's kind and wise tutelage, with his nuanced urgings, made clear the need for participation of everyone. The key was understanding that honoring our parents was a Jewish value deeper than any denomination. Josh articulated this core value—and spoke as the community's voice—every day of his career.

Josh insisted that each person involved at Kline Galland understand and believe that the delivery of care to the elderly was a personal mission, whether they were an executive, social worker, board member, kitchen worker, nurse or volunteer. So long as all in the Kline Galland family shared this mission, differences in wealth, education, title, position, or responsibility fell away.

Josh hired citizens of the world, from Africa to Korea to the Philippines. Their religions? Catholic, Protestant, Muslim, Buddhist and Jew. Josh, a stranger, welcomed and honored them all as part of the team.

One of the most touching expressions of returning that honor occurred at Josh's retirement celebration, when a Vietnamese staff person gave Josh an unexpected and deeply emotional salutation: a solemn bow from the waist. Everyone watching shared in the heartfelt gesture. Josh had earned it.

So, what about this "close encounter?" Despite our different beginnings, I grew to revere, admire, and love Josh for his adherence to mission, his skill of implementation, and for his heart. We were never really apart in what mattered.

I see Josh's footprint on the community every day, in the standards that continue almost a decade after his succession to emeritus and then into retirement.

Josh Gortler's name in Seattle is synonymous not only with providing the highest quality of care to the most sensitive and vulnerable among us, but also with honesty in business dealings, and integrity in the challenging work of negotiating a diverse political landscape. In all this, it is a name synonymous with the deepest values of Jewish tradition.

His is the story of a displaced child from a world of terror who grew up to make a home for the parents of others. He has comforted families as his own parents comforted him: by providing food and shelter and tradition, as his father did, and by mending his own and others' lives as his mother once mended torn garments for the rescued remnants of her people.

Bravo, Josh, for your story, and thank you for all that you have given me, our community, and the generations to come.

Mike Cohen
Kline Galland Board of Directors, 30-year member
Board Chair, 1989-1992
Seattle, Washington 2019

Professional Milestones

1973
Appointed Clinical Instructor, Department of Comprehensive Nursing Care Systems, University of Washington

1974
Appointed to Washington State Board of Nursing Home Administrators by Washington Governor Dan Evans

1979
Re-appointed to Washington State Board of Nursing Home Administrators by Governor Dixie Lee Ray

1982
Appointed Chairman of the Washington State Board of Nursing Home Administrators by Governor John Spellman

1987
Elected a Fellow of the American College of Health Care Administrators

1991
Appointed to Clinical Faculty at Seattle University

1992
Regional Meritorious Service Award, American Association of Homes for the Aging

1994
President's Award for Outstanding Services, Jewish Federation of Greater Seattle

1997
Award of Honor, National Association of Jewish Homes and Housing for the Aging. the Association's highest award.

2006
Washington Association of Homes and Housing for the Aging: Mentor of the Year Award,

Washington Association of Homes and Housing for the Aging: Meritorious Service Award,

American Association of Homes and Services for the Aging: The Dr. Herbert Shore Outstanding Mentor of the Year Award

May 2014
Yeshiva University, Doctor of Humane Letters

2019
Washington State House Resolution 2019-4633: "That the House of Representatives, on behalf of the people of the State of Washington, recognize and honor the life of Joshua Gortler and his monumental contributions to the understanding of remembrance, freedom, and democracy in our State."

Photo with Senator Robert F. Kennedy. *Courtesy of the Joshua Gortler collection.*

ROBERT F. KENNEDY
NEW YORK

United States Senate
WASHINGTON, D.C. 20510

January 30, 1968

Dear Mr. Gortler:

Thank you for your letter of
January 25. I just wanted you to
know how much I enjoyed my
brief visit with you.

I am pleased to autograph the
photograph you enclosed and
return it to you with my best
wishes.

Sincerely,

Robert F. Kennedy

Mr. Joshua Gortler
Assistant Executive Director
Y.M. & Y.W.H.A.
of Greater Flushing
45-35 Kissena Boulevard
Flushing, New York 11355

Senator Robert F. Kennedy Letter. *Courtesy of the Joshua Gortler collection.*

Summer 2014 "Alumni Today" page, Yeshiva University newsletter. *Courtesy of the Joshua Gortler collection.*

May 2014 Yeshiva University citation. *Courtesy of the Joshua Gortler collection.*

May 2014 photo, Josh & YU president Richard Joel. *Courtesy of the Joshua Gortler collection.*

NEWS

CAPITOL HILL TIMES   SEPTEMBER 26, 2007   **3**

Holocaust survivor puts things in perspective

Joshua Gortler reminds homeless youth that if he can do it, so can they

By Korte Brueckmann

Joshua Gortler stood out in this crowd of young people, 18 to 25, in their street clothes. Gortler was in Seattle business attire sporting a goatee and mustache, a twinkle in his eye and a yarmulke on his head. At 70, he is one of the youngest survivors of the World War II Holocaust that swept 6 million Jews into death camps where they perished.

The audience, perhaps a dozen members of the homeless youth advocacy group Peace for the Streets by Kids from the Streets (PSKS), sat in rapt attention on Wednesday, Sept. 19, as Gortler told his story. PSKS provides support and services to Seattle area homeless youth and young adults. The efforts are focused to lead homeless youth from the streets to self-sufficient and productive lives in the community.

Gortler had two major messages for the young people who gathered to hear him. The first, and most personal, is that evil was truly loose in Europe in the mid-20th century. The Holocaust truly happened, and he saw it. The second was that if he could arrive in the United States at age 16 with nothing and unable to read or write, then acquire a degree in psychology and then a masters degree in social work and administration, then so can they.

Gortler's earliest memory, he told his audience, was when the German Army occupied his village in Poland and hanged his grandfather, the village's chief rabbi, from a tree in the town square. Gortler was just 3-years-old.

"Your homelessness compared to that homelessness, there is no comparison," Gortler said. "People have no idea how bad it can be."

Gortler's father worked in his family's long-established lumber business and had many business contacts. Through those contacts the family was able to go into hiding. With the protection of their friends, when it became possible, they fled to the protection of the Soviet Army, ultimately finding refuge in Siberia. This, Gortler explained, was still a hard life because of the lack of ordinary necessities and the extreme winter cold.

From Siberia, the family was moved to Tashkent in Uzbekistan, one of the former Soviet republics that borders Afghanistan. Conditions continued to be primitive and

Joshua Gortler
Photo/Bradley Engblom

life harsh. After the end of World War II, the family moved back to Poland, but were not welcomed by government officials. They moved on to Berlin, where they lived in a displaced persons camp.

Gortler told the group that he was soused to having to scrounge dirty water or melt snow for water, that he was overcome when he saw a full, clean basin of flowing water. He put his whole face in it and drank deeply, only afterward discovering it was a urinal. This story did not get a single laugh. His audience was too wrapped in the tale to find any amusement value.

Finally, his family managed to get passage with many other refugees on a boat to the United States. He arrived with his parents, 16-years-old, completely illiterate without a day of formal education to his credit. He arranged to attend a Jewish school in New York, where he graduated high school in three years, went on to earn his bachelor's degree and then a masters degree in social

work. He proceeded to work in the Bronx with gangs. Then, 38 years ago, he came to Seattle to work with the elderly.

"I'm probably one of the youngest ones left," Gortler said of the Holocaust survivors. "I am a child survivor. My job is to tell people what happened. I am not a concentration camp survivor. My life, what I told you, was [by comparison] an easy one."

Easy for a Holocaust survivor, but not compared to life on the streets of an American city.

James Wlos, a member of PSKS who works as a longshoreman, said he is impressed with what hardships people can endure.

"My version of being homeless is just you live outside and make your way," he said. He said it helps show that if people work as a team, anything can be achieved.

"I got some knowledge that I didn't have before," said a young man who gave the name Hopper. "I got some perspective from the other side [of World War II]."

Gortler said that he kept his story to himself for many years, and it was only a half dozen years ago, when he read about the people who deny the Holocaust ever happened, that he knew he must tell his story and keep the memory of the Holocaust alive.

Gortler finished his prepared remarks with a reading from a book of the Old Testament, Ecclesiastes, in Hebrew, which he translated:

To every thing there is a season, and a time to every purpose under the heaven:

A time to be born, and a time to die; a time to plant, and a time to pluck up that which is planted;

A time to kill, and a time to heal; a time to break down, and a time to build up;

A time to weep, and a time to laugh; a time to mourn, and a time to dance;

A time to cast away stones, and a time to gather stones together; a time to embrace, and a time to refrain from embracing;

A time to get, and a time to lose; a time to keep, and a time to cast away;

A time to rend, and a time to sew; a time to keep silence, and a time to speak;

A time to love, and a time to hate; a time of war, and a time of peace.

"It is time now to speak," Gortler said.

Cal Anderson Park potluck planned

A potluck event will take place at Cal Anderson Park on Sunday, Sept. 30. The gathering is a get-to-know-your-neighbors event is planned for neighbors of the homes in the blocks immediately surrounding Cal Anderson Park.

New East Precinct commander Capt. Paul McDonagh will be on hand to meet neighbors and discuss issues. The afternoon provides a great chance to talk about neighborhood events and safety issues.

The event is sponsored by Cal Anderson Park Alliance (CAPA), Seattle Neighborhood Groups, Seattle Parks and the 11th Avenue Inn Bed and Breakfast.

Neighbors are encouraged to bring something edible to share with other neighbors. The event takes place on Sunday, Sept. 30, from 4 to 6 p.m., at Cal Anderson Park.

September 26, 2007 Capitol Hill Times "Holocaust Survivor...Perspective". *Reprinted with permission of Capitol Hill Times (Pacific Publishing Co.).*

The Seattle Times

seattletimes.com/localnews | APRIL 27, 2017

HOLOCAUST SURVIVOR WITH WORDS FOR TODAY

Jerry Large
Seattle Times staff columnist

Joshua Gortler was 3 years old in 1939 when the German army marched into his small hometown, Tomaszow Lubelski, in southeastern Poland and changed the course of his life.

JOHN FROSCHAUER / PACIFIC LUTHERAN UNIVERSITY

Joshua Gortler holds a copy of "Denying the Holocaust" at a Holocaust conference in 2013. Gortler gave several talks this week about his own survival and relevance for today.

Joshua Gortler was 3 years old in 1939 when the German army marched into his small hometown, Tomaszow Lubelski, in southeastern Poland and changed the course of his life.

He told his story Tuesday at The Summit on First Hill before an audience of mostly Jewish people old enough to know something about the pain he spoke of.

None of us knows when our world might turn upside down, but it happens to people around the world again and again. And sometimes on a scale that surpasses understanding.

Gortler is a longtime, successful Seattle resident, and he is also a survivor of the Holocaust, the Nazi attempt to exterminate the world's Jews. Six million European Jews were killed in a fit of racial cleansing. It is a horror the world should never forget, and yet there are people who deny it happened.

Monday was Holocaust Remembrance Day, so this week people have been revisiting memories and considering how the lessons of that tragedy apply to the present.

Gortler held up a copy of a book written by the historian Deborah Lipstadt, who began her career at the University of Washington in the 1970s. The 1993 book,

April 27, 2017 Seattle Times story, "Holocaust Survivor...Words for Today". *Reprinted with permission of The Seattle Times.*

"Denying the Holocaust: The Growing Assault on Truth and Memory," is one of several she wrote on the subject.

Gortler reminded his audience of a piece of graffiti scrawled just last month at Temple De Hirsch Sinai in Seattle's Capitol Hill neighborhood. The graffiti read: "The Holocaust is Fake History."

There is evidence. There are witnesses. There is his own life.

Gortler believes there are three categories of survivors and suffering. First, people who lived through the extermination camps, people who survived by going into hiding, and, finally, people like him, who escaped.

Tomaszow had a significant Jewish population, and the Germans gathered them together and issued them yellow stars. While they were being confined to one area, his grandfather, an elder in the community, arose one morning and said it was time for prayers. He said the women needed to separate themselves from the men, but there was not enough room for that, so he walked outside the space they were held in. Later he was found hanging from a tree upside down.

Gortler and everyone else were loaded onto cattle cars and taken to another town, where they were fenced in. Gortler was with his mother, father and older brother when a gentile who was a business partner of his father helped them cut the fence and escape.

Briefly they hid with gentiles, then they made their way to the Russian lines, and when the Russians retreated, his family and others went with them.

Russia, he said, was the only country that opened its doors to fleeing Jews. Once inside Russia, Jewish refugees were loaded onto trains and transported across the country to Siberia. The Russians admitted Jews, he said, because they wanted slave labor.

The refugees were plagued by diseases and had so little food that they would scavenge potato peels thrown out by Russian army cooks. He was 5 or 6 years old when they were moved again, this time to Tashkent, Uzbekistan, where they lived in a hut with a mud floor.

After the war, the family found that its home and business in Tomaszow had been taken over by non-Jews, and Jews were not welcome.

His father had seven siblings and they were all dead. His mother had eight siblings and they were all dead.

The family made their way to a refugee camp in partitioned Berlin, where they lived while countries debated their fate. Shiploads of Jewish refugees were turned away from the United States and from British-run Palestine. "No country wanted the

April 27, 2017 Seattle Times story, "Holocaust Survivor...Words for Today". *Reprinted with permission of The Seattle Times.*

Jews," Gortler said. Gortler said we should reflect on that cruelty when we think about our response to people who are displaced by tragic circumstances today.

Finally, in 1951, his family received visas to come to the United States.

Beginning in 1969, Gortler spent 38 years with Kline Galland, which runs two Seattle facilities for seniors, the Kline Galland Home and The Summit at First Hill. Ten years ago, he retired as CEO to become chairman of the Kline Galland Foundation. He plans to step down in June.

At Tuesday's event, Gortler read the famous quotation from Martin Niemoller, a Protestant minister who spoke out against Adolf Hitler. Niemoller's message was that if we don't speak up for people outside our group when they are being oppressed, we may eventually find ourselves in their shoes.

Gortler said he hopes that all of us, when we pass, will do so knowing we have made the world better.

April 27, 2017 Seattle Times story, "Holocaust Survivor...Words for Today". *Reprinted with permission of The Seattle Times.*

Dr. Herbert Shore Outstanding Mentor Award
Joshua H. Gortler
President and CEO
Caroline Kline Galland Home
Seattle, Wash.

Caroline Kline Galland Home

Joshua Gortler has shared his time and knowledge with dozens of emerging leaders in Washington state, where he is president and CEO of the Caroline Kline Galland Home. Here, in the words of some of those he has guided, is ample evidence of his achievements as an outstanding mentor:

"I met Josh in Seattle while completing my own AIT ... [He] was not my preceptor, but ... took an interest in my progress ... He has remained a colleague who, when [we] had our own survey challenge ... was one of the first to phone me and offer professional support ..."

"When I first started ... Josh was there to assist me in the development of this new facility specifically targeted at a minority population ... He always willingly shared information ... I enjoyed his leadership style and his ability to always do the right thing ... Mostly, I appreciated his advice, his style, and his kindness."

"I did not know much about the [field], so I visited Josh several times and [sought] his advice on how I should work with the community ... Josh was generous in sharing with me the Kline Galland experience and provided me with much valuable information on what to do and not to do in nursing home management. I was grateful for his advice."

Josh Gortler has demonstrated an unflinching attitude of personal and corporate responsibility and commitment to putting quality first. His staff calls the Caroline Kline Galland Home "the extension of Josh's caring and loving style."

AAHHA Dr. Herbert Shore Outstanding Mentor Award. *Photocopy courtesy of the Joshua Gortler collection.*

GARY LOCKE
Governor

STATE OF WASHINGTON

OFFICE OF THE GOVERNOR

P.O. Box 40002 • Olympia, Washington 98504-0002 • (360) 753-6780 • TTY/TDD (360) 753-6466

June 13, 1999

Josh and Sarah Gortler
c/o Seattle Hebrew Academy
1617 Interlaken Drive East
Seattle, Washington 98112

Dear Josh and Sarah:

I was delighted to learn you will be honored this evening with the Seattle Hebrew Academy's 1999 Distinguished Community Service Award. You are most deserving of this tribute.

While I am unable to join you on this special occasion, I am extremely pleased to recognize your important philanthropic endeavors and outstanding contributions to the Seattle Jewish community. I commend both of you for the invaluable leadership you have provided to a variety of worthwhile organizations, especially the Seattle Hebrew Academy and the Washington State Board of Examiners for Nursing Home Administrators.

Josh, I have thoroughly enjoyed working with you on quality of care issues, beginning when I was a member of the state House of Representatives. I send my warmest regards as you celebrate 30 years of dedicated service to the Kline Galland Center and Affiliates. The facility's success and fine reputation are due in large part to your tremendous efforts. Congratulations on reaching this significant milestone!

As we prepare to meet the promise and challenge of the 21st century, we must strive to adopt a more basic philosophy of taking care of one another. Through your renowned commitment to volunteerism, both of you have demonstrated a pledge to establishing a greater sense of fellowship among all people. By sharing your wisdom, time, and talents with others, you are helping to create hope for a brighter future in the new millennium.

On behalf of the citizens of the state of Washington, I thank and applaud you, Josh and Sarah, for your generosity. Please accept my best wishes for a most enjoyable and memorable event.

Sincerely,

Gary Locke
Governor

June 13, 1999 Gov. Gary Locke to Josh, congratulations on SHA award. *Courtesy of the Joshua Gortler collection.*

With Gov. Christine Gregoire (center) and Jeannie Alhadeff, KGC Board Chair. *Courtesy of the Joshua Gortler collection.*

April 11, 2019. On the occasion of the passage of WA State House Resolution 2019-4633, Josh proudly displays the resolution, accompanied by, from left: 23rd District Representative Sherry Appleton; Sarah; Dee Simon, Executive Director, Holocaust Center for Humanity of Seattle; and 41st District Representative Tana Senn. *Courtesy of the Joshua Gortler collection.*

HOUSE OF REPRESENTATIVES

RESOLUTION

HOUSE RESOLUTION NO. 2019-4633, by Representative Appleton

WHEREAS, Joshua Gortler, a longtime resident of Washington State, has tirelessly shared his experiences as a Holocaust survivor with citizens of our state, especially students of all ages, in the service of truth and understanding, and has brought honor to Washington State by his visionary leadership of award-winning services to the elderly; and

WHEREAS, Joshua's childhood was disrupted, as a 3-year old Jewish boy, by the Nazi invasion of his Polish hometown, Tomaszow Lubelski, in 1939; and

WHEREAS, Joshua and his family barely escaped one of the most horrific genocides the world has ever known by fleeing across a border, finding refuge in Siberia and Uzbekistan; and

WHEREAS, Joshua and his family tried to return to their home town of Tomaszow but found themselves unwelcome, spent six years in displaced persons camps in Germany, and finally received visas to come to the United States in 1951; and

WHEREAS, After arriving in the United States as a 15-year old with no English skills and limited formal education, Joshua went on to earn his Bachelor's and Master's degrees in social work from Yeshiva University, which granted him an honorary Doctorate in 2014 for his work in elder care; and

WHEREAS, Since 1969, Joshua has served Seattle senior citizens by building the Kline Galland Home and The Summit at First Hill into award-winning facilities. Upon his retirement in 2007 as CEO of The Kline Galland Center and Affiliates, he became President of The Kline Galland Foundation to ensure the continuation of this high-quality care; and

WHEREAS, By volunteering as a speaker for Seattle's Holocaust Center for Humanity, Joshua is sharing with young people, including at-risk youth in detention centers in King and Kitsap Counties, his lifetime experiences as a Holocaust survivor who turned a life of hardship into a successful career as a community leader; and

WHEREAS, Joshua is a living survivor of the Holocaust and is a renowned humanitarian and author who understands the importance of protecting our freedoms and caring for people at risk in our society; and

WHEREAS, Joshua has dedicated his life to helping others who have experienced oppression, and conveyed the message that each person can make a positive difference in this world;

NOW, THEREFORE, BE IT RESOLVED, That the House of Representatives, on behalf of the people of the State of Washington, recognize and honor the life of Joshua Gortler and his monumental contributions to the understanding of remembrance, freedom, and democracy in our State; and

BE IT FURTHER RESOLVED, That copies of this resolution be immediately transmitted by the Chief Clerk of the House of Representatives to Joshua Gortler.

I hereby certify this to be a true and correct copy of
Resolution 4633 adopted by the House of Representatives
April 5, 2019

Bernard Dean, Chief Clerk

WA State House resolution 2019-4633. *Courtesy of the Joshua Gortler collection.*

After Josh's PowerPoint presentation on behalf of Holocaust Center for Humanity of Seattle, at Mercer Island Rotary, November 2017. With Petra Heussner-Walker, Emerita Honorary Consul, Federal Republic of Germany, and Khalit Aisin, Deputy Consul General, Russian Federation. *Courtesy of Gigi Yellen.*

September 7, 2017. On the occasion of their donation of a Torah scroll in honor of their parents, Josh and Morris Gortler celebrate with family at Makor Synagogue in Scottsdale, AZ. Josh performs the traditional celebratory act of inscribing the final letter in this Torah. From left: Nina Gortler Blockman, Sarah Gortler, Josh (seated), Morris Gortler, Marcelle Gortler. *Courtesy of the Joshua Gortler collection.*

AN APPRECIATION: THE GIFT
By Tom Leavitt
President, Kline Galland Center 1997-2000

I was introduced to Josh Gortler in the early 1970's by my father, Robert Leavitt, who was active as a volunteer in the real estate and facilities work of the Kline Galland Center. He told me about the relatively new executive director of the Home (just a nursing home at the time), a young immigrant from Nazi-overrun Poland, a graduate of the yeshiva in New York. He told me I had to meet this guy, as he was one of the brightest and most capable people he had ever met.

My father was a University of Chicago Law School grad who became very enthusiastic upon meeting and knowing ultra-bright people. He made it abundantly clear he thought Josh was at the top of that list. But I was just starting law school in another city and didn't have time to meet my father's new friends.

I moved back to Seattle, began my professional career, and devoted my volunteer energy to helping traditionally under-represented communities. Then I began to think I needed to volunteer with an organization in "my own" Jewish community. I finally agreed to join my father at Kline Galland for coffee with this fellow Josh. As though it was yesterday, I remember walking toward Josh Gortler's office just inside the main entry at the Home, following the sound of that now familiar high-pitched laugh one never forgets after hearing it just once. Entering his office, I saw the photo of a young Gortler walking along with Bobby Kennedy, and thought, "oh, this is my kinda guy!" This Gortler fellow was not only exceptionally bright, but also affable and immediately likable.

A few years later, another invitation from my father, to a planning meeting for a badly needed expansion at Kline Galland. My dad had been the committee-of-one who had overseen the previous expansion, and it was easily the activity he was most proud of in his adult life. He wanted me involved in the next one. I did attend the 1978 exploratory meeting, and never left.

The expansion project required a lot of neighborly visits. We sat in the living rooms and sun porches of the homes of people who lived closest to

Kline Galland, but who were the most vocal opponents of our proposed expansion. We listened as they expressed respect for Josh, and for the work of the Home, even as they voiced their emphatic opposition. I wondered how he had won the affection of neighbors who were openly hostile to the expansion? Neighbors who had sued and lost over the previous expansion! They opposed expansion, but admired Josh.

Josh always made certain that neighbors were invited to major events at the Home, and he worked very hard to gain their appreciation for the quality of care the nursing home residents received.

To build on that personal goodwill, we met countless times with neighbors, over a period of months, until the first domino fell: the property owner between the Home and Lake Washington agreed to sell to Kline Galland. It was economics, of course, but the neighbor, knowing he would potentially come under a great deal of criticism from the others, expressed the confidence that Kline Galland under Josh's leadership would continue to respect its neighbors' desire for privacy and quiet.

After that first sale, other neighbors were relieved of the pressure not to sell. We ended up with enough property for a comfortable buffer between the Home and the adjacent single-family dwellings. This was a monumental accomplishment for the organization, and although I received credit for having made these deals, I always knew that the true genius was Josh, who had the foresight to welcome the neighbors in, and to empathize with their concerns about the effects of living next door to this nursing home.

As vice president of the board and chair of the real estate committee, I made the mistake no one should ever make when working with Josh Gortler: I underestimated his ability to add expertise to this effort. Certainly, he had more experience than anyone in operating a nursing facility, but his acute awareness of what makes people comfortable, and how pieces of a complex building fit together, was apparent every day of the project. I spoke with Josh on the phone several times a week, as I visited the construction site and directed the design team. I cannot recall one problem where Josh couldn't come up with a good solution. He is not an architect, engineer or commercial construction expert, but he just innately "got it".

Not only did Josh have his fingers on the pulse of Kline Galland, but he earned the absolute respect of the staff. That's one reason that

Kline Galland had so little staff turnover: respect and admiration for the boss. He treated everyone with dignity. Each staff member seemed to feel appreciated and valued for their contribution to the successful care of the residents.

Josh generously shares his wisdom, his acute awareness of how human beings approach the world and each other. He can weave his analysis of a problem together with his mind-boggling depth of understanding of the Orthodox teachings of the Talmud. This was something I had not been exposed to before. Often, I felt like a character in a story, sitting at the feet of the wisest person in the land, learning from him. Josh was never dismissive of how little I knew. He spoke with me with respect for my curiosity: I was a student eager to learn. And he, too, expressed an interest in learning a bit himself along the way.

One day, during a discussion in Josh's office, I watched as he opened and read EVERY single piece of business mail that came in. He told me this was how he kept track of all the departments and business of the organization.

The Home's expansion could not have happened without raising more money than had been raised before by any other organization in the Jewish community, and Kline Galland had never before even had to solicit donations. It had been a self-sustaining organization. The fundraising committee did a wonderful job, but the money was raised both directly and indirectly by Josh. His reputation in the community made fundraising much easier: he personally called on major donors, and secured pledges far in excess of what anyone had anticipated. I loved going on these calls with Josh. In my own business I raised investment dollars for real estate projects, and thought I was pretty good at it. But this was like watching a great artist work.

As board chair, I marveled over Josh's masterful work with the design and construction team to create a comfortable and efficient facility with room to expand. Beyond the skilled nursing home, adult day-care and meals on wheels, Josh brought us into a beautiful new facility for independent retirement and assisted living, The Summit at First Hill. Kline Galland became a service delivery conglomerate.

One of the most poignant and meaningful experiences of my adult life happened thanks to Josh. He and I were in Los Angeles, attending a conference of Jewish organizations addressing the needs of the elderly, when he suggested that we visit the recently-opened Holocaust museum there. We spent hours looking through rolls of microfiche photos taken in the German Displaced Persons camps where Josh had lived.

He was looking for pictures of himself and his family. Although we did not find any, his description of what we were viewing simply took my breath away. I came to understand how Josh, who had survived all that, could find so much comfort in living according to Jewish tradition. What emotional strength and intellectual power he obviously had, to make the transition from such a past to running a complex organization like Kline Galland. When my wife and I later took our children to other Holocaust memorial sites, I was able to relate some of what I had learned from Josh that afternoon.

I had my own experience as a family member of a Kline Galland Home resident. My mother, suffering from increasingly debilitating dementia, moved in and lived there for the balance of her life, about 8 years. I visited her each time I was at the Home for board work, and often on the weekends with our children. I saw firsthand the care that Josh insisted on. My mother was treated with dignity and respect, as one would treat a beloved family member in one's own home. Even after all the years of seeing Kline Galland from an organizational development viewpoint, we were still just astounded by the professionalism and personal attachment shown by the staff to our mother and every other resident.

I felt Josh's personal pride was always subordinate to his desire for Kline Galland to be successful. Upon his retirement as CEO, Josh headed up the new Kline Galland Foundation, using his magical powers to continue raising a lot of money, leaving his legacy even broader and more successful than when he "retired."

Josh made a welcoming environment for a diverse Jewish community. He gave the jobs with the greatest responsibilities to women. He developed probably our most effective asset: a most remarkable volunteer organization. Through the sheer power of personality and persuasion, Josh opened the doors of the Home to rich and poor; Ashkenazi and Sephardi; young and old; Orthodox, Conservative, Reform or non-religious. Everyone was welcomed and encouraged to bring their time and talents to improve the lives of the residents in every respect.

I have found inspiration in Josh's self-deprecating sense of humor; in his combination of informal approach to management with a demand for perfection from a diverse staff; in the respect he showed to people of so many different backgrounds and ethnicities who made careers caring for the residents; in the skill with which he handled even the most difficult and anxious families of residents.

Josh has treated all people with sensitivity, but particularly those residents who had survived the Holocaust and were suffering from the dementia that had them reliving those terrors. These were frightened people, living out the end of their lives under his care, and he refused to let them suffer. During countless meetings in the Home's conference room, we would suddenly be interrupted as the hall reverberated with a resident's screaming. Josh would drop everything and rush to the resident; within a short time, that person would be quiet and calm again.

It is a gift. It is his magic. I had the great honor of observing and learning so much over the years from him. From that experience, I truly believe I am a better person. I will forever be grateful. Our community is and will forever be a better place for having been touched, and taught, by Joshua Gortler.

Tom Leavitt
President, Kline Galland Center 1997-2000
Seattle, Washington 2019

References

Ander, Heike and Michaela Melian. *Föhrenwald*. ©2005, Revolver: Archiv für aktuelle Kunst, Frankfort am Main

Altshuler, David A. *Hitler's War Against the Jews: A Young Reader's Version of The War Against the Jews 1933-1945 by Lucy S. Dawidowicz*. ©1978, Behrman House

Goldsmith, Seth. *Choosing a Nursing Home*. ©1990, Prentice Hall Press

Holocaust Center for Humanity, Seattle
https://www.holocaustcenterseattle.org/josh-gortler

Jewish Virtual Library
https://www.jewishvirtuallibrary.org/

"Music and the Holocaust"
http://holocaustmusic.ort.org/

POLIN Virtual Shtetl
https://sztetl.org.pl/en

"Saved by Deportation: An Unknown Odyssey of Polish Jews." 2006 documentary film by Slawomir Grunberg and Robert Podgursky.
https://www.kanopy.com/product/saved-deportation

http://www.hebrewsongs.com

http://www.klesmer-musik.de

United States Holocaust Memorial Museum
https://www.ushmm.org

Washington State Jewish Historical Society archives at the University of Washington. Joshua Gortler interviews:
https://digitalcollections.lib.washington.edu/digital/collection/ohc/id/2252/rec/186

World History Project
https://worldhistoryproject.org/

Yellen, Gigi. Audio interviews April 2017-June 2019. Private collection.

Acknowledgments

I would like to express my gratitude to the following individuals, who helped to make this book a reality:

Roselyn Bell, Aliza Blockman, Nina Blockman, Moshe Blockman, Yosef Blockman, Linda Clifton, Jeff Cohen, Laurie Cohen, Michael Cohen, Howard Droker, Annie Fairchild, Seth Goldsmith, Sarah Gortler, Shlomo Gortler, Richard Green, Petra Heussner-Walker, Nancy Hood, Ilana Cone Kennedy, Rivy Poupko Kletenik, Wolf Kohn, Mardell Kromer, Tom Leavitt, Jacob Menashe, Dan Ozog, Dee Simon, Julia Thompson, Luci Varon

Special thanks: To our tireless and supportive publishing consultant, Jennifer McCord,to our diligent copy editor, Megan Stills, and to our inventive graphic designer, Rudy Ramos.

I am especially grateful to Gigi Yellen, whose hours of interviews with me refreshed my memories very gently, and helped me express them in words. –JG

Thanks beyond measure to Dr. Wolf Kohn, who made room in our life for my work on this project, and whose affection for Josh made it hardly seem like work at all. -GY

Joshua Gortler currently lives in
Seattle, Washington.